MAKING THE EARLY MODERN METROPOLIS

EARLY AMERICAN HISTORIES

Douglas Bradburn, John C. Coombs, and S. Max Edelson, Editors

MAKING THE EARLY MODERN METROPOLIS

Culture and Power in
Pre-Revolutionary Philadelphia

DANIEL P. JOHNSON

UNIVERSITY OF VIRGINIA PRESS

Charlottesville and London

University of Virginia Press
© 2022 by the Rector and Visitors of the University of Virginia
All rights reserved
Printed in the United States of America on acid-free paper

First published 2022

9 8 7 6 5 4 3 2 1

Library of Congress Cataloging-in-Publication Data

Names: Johnson, Daniel P., author.
Title: Making the early modern metropolis : culture and power in pre-
    revolutionary Philadelphia / Daniel P. Johnson.
Other titles: Culture and power in pre-revolutionary Philadelphia
Description: Charlottesville : University of Virginia Press, 2022. | Series:
    Early American histories | Includes bibliographical references and index.
Identifiers: LCCN 2022013445 (print) | LCCN 2022013446 (ebook) |
    ISBN 9780813945408 (hardcover) | ISBN 9780813945415 (paperback) |
    ISBN 9780813945422 (ebook)
Subjects: LCSH: Philadelphia (Pa.)—Social life and customs—To 1775. |
    Philadelphia (Pa.)—History—Colonial period, ca. 1600–1775. |
    Urbanization—Pennsylvania—Philadelphia—History—18th century. |
    Philadelphia (Pa.)—Social conditions—18th century. | Philadelphia (Pa.)—
    History—18th century.
Classification: LCC F158.4 .J64 2022 (print) | LCC F158.4 (ebook) |
    DDC 974.8/11—dc23/eng/20220323
LC record available at https://lccn.loc.gov/2022013445
LC ebook record available at https://lccn.loc.gov/2022013446

Cover art: Details of "The South East Prospect of the City of Philadelphia," Peter
Cooper, ca. 1718. (Photo courtesy of the Library Company of Philadelphia)

For Mike (1969–2017)

CONTENTS

ACKNOWLEDGMENTS

Writing this book has been a long journey made possible by the support of many people and institutions. While I was a graduate student at Binghamton University, my advisors, professors, and dissertation committee members gave invaluable advice and inspiration during the book's formative stages. I am forever grateful to Doug Bradburn, Tom Dublin, Diane Sommerville, Rifa'at Abou-El-Haj, and Simon Middleton for their direction. Fellow graduate students David Gutman, Gül Karagöz Kızılca, Todd Goehle, Kolya Abramsky, Fulya Özkan, Nurçin İleri, Sandra Sánchez López, Carlos Cortissoz, Chris Pearl, Can Nacar, Nilay Özok-Gündoğan, and Azat Gündoğan helped make learning how to research and write history at Binghamton a truly collective and joyful experience. My friends and colleagues at Bilkent University—William Coker, Ayşe Çelikkol, Andy Ploeg, Mihaela Harper, Rachel Bruzzone, Douglas Olson, Joshua Bartlett, Kara McCormack, Tara Needham, Cory Stockwell, and Buffy Turner—have stimulated my thinking on history and the humanities in innumerable ways. At the University of Virginia Press, Dick Holway, Nadine Zimmerli, and Leslie Tingle expertly guided the work from manuscript to book.

Institutional support was also indispensable. Binghamton University's Department of History, the Gilder Lehrman Institute, Bilkent University, and the William Reese Company at the University of Minnesota's James Ford Bell Library provided financial support without which this book could not have been written. A semester sabbatical from Bilkent in 2017 was essential in turning a very rough draft into something resembling a book. The Center for Early Modern History at the University of Minnesota provided a welcoming and stimulating research home during the sabbatical, and the Consortium for the Study of the Premodern World generously offered a visiting professorship. At Minnesota, J. B. Shank, Jon Butler, Katherine Gerbner, Dave Hacker, Margaret Carlyle, and Marguerite Ragnow graciously gave their time and knowledge to a visiting scholar.

Most important has been the love and encouragement of my family. My parents Robert and Carol, my brother Michael, my partner Hande, and my daughter Eda have been fundamental supports from this book's inception. It is dedicated in loving memory to Brother Mike.

MAKING THE EARLY MODERN METROPOLIS

INTRODUCTION

Sometime in the 1760s a man named John, a local prophet from Blockley Township in western Philadelphia County, recorded a recurring dream in his journal. In the dream John began a journey to the city of Philadelphia at dusk; when he arrived at the town's entrance at the gable-end of the State House on Chestnut Street, he was met by a winged man in bright clothing. The angel beckoned John to come closer and told him: "I will shew [you] the calamity that is coming upon this City of Philadelphia for their Pride, Deceit, & other backsliding." As darkness overtook the town, John and the angel observed from city rooftops a multitude of black wagons, each pulled by four black horses accompanied by two workmen in black caps. The carts were filled with dead bodies, while the screams of men, women, and children filled the country-dweller's ears. The angel responded to his query regarding the meaning of this frightful scene by bringing John to Front Street along the Delaware River, where there were seventy-five more wagons. In the center of the caravan was a black cart with eight black horses containing a large tub, out of which issued a column of black smoke "so thick and so Dark that it put me in mind of the Darkness of Egypt." The angel then told John that the eight black horses were the plagues and pestilence visited on the people of Philadelphia for, once again, their pride, deceit, and backsliding. After the pair visited city cemeteries and saw the suffering of all inhabitants (Quakers as well as Anglicans), the angel bid John to "Return to the Country." Though he then thankfully awoke, John remained haunted by the "dismal Lamentations of the People in mine Ears."[1]

John of Blockley's nightmare vision may have been an especially vivid one, but he was not alone in criticizing conditions in Philadelphia and the mid-Atlantic in the 1760s. In September 1763, in the midst of a severe economic slump following the Seven Years' War, Philadelphians protested the high cost of food, leading the city government to require provisions be sold only at the town market at publicly listed prices.[2] The following year, inhabitants of neighboring Chester County requested that the provincial assembly issue new bills of credit. The scarcity of money in the colony had led to the daily seizure of debtors' properties in town and country, forcing many defaulters and their families onto public relief.[3] A broadside promoting the construction of a linen manufactory pointed to the growing numbers of poor in and around Philadelphia, many of whom had become "burthensome to their Neighbours"—a reference to growing public relief rolls.[4] John of Blockley was not the only apocalyptic prophet in Pennsylvania: one backcountry hermit predicted in 1763 that "great and terrible events" were in store for the people of the colony.[5]

Yet these tales of woe stand in opposition to more familiar accounts of colonial Philadelphia as a unique site of tolerance, enlightenment, and prosperity. European visitors and civic-minded Philadelphians often celebrated the city's transformation from a remote colonial outpost in the 1680s to a thriving imperial metropolis by the mid-eighteenth century. Observers like the Swedish naturalist Peter Kalm, as well as Britons like the English clergyman Andrew Burnaby and the Scottish general Lord Adam Gordon, were impressed by the city's straight and wide streets, neoclassical buildings, numerous churches, and spacious quays and docks. In 1764 Gordon suggested—with great exaggeration—that Philadelphia was "one of the wonders of the World," while Burnaby reflected on the "progress of cities and empires" after visiting the city.[6] Philadelphians prided themselves on their civic consciousness and commitment to science and the arts, embodied in urban institutions like the Library Company, the Pennsylvania Hospital, and the College of Philadelphia. On the eve of the American Revolution, the physician and social reformer Benjamin Rush called his city "the capital of the new world."[7]

Educated people in the eighteenth century increasingly characterized protests and criticisms regarding backsliding and unjust economic practices like those cited above as "errors," beliefs deeply rooted in custom. Intellectuals regularly expressed sentiments similar to that of a midcentury New Yorker, who claimed there was nothing "more difficult than to eradicate popular Prejudice. Errors, like Families, demand Respect on Account of their Antiquity."[8] The need to break historical bonds of ignorance and error was a defining challenge for eighteenth-century thinkers. From this perspective John's nightmare recalled the archaic and superstitious dream vision, in which a protagonist (usually a knight or peasant), guided by a saint or angel, visits hell and encounters fiery rivers and lakes as well as monstrous creatures and demons.[9] Demands for market regulation to prevent engrossing and forestalling (buying up and withholding goods to enhance prices) were couched in a language of seller "avarice" and recalled a traditional moral economy at odds with new liberal economic theories.[10] Complaints involving debt and currency scarcity similarly evoked a customary discourse of usury and money hoarding with roots in a commercializing medieval Europe and Renaissance arguments over legitimate rates of interest.[11]

Whereas John of Blockley expressed a popular association of cities with greed and corruption (and implicitly connected country living with innocence and virtue), Burnaby and Gordon voiced classical and Renaissance notions of cities as centers of knowledge, civility, and wealth. Rather than religious backsliding or hypocritical worldliness, these writers saw in Philadelphia the industriousness and improvement that had made Great Britain a wealthy global power. Cities equated civilization in this view (in contrast to rural backwardness), and for many colonists the growth of American metropolises meant that they had joined the British Empire as members of the freest and richest state in the world. And visiting travelers were not alone in celebrating the virtues of Pennsylvania's New World commonwealth: French philosophers like Montesquieu and Voltaire, though they never set foot in the colony, were enthusiastic admirers of William Penn and his liberal experiment in America.[12]

Though modern historians have complicated the picture, they have generally endorsed contemporaries' view of early Philadelphia as a uniquely enlightened place. Scholars have shown how William Penn's plan for Philadelphia was influenced by new urban principles of perspective and geometric order, often in contrast to unplanned, medieval-looking towns like Boston and New York.[13] They have also framed early conflicts between the proprietor and settlers as differences between Penn's "radical vision" and colonists' "tradition-bound expectations."[14] Religious tolerance and economic opportunity led to rapid growth in both population and economy in town and country in the two decades after the colony's founding. By the 1720s Philadelphia had become the primary port of disembarkation for free migrants to North America; by the 1760s it was the continent's largest city, with a population of twenty thousand.[15] Between these decades the city became a center of Atlantic print culture, with the towering figure of Benjamin Franklin embodying a thriving British American public sphere.[16] Social historians have also demonstrated that widespread poverty emerged in Philadelphia only in the 1760s, in contrast to the era of relative material comfort between the 1680s and 1750s.[17]

Recent scholarship has focused on everyday life in early Philadelphia, placing particular emphasis on how individuals and collectivities addressed the challenges of living in a growing American city. The relationship between tavern culture and politics, the creation of municipal reforms to address urban health issues, and the formation of associations and clubs are important examples of how historians have analyzed Philadelphia's early development.[18] *Making the Early Modern Metropolis* builds on recent work on social life in Philadelphia, though with an expanded temporal and geographical framework. Whereas literature on colonial Philadelphia tends to emphasize the city's modern, liberal features, I situate the city's early development in a longer and wider history of early modern urban transformation.[19] Rather than a contest between old and new, I argue that it was in the interplay of inherited and often competing systems of belief during a period of profound growth and change that early modern cities like Philadelphia were made. Novel social conditions intersected with patterns of thought and practice from a rich variety of traditions to forge British America's most dynamic city.

In the century after 1660 English towns grew at unprecedented levels while traditional forms of apprenticeship and market regulation declined.[20] In England's American colonies small villages grew into substantial commercial cities, though colonial urban society differed in fundamental ways from that of the metropole. Most important was colonists' enslavement of large numbers of people of African descent, whose labor was crucial to the development of cities like Boston, Bridgetown (Barbados), New York, Philadelphia, Port Royal (Jamaica), and Charleston. At the same time, urban institutions and social systems in England and British America remained largely governed by norms originating in the late medieval period, roughly between the thirteenth and sixteenth centuries. In the High Middle Ages charters of incorporation first granted European towns self-governing "free" status, and a key concept that would animate late medieval urban society was that of the *bonum commune*, or *communitas*. Though as a formal political idea the notion of the common good dates to Greco-Roman antiquity, its medieval manifestation first developed in towns, passing from merchant associations to urban leagues and eventually to larger political entities.[21] In early modern European cities the notion of the common good provided a "normative regulative idea" of "unquestionable axiomatic value."[22] By the 1500s honesty, reasonableness, convenience, justice,

and Christian charity comprised the main keywords of the urban bonum commune, and these terms continued to pervade social and political discourse in
cities on both sides of the Atlantic through the eighteenth century.

While the centrality of the notion of the public good is well-known to
political and intellectual historians, the concept pervaded every level of early
modern Western culture, and its prominence in everyday social relations warrants closer scrutiny. The ubiquity of the notion of the communitas meant that
residents' claims to act for common good could be expressed in competing
ways—for example, in arguments for maintaining the corporate status quo or,
conversely, in demands for the redistribution of resources.[23] Alleged violations
of the common good were articulated in a language involving the abuse of
power and, consequently, the "oppression" of one group over another. Whereas
principles of honesty, neighborliness, and hospitality ideally conditioned social
life, in times of conflict some townspeople believed those seeking power acted
in their own private interests. Urban disputes therefore often involved discursive contests over who spoke truthfully in the interest of the public, whether in
petitions or testimonies before authorities or, increasingly in the seventeenth
and eighteenth centuries, in an expanding print culture. The expression of conflicts over immediate material concerns could also alter the balance of social
power with potentially long-lasting consequences.

By sixteenth-century European standards England was a highly centralized
state. Yet urban corporate identities were reinforced by, and not opposed to,
the formation of a national political consciousness. Levels of craft and guild
apprenticeship rose at higher rates than population at a time of sharp demographic increase in the late sixteenth and early seventeenth centuries. Laws like
the Statute of Artificers (1563) created a national system of labor regulation
while also encouraging urban freemanship and corporate identification with
a seven-year apprenticeship requirement for the practice of crafts.[24] A connection between local and national identities was also strengthened by office-
holding opportunities; political participation as constables, justices, and grand
jurymen among a growing middling sort fostered a popular view of England as
a uniquely participatory and law-based state.[25]

The most famous expression of commonwealth social thought in the sixteenth century, Thomas Smith's De Republica Anglorum, emphasized the
importance of urban and national identities as well as changing social relations to explain England's growing wealth and power. Smith pointed out that
urban burgesses and citizens, those who possessed the freedom of the city as

well as the "substance to beare the charges," followed the gentry in England's four-class social hierarchy. What distinguished the English commonwealth from other European polities, according to Smith, was its large population of yeomen, a prosperous group of tenant farmers.[26] This industrious class contributed significantly to England's "improvement," a concept historians have associated with changing humanist ideas concerning value, national wealth, and "projects."[27] Smith was also an early promoter of Irish colonization, and by the 1580s some improvers argued that establishing plantations in America would enrich the English commonwealth while reducing unemployment and social unrest at home. Accelerating with the creation of the Virginia Company of London in 1606 and continuing through the seventeenth century, a literary genre promoting settlement in a new language of improvement and the public interest accompanied the creation of English colonies in America.[28]

William Penn and other Philadelphia founders were strongly influenced by Elizabethan and early Stuart ideas of improvement, liberty, and the benefits of colonization for the commonwealth. The creation of a colony founded by Quakers would not have been possible without the English Civil Wars of the 1640s, however. Parliament's defeat of Charles I and the execution of the king in early 1649 were followed by the abolition of the House of Lords, the disestablishment of the Church of England, and the creation of a republic. Yet for some the new Commonwealth did not go far enough. One group arising during the 1650s, called Quakers by their critics, vociferously opposed any church establishment, sharing with other radicals a hostility to tithes and "hireling" clergy. They disrupted church meetings and railed in print and public against the continuance of England's corrupt legal and educational systems. As early as 1657 the Protectorate government under Oliver Cromwell enacted anti-Quaker laws, but large-scale state repression began following the restoration of the monarchy in 1660, when dissenters were subjected to waves of persecution. Between the 1660s and 1680s thousands of Quakers were imprisoned; hundreds died. In the midst of persecution and internal dissension, in the late 1660s George Fox assumed primary leadership of the Quakers and proceeded to establish a centralized organizational structure for the group.[29] William Penn and other converts to the new Religious Society of Friends purchased West Jersey as a refuge for persecuted Quakers in 1677, and four years later Charles II awarded Penn a neighboring mid-Atlantic colony as repayment for a debt owed to Penn's father.

The establishment of Pennsylvania is inseparable from the preceding era of revolution, republic, and restoration. As we will see, this period would also loom large in culture and politics in Philadelphia well into the eighteenth century. But the longer history of European urban growth and socioeconomic transformation in England was equally important to Philadelphia's development. Penn's 1685 account of Philadelphia's first three years emphasized the creation of urban institutions like markets, ordinaries, a town bell signaling work and mealtimes, a nine o'clock curfew enforced by a public watch, and the furnishing of the town with numerous "convenient"—a fundamental term in the urban commonwealth lexicon—mills. Penn also celebrated the many "improvements" already made in the town. A local shipbuilding industry was quickly established, and rapid settlement and the construction of well-made houses resulted in rising land prices, which were the best measurement of the "Improvement of the place."[30] A traditional, well-regulated urban order was fully compatible with contemporary ideas about economic development and personal enrichment.

Yet the American mid-Atlantic environment presented significant problems to Penn's vision. In his enthusiastic 1685 account, he claimed that the natural abundance of the area's soils and waterways allowed farmers to maintain themselves and pay for other necessities with their own produce.[31] Within a decade, however, this idealized barter economy was belied by complaints of scarce currency and serious tensions between creditors and debtors. Recognizing the important role credit would play in the colonial economy (as it had in England for well over a century), founding assemblymen enacted novel debt laws that reflected this dependence. Debtor-creditor relations and the money supply would continue to be primary drivers of social and political conflict in the city into midcentury and beyond. The availability and cost of labor in the Americas in the 1680s also led Pennsylvania's first representatives to draw on other colonies' labor laws, specifically regarding servitude and slavery. Departures from the colony's founding legal code were further evidenced in penal law, as lawmakers adopted English corporal punishments for property crimes early in the eighteenth century. Beginning in the 1720s Philadelphia's urban print culture played a key role in representing crime to townspeople; it was also crucial to conveying political conflicts and ideological contests over who were the true defenders of the public good. As Philadelphia grew from a small colonial port to a large British metropolis between the 1680s and 1760s, the enlightened and prosperous city admired by many had also become a site of pronounced social and political conflict. It was a place in which the very different experiences of Burnaby, Gordon, and John of Blockley could find expression.

The ways in which colonists articulated these differences indicate how older patterns of thought and belief fused with the novel exigencies of a growing Atlantic world. Recognizing the importance of commerce to the future prosperity of his colony, Penn encouraged wealthy urban merchants like James Claypoole, Robert Turner, and Griffith Jones to settle in the city.[32] Yet Penn's vision for Pennsylvania recalled a classical rural ideal, and the social and political ideas of the proprietors and of allies like Robert Barclay in the 1670s resembled the early sixteenth-century writings of conservative humanists like Thomas Elyot far more than they did those of Commonwealth-era Quakers like James Naylor and Edward Burrough.[33] The importance of the past to contemporary problems was further evidenced in the 1720s, when proprietary Quakers represented criticisms of local government as akin to those of Parliament toward the Crown in the 1640s and as leveling threats to the rule of the colony's "best men"—meaning wealthy Friends. Similarly, in public arguments over currency, opponents of paper money deployed traditional arguments about the "intrinsic value" of silver and gold, while some of these same supporters of conventional ideas about money applied a new liberal language of property to servants and enslaved laborers.

Philadelphians suspicious of the power of the colony's "best men" drew on different traditions and values. Like Friends' seventeenth-century critics, some scholars have placed early Quaker ideas in a long tradition of English anticlericalism, a thread connecting late medieval Lollards to early Reformation Anabaptists and continuing into the seventeenth century with Familists, Seekers, and Ranters.[34] The presence of "Singing" and "Ranting" Quakers in the mid-Atlantic indicates that this antiauthoritarian tradition persisted into the eighteenth century despite the Society of Friends' official moderation and the creation of disciplinary mechanisms in the church. Non-Quaker criticisms of hypocritical "worldly" Friends in the late seventeenth century coincided with debtor claims of creditor usury and merchant money hoarding. Petitions to provincial authorities similarly complained of the oppressive exactions of urban creditors and landlords, while beginning in the 1720s satirical dialogues and letters deployed medieval allegorical figures like the virtuous Plowman to criticize urban and provincial society.[35] In the decades after the 1720s some Philadelphians even resorted to customary methods of direct action—street demonstrations and riots—to protest what they felt were violations of the common good.[36]

It was in these mid-eighteenth-century decades that Philadelphia was fully integrated into an Atlantic economic and cultural system. The city's evolution was shaped by external forces as well as by the ways in which local groups—creditors and debtors, men and women, free and unfree, learned and unlearned—appropriated past ideas and practices to make claims for legitimacy and authority, in Philadelphia as elsewhere in the Americas.[37] While the story of early Philadelphia is therefore undoubtedly unique, it is also symptomatic of a general early modern process of urbanization and Atlanticization whose foundations lay in late medieval and Renaissance Europe and expanded outward as European states established large colonial empires between the sixteenth and eighteenth centuries. The distinctive manifestations of these changes in Philadelphia speak to the myriad global forces that made the early modern world.

Characterizing Philadelphia as an early modern city, as I do in this book, brings up the question of definition. The category of "early modernity"—generally the period between the early sixteenth and late eighteenth centuries—first appeared in mid-Victorian England but did not come into wide usage by historians until the 1970s.[38] While critics have seen the imprecision and inconsistent application of the term as a liability, proponents have argued that one of early modernity's virtues lies in its ability to trace continuities and gradual transformations as well as sudden breaks. Keith Wrightson has argued that contemporaries of the early modern period believed themselves to be living in new and changing times, and numerous nineteenth-century thinkers agreed.[39] Proponents and critics alike acknowledge that the growing preference for the concept in the late twentieth century was part of a conscious effort among scholars across disciplines to be more inclusive of nonelite sources, as well as to undermine the Eurocentric categories of the Renaissance and Enlightenment.[40] While the notion of early modernity might also imply a Eurocentric teleology, scholars specializing in non-Western regions and comparative global histories have deployed an early modern periodization with fruitful results.[41]

Although the proliferation of Atlantic and global histories in recent decades has encouraged the expansion of the early modern concept, scholars of North America before 1800 have yet to fully embrace the term.[42] There was, of course, no medieval period bracketing the fall of Rome and the Renaissance in the Americas, with European empires in the Western Hemisphere coinciding with the onset of "early modernity." Yet the fact that numerous societies inhabited the Western Hemisphere for millennia prior to the arrival of Europeans arguably raises even more problematic conceptual problems for the common generic category of "early America."[43] Terms like "colonial," "revolutionary," and "early republican" may be more temporally precise, but they are also political categories that may not correspond to economic, social, or cultural changes. Douglass Bradburn and John Coombs have argued that "colonial America" suggests colonies were self-contained and closed off from larger trends and cultural patterns in the contemporary world. Embracing the early modern, by contrast, can "break down the artificial barriers that too often separate early American histories from the great problems and literature of the early modern world."[44]

The history of early Philadelphia is part of a larger story of colonization, merchant capitalism, imperial war, state formation, and the "unprecedented mingling and mixing of peoples, ideas, worldviews, and cosmologies from around the globe."[45] The cosmopolitan city of Philadelphia exemplifies this mingling and mixing of peoples, beliefs, and practices as well as any place in the early modern Americas. Focusing on the eight decades between the city's 1682 founding and the mid-1760s, *Making the Early Modern Metropolis* is interested in Philadelphia's pre-revolutionary "making." A number of scholars have examined early Philadelphia from the colonial through the revolutionary era, and the period between the 1760s and early 1800s has been extensively studied.[46] The mid-1760s mark a decisive break in Philadelphia's history, however: the ending of the Seven Years' War in 1763, Benjamin Franklin's unsuccessful campaign to make Pennsylvania a royal colony in 1764, and the outbreak of the Stamp Act controversy in 1765 ushered in an era of new challenges.[47] More broadly, while some scholars terminate the early modern period in 1660, 1688, 1750, 1776, 1789, 1800, or even 1815, by ending this study in 1764, I follow those who argue that self-perceptions of living in yet another new age began with the Age of Revolutions and industrialization between the 1760s and 1840s.[48]

Before notions of individual liberty and rights became hegemonic in the late eighteenth century, most people regarded communities and societies as interdependent entities in which reciprocal relations and a just social order were paramount.[49] Early modern people did not see inequality, a lack of rights, or an absence of order as resulting from large, impersonal economic or political structures. Rather, "oppression" resulted from imbalances of power within disordered communities and governments in which a proper equilibrium was upset—usually by a few designing individuals who placed their own interests over that of the public. John from Blockley Township believed powerful Philadelphians had become obsessed with worldly gain and therefore had lost a Christian sense of true religion and humanity. Many agreed, believing the concentration of economic, legal, and political power placed the public good in peril. Others believed that common people possessed inordinate power in

Philadelphia and Pennsylvania. In this view high wages for free workers and the formation of a political culture in which common people freely engaged in political discourse signaled ordinary townspeople's excessive power. When appropriated by demagogues who utilized a populist rhetoric to advance their interests, this strength portended anarchic disorder. That these contradictory ideas regarding the distribution of power existed in the same place testifies to the importance and flexibility of a concept that, like that of the commonwealth, was fundamental to early modern life.

Making the Early Modern Metropolis examines how, in a particular place and time, individuals and groups competed for power in institutions as well as in public contests over meaning.[50] In addition to analyzing the beliefs and practices emphasized by cultural historians in recent years, I pay additional attention to the rhetoric, genres, and conventions that framed these contests. The form as well as the content of petitions, indictments, grand jury addresses, broadsides, newspaper articles, and pamphlets mattered to their production, reception, and success (or failure). The keywords of the early modern commonwealth discussed above—justice, reasonableness, convenience, neighborliness, the public good—tell us much about the values of early Philadelphians; the forms in which they were expressed are equally significant. Also important, however, is locating changing languages of power in social and material contexts—whether this context was the home, the courthouse, the public sphere, or city streets and squares. Culture was neither autonomous nor simply a reflection of social structure. It was the space in which social reality was constructed, the nexus between economic structure and the making of meaning.[51]

The book is written thematically: the three themes of "Work and Economy," "Law and Disorder," and "Spaces of Pleasure and Danger" constitute the work's tripartite structure. Exploring these interconnected areas of social life in colonial Philadelphia provides a comprehensive analysis of the relationship between social change, institutional development, and cultural formation. This organization also implicitly problematizes the notion of separable orders—the idea that political and legal institutions are of a wholly different order than, for example, print or festive culture. In reality, society and culture are in constant interaction and are ultimately inseparable; laws are created by legislators in response to constituents' demands which, while rooted in material interests, are inevitably informed by systems of belief.[52]

At the founding in the 1680s, Pennsylvania settlers were acutely aware that access to labor power and credit would determine the colony's economic future. Part I, "Labor and Economy," contains the first two chapters, which analyze the development of the Philadelphia economy. Contemporaries frequently commented on the general prosperity in the mid-Atlantic and on the favorable position of artisans in Philadelphia in an urban context of labor demand. Yet the scarcity of currency in the commercial port led to frequent clashes between debtors and creditors, and the formation of an economic culture in which debt and the virtues (or vices) of paper money figured prominently is the subject of the chapter 1. The demand for labor also led colonists to purchase indentured servants and enslaved people, and in Pennsylvania bound workers were concentrated in Philadelphia. The development of unfree labor in Philadelphia—as viewed in a wider Atlantic context of labor commodification, ideological and legal sanctification of property, and imperial war—is the subject of chapter 2.[53]

For many in England and the colonies, adherence to the rule of law distinguished freeborn English people from those who lived in tyrannical systems of absolute rule. The evolution of law and the culture of legalism in Philadelphia is the focus of part II, "Law and Disorder." Chapter 3 examines how traditional attitudes toward law were adapted to the colonial urban environment. While many Philadelphians celebrated their membership in an imperial polity based on law and the English constitution, townspeople regularly ignored provincial statutes and assaulted law enforcement officials. Public criticisms of powerful economic and political interests drew on citizens' longstanding suspicions of law and legal professionals, moreover, and emphasized law's function as an instrument of power. Law's power was equally consequential in terms of crime, the focus of chapter 4. Though Pennsylvania's founding laws were incomparably progressive by seventeenth-century standards, by the 1720s criminal statutes resembled those of colonies throughout the Americas. The exchange of goods and ideas throughout the Atlantic world led Pennsylvania lawmakers to adopt dominant Anglo-American norms concerning the inviolability of property and the concomitant need to mete exemplary punishments to offenders.

The importance of law to English and Anglo-American culture was related to another pervasive early modern concept: that of order. The book's third and final part, "Spaces of Pleasure and Danger," explores how different ideas of order were manifested in Philadelphia's print culture and in the physical spaces of the city. William Penn's founding ideal of order was challenged by religious schism within the Society of Friends as early as the 1690s, and print played an essential role in transmitting this division to the wider urban and provincial population. Despite the creation by the 1730s of a print culture superficially in agreement over the supremacy of British institutions, ideological conflict persisted through the middle of the century and is the focus of chapter 5. The perennial early modern obsession with order as manifested in disputes arising out of the uses of the physical spaces of the city is analyzed in chapter 6. As Philadelphia elites applied metropolitan notions of refinement to the growing city, autonomous "lower-sort" spaces and practices threatened an ideal of genteel order. It was arguably in public sites such as taverns, streets, and squares where competing claims to legitimate practices were most fiercely fought over.

PART I

LABOR AND ECONOMY

1

"NOTHING WILL SATISFY
YOU BUT MONEY"

Community, Credit, and the Politics of Money

By the middle of the eighteenth century, Philadelphia was a famously prosperous British American city. The bustling town was the port through which
much of the produce of the large and fertile Delaware Valley, as well as that of
parts of Maryland and New Jersey, passed on its way to points throughout the
Atlantic world. Colonists continued to send the grains that were Pennsylvania's staple crops mainly to the West Indies, though after the 1730s the colony
increasingly exported foodstuffs to continental Europe and other mainland
American colonies. Growing numbers of immigrants flocked to Philadelphia
and its hinterland between the 1720s and 1760s, as the city came to rival
Boston and New York for economic and cultural urban supremacy in North
America. Farmers from neighboring counties brought fruits and vegetables,
livestock, dairy products, and beef and pork to the biweekly Philadelphia
market. Staves, shingles, iron, pig iron, barrels, and other manufactured goods
passed through the city to coastal and overseas destinations. From England
came an ever-increasing volume of manufactured goods, while rum, sugar,
molasses, cotton, indigo, specie, and bills of exchange and credit arrived from
other American colonies.[1]

General prosperity did not produce an environment free of economic
adversity and political conflict, however. A 1764 petition from inhabitants
of Chester County (bordering Philadelphia to the west and one of the three
original counties Penn created from land purchased from the Delaware tribe)
illustrates the main economic difficulties colonists encountered between the
founding and the 1760s. According to petitioners, the absence of a sufficient
medium of exchange in recent years had produced significant hardship for

most people in the colony. The provincial assembly's emissions of provincial bills of credit beginning in the 1720s had made it possible for merchants, farmers, and mechanics to repay debts and make internal improvements, and since the bills could not be remitted to England they remained in circulation in Pennsylvania. Paper money thus greatly reduced the economic "Hardships and Inconveniences" experienced by ordinary colonists and importantly enhanced the "Welfare and Interest of this City and Province" by facilitating exchange and stimulating development.

Yet the absence of provincial bills in recent years led once again to serious economic difficulties, most importantly the seizure of debtors' properties. Debtors and their families were forced to resort to public charity as a result—a humiliating fate deeply resented by laboring people in the early modern English world.[2] Though petitioners were aware that Parliament's new currency act prohibited colonial governments from printing paper money, they claimed that colonists would nevertheless accept provincial bills "with the utmost Chearfulness" in all contracts.[3] As new and competing ideas about money circulated throughout the British Atlantic world and as colonies printed growing volumes of bills of credit, many Philadelphians believed paper currency uniquely embodied freedom. If monetary scarcity and indebtedness signified oppression and the loss of liberty, paper money connoted independence, improvement, and the common good.

Social historians have noted the growing importance of wage labor and the corresponding decline in servitude and slavery in Philadelphia in the second half of the eighteenth century.[4] Though many people in Philadelphia worked for wages before the 1760s, in a preindustrial system of production in which currency was scarce, the relationship between creditors and debtors was a fundamental determinant of social relations. Daniel Vickers has argued that social tensions in early America were rooted not in markets and issues of property rights but in the "exercise of power," and that these tensions were primarily located in "the instrumentality of credit."[5] Though Vickers's scholarship focused mainly on rural New England, in commercial ports like Boston, New York, Philadelphia, and Charleston access to credit was essential for economic survival. Credit also functioned as a key source of social power, and wealthy urban merchants had most access to regions' cash. Conversely, the condition of indebtedness was a form of dependence, with the specter of default portending a damaging loss of property and bodily freedom. If laboring people, especially those with craft skills, were able to command high wages in early Philadelphia, the absence of money and the possibility of default constituted serious threats to many colonists' liberty.

Economic and social changes in late medieval and sixteenth-century Europe strongly informed Pennsylvanians' beliefs about money and credit, though new economic theories in seventeenth-century England and the dearth of coin in the colonies contributed to a novel colonial monetary environment. The expansion and commercialization of agriculture in Europe beginning in the High Middle Ages, together with the rise of long-distance trade, produced new demands for a medium of exchange. Despite the unique development of agrarian capitalism in England in the fifteenth and sixteenth centuries, the English state remained committed to a "strong money" policy and applied this policy to new American colonies in the seventeenth century.[6] Monetary scarcity in the Americas and colonists' subsequent dependence on complex credit networks were outgrowths of English laws and new methods of exchange based on credit and trust. When the Chester petitioners claimed that after Pennsylvania's founding the "industrious Poor" were often "left to the Mercy of those few Persons who stood possessed of the principal Part of the Gold and Silver in the Colony," they implied powerful men hoarded coin to the detriment of the populace.[7] Hoarding money, like other goods, was a practice that threatened the common good. Many Philadelphians would have agreed with the medieval proverb still prominent in eighteenth-century England: "*Riches* are like muck which stink in a heap, but, spread abroad, make the earth fruitful."[8]

Francis Bacon similarly wrote in the early seventeenth century that in addition to the need to distribute money widely, state regulation of the "devouring trades of usury, ingrossing, great pasturages, and the like" was essential for the maintenance of social peace.[9] The Pennsylvania assembly passed laws regulating interest rates and debt law in the early 1680s, and after its incorporation in 1701 the City of Philadelphia controlled urban markets and the sessions courts where debt cases were heard. After incorporation some Philadelphians thought municipal court fees were as "devouring" as the lending practices of urban merchants. Moreover, the assembly's policies of land seizure and labor service as legal forms of debt repayment led many colonists to believe provincial statutes favored creditors over debtors. Between the 1680s and 1760s mid-Atlantic colonists developed a theory of dispossession according to which powerful interests intentionally kept money scarce in order to appropriate borrowers' land and labor.[10]

Chester inhabitants also published their petition in Philadelphia as a broadside, a cheap publication passed from hand to hand and posted on tavern walls, buildings, and in public squares. Though English people had petitioned the Crown over a scarcity of coin as early as the thirteenth century, it was in the context of the English Revolution in the seventeenth century that printed petitions—some of them protesting the "slavery" of debtors' prison—became key instruments of political propaganda.[11] The Pennsylvania assembly's decision to issue paper money in the 1720s eased many colonists' economic burdens, but it also made locally produced money a crucial issue of social and political contestation. Pamphleteers' plain language in support for paper money confirmed many inhabitants' beliefs in the need for more money; populist publications also lent legitimacy to a theory of merchant dispossession that had developed over the preceding four decades. Some even argued, in contrast to those who maintained a belief in gold and silver's "intrinsic value," that value was actually determined by human labor and that the public good was best served by an abundant supply of paper money. The Chester petition was simultaneously an ancient form of protest as well as a new mode of popular politics reflective of fundamental changes in colonial and early modern society.

Commonwealth, Currency, and Debt at the Founding

At the time of Pennsylvania's founding, English thought concerning colonies and trade was undergoing a significant shift. Between the 1580s and 1640s, advocates for the establishment of overseas colonies argued plantations would enrich the English commonwealth while providing a place for the country's growing population of "wandringe beggars."[12] However, after the mid-seventeenth century, falling prices, increasing wages, and demographic stabilization led economic thinkers to reassess the value of the national population. The statistical studies of John Graunt and William Petty (especially the latter's concept of political arithmetic) exemplified a new belief that the greater part of the nation's wealth lay in "the Value of the People." Rather than the "idle" English population who could be put to better use at home, they suggested unfree laborers—English felons, Irish rebels, and enslaved Africans—should constitute England's New World workforce.[13] During the same period some writers abandoned a traditional consensual model of the commonwealth in favor of theories favoring a "public"—rather than "common"—good, according to which the pursuit of private interest could enrich the nation.[14]

William Penn addressed these intellectual currents in *Some Account of the Province of Pennsylvania*, a 1681 promotional pamphlet dedicated to "such as are or may be disposed to transport Themselves or Servants" into the new colony. Penn prefaced his account with general thoughts on the benefits of colonies in a fusion of classical political philosophy and newer economic ideas concerning profit and improvement. In contrast to those who claimed plantations drained commonwealths of people and wealth, Penn argued colonies were in fact the "Seeds of Nations," citing the ancient Hebrew, Greek, and Roman empires. The cause of great empires' decay was not colonies, but rather domestic "Luxury and corruption of Manners." Neglecting the ancient virtue of industry and instead becoming addicted to "Pleasure and Effeminacy" led to economic ruin, which inevitably followed the people's spiritual degradation and moral debauchery. Similarly, in contemporary England husbandmen and the gentry neglected agriculture, as an urbane and effeminate love of superfluous trifles had replaced a culture that previously prized honest, "Manly-labour." Colonies like Pennsylvania, where labor commanded high wages, offered material comfort to the English poor while also making possible the revival of national greatness—and manliness. Though industrious workers would be the foundation of colonial prosperity, they required the supervision of "Men of universal Spirits" who resembled Greek and Roman colonists of great "Wisdom, Virtue, Labour, and Constancy."[15]

Patriotic idealism was not antithetical to personal enrichment. Penn claimed that overseas plantations had greatly enriched the home country. Cultivated land in Jamaica and Barbados was worth three times that in England, and colonial imports fueled the growth of domestic industry. Plantations created employment for thousands of English workers in the maritime trades, while "many thousand Blacks and Indians" received cloth, tools, and utensils from England. The products of the labor of Africans and Native Americans in turn came back to England, "which adds Wealth and People to the English Dominions" in a virtuous—and evidently free—circle of transatlantic trade.[16] Penn published his plan for Philadelphia privileging initial investors (First Purchasers) around the same time he wrote *Some Account*; 1681 was also the year in which he famously remarked that while his primary goal was to extend religious freedom in his colony, "yet I want some recompense for my trouble."[17] The idea that colonial investment led to improvement and the public good as well as individual enrichment was echoed by Thomas Budd in 1685, when he informed readers that by investing in Pennsylvania and New Jersey "the Rich may help to relieve the Poor, and yet reap great Profit and Advantage to themselves by their doing so."[18]

The public good, social order, industry, and individual profit formed a harmonious whole for the proprietor and other promoters of settlement, and the desired relationship between liberty and material prosperity was borne out by Pennsylvania's unprecedented late seventeenth-century growth. By the end of 1685 approximately eight thousand settlers had arrived in the colony aboard ninety ships, and the population of Philadelphia reached two thousand before the turn of the eighteenth century.[19] Penn wrote shortly after the founding that numerous tradesmen had already constructed a vibrant and bustling town. National diversity (French, Dutch, German, Swedish, Danish, Finnish, Scotch, Irish, and English colonists—the latter equal to the rest—populated the province) and rapid growth had not hindered the creation of an orderly and industrious commonwealth, however. Rising property values—the original meaning of "improvement"—seemingly demonstrated the compatibility of personal enrichment and general well-being.[20]

Pamphlets emphasizing material opportunities for settlers avoided discussion of the economic difficulties that confronted English colonists in America. Though in Elizabethan England a new culture of credit often compensated for a scarcity of coin, debt litigation grew significantly in the late sixteenth century and continued to expand in the seventeenth. Creditors increasingly placed borrowers unable or unwilling to repay loans in debtor's prison, while the conditional (or "penal") bond, in existence for centuries, was put to a variety of new uses, including for debt.[21] One type of bond, the indenture, in which a debtor's body served as a surety against future loss, would be essential in the creation of a labor force in England's American colonies. The abuses this system gave rise to, however—particularly servants' belief that laboring in America was a form of slavery—lessened many people's willingness to emigrate by the 1660s and 1670s.[22] Founding Pennsylvanians were acutely aware of the importance of credit and labor power to colonial economic success.

The idea of legally requiring labor services for the repayment of debts had long been socially unacceptable in England. A polemic against usury published in 1578 (seven years after the Parliament's legalization of usury) made the Aristotelian argument that not only was the breeding of money unnatural, but in ancient Rome "men in debte were compelled to give their bodies into slaverie." The enslavement of debtors led to popular uprisings and the abolition of the practice, a situation—it was implied—likely to occur again should freeborn Englishmen be forced into debt bondage.[23] However, between the 1640s and 1660s Maryland, Barbados, Jamaica, New York, and a number of New England colonies passed laws allowing labor service for the recovery of debts.[24] Though the extent of debt servitude is impossible to quantify, by the 1670s the English practice of selling debtors into servitude was evidently a common feature in some of England's American colonies. Alexander Exquemelin, a former French West India Company employee-turned-pirate, wrote in his best-selling *Bucaniers of America* that an especially "rigorous" practice among the English in the West Indies was the selling of men owing above twenty-five shillings for between six and eight months. According to Exquemelin, in Jamaica the English "do easily sell one another for debt."[25]

William Penn's founding charter for Pennsylvania was a result of negotiations with Friends and investors in London and reflected Renaissance and Restoration-era Quaker reformist thought. Political representatives in the new colony, many of them having had previous trading experience in other English colonies, addressed conditions on the ground in early provincial legislation.[26] Debt repayment and the regulation of labor figured prominently in the new colony's laws. Assemblymen followed English precedent in allowing the seizure of moveable property for debt, though they departed from the common law in also permitting the confiscation of land, likely following a practice established in Massachusetts. Legislators borrowed from neighboring New York when they approved a law allowing those without property to repay debts through servitude, if desired by the creditor.[27] The importance of settlers' investment in labor on credit, possibly motivated by assemblymen's experiences elsewhere in the Americas, was indicated by a ban against the seizure of bound laborers ("white or black") for debt, as bought servants constituted many colonists' principle "means of Livelihood."[28]

Colonists' desire to attract money by raising the value of local currency had frustrated imperial officials prior to Pennsylvania's founding. In 1676 colonial administrator Edward Randolph compared colonies' "liberty of coinage" with the dangerous licentiousness tolerated in the republican 1650s.[29] Despite Randolph's complaints and other colonies' use of "Boston shillings" and Spanish pieces of eight—the latter the most important coin in the Americas—specie remained scarce in the colonies. The Puritan military officer John Blackwell, a Cromwellian supporter of the Commonwealth, immigrated to New England and speculated in land after his Irish properties were revoked during the Restoration. Blackwell advocated for the establishment of a land bank in

Massachusetts to remedy the scarcity of currency, and the Bay Colony's printing of paper money worth £7,000 in 1690 and £40,000 in 1691 set a key precedent for colonial monetary development.[30]

While Blackwell was supportive of a temporary colonial currency to facilitate trade, he was shocked by the economic chaos he found in Pennsylvania
after landing in Philadelphia as lieutenant governor in 1688. Historians have
emphasized Blackwell's inevitable political conflicts with leading Pennsylvania
Friends; his critique of Philadelphians' economic practices has received less
attention.[31] Shortly after his arrival Blackwell wrote to Penn, then in London,
that town merchants sold goods for three to four times the price in England.
This was particularly hard on the "poore people" of the city, who, when they
were fortunate enough to obtain money to purchase imported commodities,
paid four shillings for items costing twelve pence in London—a 400 percent
increase. Prices in Philadelphia were double what they were even in Boston
and were not limited to luxuries but included everyday goods like linen, wool-
ens, hats, and other necessities. In addition to the predatory practices of urban
merchants, lawmakers' practice of raising the value of local money was highly
damaging to the wider system of colonial trade. Blackwell also emphasized that
altering local currency values reduced the value of Penn's quitrents.[32]

Blackwell's letters to the proprietor were phrased in a commonwealth rhetoric that displayed a special concern for common people, who in this case suffered
at the hands of a clique of town merchants. Yet Blackwell's criticism of economic
disorder in the colony paradoxically echoed the promotional pamphlets of the
Welsh Friend Gabriel Thomas. In a tract addressed to England's poor, Thomas
noted wages for laborers of all sorts were much higher in Pennsylvania than in
England, while taxes were low and tithes (a primary object of Quaker hostility
in the 1650s) were nonexistent. Work was available year-round, and skilled
construction workers like carpenters, bricklayers, and masons could earn as
much as five or six shillings a day.[33] For Blackwell, however, laborers' wages
contributed substantially to the colony's economic disorder.[34] For example,
sawyers—traditionally lower-status workmen in England who were in high
demand in new seaports in which ship and home construction were crucial
industries—in Philadelphia obtained three pounds per thousand feet of pine
boards, whereas in Boston the artisans earned between twenty and twenty-five
shillings for the same work.[35] Philadelphia sawyers therefore received wages
approximately three times higher than those in Boston, a good example for
Blackwell of how laborers "consumed" the profits of local traders.[36]

While the cost of living in Philadelphia may have been high—Blackwell claimed he could live more comfortably at half the cost in London—for many potential migrants the prospects for a better life in the new town outweighed potential hazards. In less than a decade the city contained 22 shopkeepers and 119 craftsmen; thirty-five different trades and businesses were conducted in the town. Most craft workers in Philadelphia had previously labored in London, Bristol, Dublin, and other British towns; a number hailed from depressed northern and western English counties where there were large numbers of Friends.[37] Blackwell's representation of economic chaos and antagonisms in the 1680s nevertheless provided a glimpse of power struggles that would persist through the first six decades of the eighteenth century.

Incorporation, Communitas, and Credit

After returning to power in 1660, Charles II revoked and reissued numerous borough charters in an effort to strengthen Crown control over Parliament. A growing chorus of economic writers argued against restricting trades to local freemen and opposed traditional regulations like mandatory seven-year apprenticeships for skilled crafts.[38] Between the Restoration and the mid-eighteenth century, English urban society grew more stratified and its governance increasingly oligarchic. Over the same period, the significance of customary institutions of apprenticeship and guild membership gradually declined. While by the early eighteenth century guilds were generally unable to regulate urban English workforces, they continued to be important social institutions as markers of status, with membership available through purchase or patrimony. Royal officials remained committed to colonial town-building, however, as cities would ideally serve as imperial instruments of civilization and order in sprawling and disorderly American colonies.[39]

The first evidence of Philadelphians' desire for incorporation appeared in a 1684 remonstrance delivered to Penn. Sent by a number of First Purchasers, the document claimed that the proprietor had given them less land than agreed in the "Conditions and Concessions" of 1681, had withheld access to natural resources, and had levied quitrents to which they had never consented. Though founding emigrants braved numerous risks in their travels across the Atlantic and landed in a New World wilderness, through their diligence and industry colonists had done more in two years to advance Philadelphia than had neighboring settlers in decades. Yet "to this day" Philadelphia was "onely a Nominall Citie, having no Charter to Incorporate them, Or grant of the least priviledges of a Corporation."[40]

Colonial merchants and artisans desired incorporation in large part because corporate charters typically granted trading privileges. A key reason New Yorkers wanted a charter for their city was to control the export of grain from the Hudson Valley to the West Indies, for example.[41] In 1691, in response to a "humble Petition" from Philadelphia townspeople that included a number of founding settlers and First Purchasers, Penn granted a charter of incorporation for good government and the "better Regulation of Trade" in the town.[42] Likely abrogated when Pennsylvania was temporarily made a royal colony in 1693, Philadelphia's merchant elite extracted another charter from the proprietor during negotiations for a new provincial constitution in 1701. The broader oligarchic turn in English urban governance was displayed in Philadelphia when the charter made membership in the city's common council hereditary and required two years' residence and property valued at a substantial fifty pounds for urban freemanship. While negotiators received the customary privileges of corporate control over land, courts, and markets, they failed to obtain (or unwisely overlooked) the right to levy taxes. Municipal income would therefore come from fines, fees, rents, and subscriptions. With no regular source of revenue in the cash-poor colonial context, the corporation was, like many inhabitants, regularly in debt.[43]

Historians generally agree that the Philadelphia corporation was ineffectual, and that its oligarchic structure alienated most inhabitants from municipal government. Many Philadelphians undoubtedly resented the corporation, and by the early eighteenth century, residents looked to the provincial assembly rather than the urban common council for the remedy of most civic problems. Incorporation did, however, institutionalize customary urban norms that benefited many inhabitants. In addition to establishing market regulations in weights and measures in the interest of consumers, city government provided employment for a number of urban tradesmen. Meatpackers obtained work measuring grain; masons, bricklayers, carpenters, joiners, and others repaired town wharfs, built a new watch house, and constructed and repaired market stalls.[44]

The charter also granted the city the right to regulate urban trades. In December 1704 the common council ordered that the town's eight carters (which included a "Widow Bristow") "take care" how they drive their carts in the city after some "mischief" from the traditionally unruly transport workers—possibly one or more accidents involving speeding carters. Some months later the council ordered a committee to negotiate with carters for carrying gravel to the city market, with wages to be paid out of public funds. A different committee was ordered to meet and consider standardizing rates for moving goods in the city. Whether rate standardization initially raised or lowered wages, carters and other transportation laborers protested the city's adjustment of their pay in 1719. Carters, draymen, and porters delivered a number of petitions to councilmen "Complaining of the Smallness of their Wages Settled by ye late Ordinance." The council agreed to adjust rates upward for the goods carters transported (the workers were paid by the piece) in Philadelphia's first municipal labor protest.[45]

In an environment of monetary scarcity and lacking the right to tax, the city found it hard to come by even the pence and shillings needed to pay carters. Early in 1705 Mayor Griffith Jones, a Penn appointee, provided overseers of the poor £3 16s 8p out of his own pocket, "they having no money in theire hands."[46] Though membership in the common council was self-perpetuating, the corporation could sell the freedom of the city to local tradespeople to raise money. In July 1705 the city awarded urban freemanship to twenty inhabitants for between 2s 6p and £2 2s 6p. Seven of those admitted (35 percent) were women. That the revenue gained from the admittance was paramount is suggested by councilmen's ordering a committee of aldermen to examine and report on money received from "fines, freedoms or otherwise" immediately following the first collective granting of urban citizenship. Some of the money received by the corporation came from members themselves, who were fined three shillings for missing municipal meetings.[47]

A number of artisans hoped the Philadelphia charter would lead to the incorporation of trades. A municipal committee responded favorably to a petition from coopers requesting incorporation in February 1705, stating the petition was "very reasonable," and that since "large p'gress" had been made by several trades in the town, guild status for coopers would set a good precedent for other city workmen. From the perspective of craftsmen incorporation would regulate wages and provide corporate protection from strangers; for the common council the creation of guilds in Philadelphia would aid in the maintenance of a disciplined and skilled labor force. There is, however, no evidence coopers actually obtained craft privileges. Yet in December the council did concede to petitions requesting that nonfreemen be prohibited from opening shops or working as master tradesmen in the city.[48]

It is probable that there were factions within the municipality that differed over the merits of craft incorporation. Informal and formal organizations of

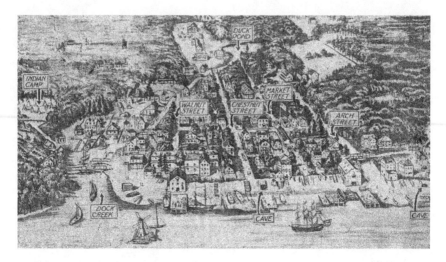

FIGURE 1. Nineteenth-century reproduction of a bird's-eye view of Philadelphia from Camden, New Jersey, circa 1702. The mouth of Dock Creek on the Delaware River is represented at the lower left. Tanneries were located slightly upstream, toward Dock Pond. (*Bird's Eye View of Philadelphia from Camden, N.J.;* courtesy of the Free Library of Philadelphia, Print and Picture Collection)

carpenters, tanners, and others would exist in Philadelphia into the revolutionary era despite the decline of urban regulations, and as the petitions cited above suggest, master craftsmen wanted to maintain the English system of freemanship in Philadelphia. Of the twenty persons admitted in the summer of 1705, Thomas Coleman and George Clark were shoemakers; builder Edmund Woolley (father of the Edmund Woolley who would build the State House in 1753) also joined at this time.[49] The most powerful artisan in Philadelphia, and likely one of the common council's supporter of guilds, was the tanner William Hudson. After emigrating from Yorkshire in 1684, Hudson set up a number of tanneries along Dock Creek, a tributary of the Delaware River that ran through the center of town. In addition to his tanning business, Hudson became a substantial Philadelphia landholder, merchant (which included providing local credit and trading in slaves), and eventually mayor. By the early eighteenth century a close group of powerful and prosperous Quaker tanners, most related to Hudson, inhabited tanyards along "the Dock."[50]

The tanners along the Dock would play a prominent role in Philadelphia's early history, demonstrating how economic opportunity in the New World could clash with customary commonwealth norms.[51] Tanneries were established in Massachusetts, New Netherland, and Virginia by the mid-seventeenth century, and Pennsylvania colonists Gabriel Thomas and Daniel Pastorius noted that the demand for finished leather and the relative abundance of animal hides made leatherworkers in America especially prosperous.[52] Philadelphia tanners' involvement in foreign markets made them objects of censure from other craftsmen, however. In 1704 Philadelphia shoemakers, saddlers, and others sent a petition to the assembly requesting a bill for the "true Tanning of Leather" and a ban on the exportation of locally manufactured leather. Feltmakers wanted a law prohibiting the export of beavers, furs, and match-coats that were "proper and needful to be work'd up" in Pennsylvania, suggesting a belief in the primacy of local employment needs over tanners' market opportunities abroad.[53]

Some years later residents of neighboring Chester County claimed Philadelphia tanners formed an illegal combination for the purpose of sending their goods out of the colony—and therefore raising the price of leather in Pennsylvania. Around the same time Philadelphia curriers protested that city tanners curried their own leather to the detriment of those trained in the craft. The leatherworkers' feud resurfaced again in 1721, when curriers complained of the "irregular practices" of city tanners and asked that the assembly confine the workmen "to the Customs and Practices of *Great-Britain*."[54] Regulatory appeals to the provincial legislature suggest a number of city craftsmen and regional consumers saw some artisans' participation in the wider Atlantic economic system as a threat to just economic practices. These customs privileged craftsmen's right to employment as well as local consumers' access to quality goods and fairly priced products.

Tensions between the Philadelphia corporation's desire to raise revenue and townspeople's protectionism surfaced after the arrival of large numbers of immigrants in the late 1710s. Immigration to Pennsylvania slowed during the War of Spanish Succession (Queen Anne's War in the colonies, 1702–13), but beginning in the late 1710s thousands of German and Irish immigrants arrived in the city seeking relief from religious persecution, the declining availability of land, and rack-renting landlords.[55] Possibly seeing a revenue opportunity in the newcomers, in March 1717 the city ordered the drawing of new statutes for the better ascertaining of terms of freemanship and new fees for the use of public wharfs in the city.[56] Between April and May the corporation granted 424 persons the freedom of the city, only 11 of whom (2.6 percent) were women—a stark contrast to the prominence of women who obtained urban freedom two decades earlier.[57] Though most new freemen arrived from abroad, a number of those admitted—men like Andrew Bradford (son of printer William Bradford),

Edmund Woolley (son of carpenter Edmund Woolley), and Samuel and William Hudson (sons of tanner William Hudson)—were from powerful local families. New arrivals paid between 5s 6d and 15s 6d for urban citizenship; the monthlong event netted the government approximately £220, a considerable sum for the cash-poor town government.[58]

If the money brought by new citizens of Philadelphia in the summer of 1717 eased some of the city government's financial problems, some urban tradesmen saw in the council's plan a threat to their livelihoods as well as to the public good. Artisans complained that strangers who settled in the town were "not Qualify'd" to practice their trades, "notwithstanding their taking out their freedoms." This led to great damages accruing not only to tradesmen who lost work or whose wages declined but also to the public—presumably because of the inferior quality of goods produced by newcomers.[59] The violation of customary norms that protected local producers and consumers through the mass admittance of outsiders to urban freedom closely resembled the language used by leatherworkers in their petitions against city tanners. In this view, consumers' right to quality products were as important to petitioners as were tradesmen's living standards. Indeed, the form of the petition itself required privileging the common good for success.

Another response included a request from city tailors and cordwainers for the incorporation of their trades, "the better to Serve ye Publick in their respective Capacities." Though in his classic history of early American labor law Richard Morris assumes the common council granted the artisans' petition for incorporation, as with coopers earlier in the century there is no evidence the artisans obtained craft privileges.[60] Rather, the council ordered those who desired trade rights to hire legal counsel for the drafting of an ordinance of incorporation, which was to be "Agreeable to ye Laws of England & this Governm[en]t, and for a Publick Good."[61] Rather than simply approve the petition, councilmen required artisans go through a costly legal process for corporate privileges. After the corporation's recommendation no more was heard of the mechanics' request, and after the tabling of a 1727 proposal to better ascertain and establish the privileges of freemanship in the city, municipal regulation of trades—historically lax in Philadelphia and in decline throughout the British world—effectively ceased.[62]

For some recently arrived immigrants, economic challenges came from a different quarter. In early 1723 "poor and honest" people who had left Europe to "obtain a livelihood" in America petitioned the assembly (not the common council) over the hiring out of enslaved inhabitants to do "servile Work" in the city. Petitioners were unable to find employment because of the practice "to the utter ruin of themselves and Families." After a second reading legislators rejected petitioners' request that enslaved people be barred from working "House to House," claiming the request was "injurious to the Publick, as well as to the Right and Privilege of such as keep Negroes."[63] For petitioners, the "ruin" of laboring men and their families signified the necessity of resorting to public relief; implied was the rise in poor rates that would result. Assemblymen's notion of the public good concerned the desire of the urban public for cheap and flexible labor. Granting the petition would moreover be a violation of the property rights of slaveholders, whose privilege of disposing of their goods as they desired was, from assemblymen's perspective, inviolable.

Severe poverty and the need for public relief was rare in Philadelphia before the 1760s, however. The most persistent economic peril for most Philadelphians, as for free colonists throughout the Americas, was the inability to repay debts. While debtors comprised a cross-section of mid-Atlantic society—men and women, merchants and farmers, artisans and day laborers, and even servants and the enslaved—access to credit and cash varied greatly by status, occupation, gender, and race. Many Philadelphians understood that the scarcity of money in the city and region made their economic independence tenuous and that their position was made yet more precarious by government policy at the urban, provincial, and imperial levels. Over the first two decades of the eighteenth century, some townspeople came to view the urban corporation and provincial assembly not as protectors of the commonalty but as defenders of powerful individuals.

A key right granted to Philadelphia with incorporation was control over county courts, and in the absence of taxes, court fees provided an important source of revenue for the municipal government. In early 1705 the common council discussed a new ordinance for determining debts under forty shillings and for ascertaining fees for debtors' court.[64] Six months after the council issued a proclamation raising the fees for the execution of a warrant for debt from three to seventeen shillings, jailed debtors petitioned the new governor, John Evans, in protest. With no money in circulation, petitioners wondered how they were to pay "extravagant" court fees, let alone creditors. "Extravagant" was an important keyword in early modern discourse, signifying the surpassing of the bounds of propriety and in opposition to another essential term: what was "reasonable." Debtors requested—unsuccessfully—that Evans deliver them "out of the Jaws of that pernicious devouring and Extravagant Court."[65]

Hostility to imprisonment for default was not unique to early Philadelphia. The institution of debtors' prison became more prominent with the expansion of credit relations in late sixteenth-century England, and regular debtor petitions and investigations into prison conditions in the eighteenth century culminated with a successful reform campaign in the 1770s.[66] Philadelphia debtors' early eighteenth-century petitions differed from those in England, however. Whereas English debtors typically complained of exploitative jailers, Philadelphians informed Evans that with no money to repay creditors and with excessive new court costs, borrowers were confined until "they could find a person to sell themselves unto for Term of Years to Pay the same and Redeem their bodies to the great Ruine and Destruction of themselves and families."[67] According to petitioners the city government raised court fees with the aim of making payment impossible and thus obtain the labor of debtors or their children.

The amounts Philadelphians borrowed ranged widely, suggestive of the importance of credit to Atlantic commerce as well as to everyday economic life on the local level. In the early 1700s transatlantic traders like the merchants Thomas Callowhill and Jeffrey Pinnoll, originally of Bristol, were "bound" to the draper John Hall and the merchant Thomas Moss, both from London, for the considerable sum of £1,600. More common were artisans like the skinner Thomas Davis, the baker Abraham Roe, and the cooper Thomas Shelley, who bound themselves to creditors for smaller (though not insubstantial) amounts of between fifty and sixty pounds.[68] Wealthy tradesmen like the brickmaker Thomas Sisom, and especially silversmiths like Cesar Ghiselin and Joseph Richardson, provided credit to relatives and laboring townspeople.[69] While such men were essential for the circulation of credit in early Philadelphia, for small borrowers like Joseph Stevenson, Sarah Radcliffe, Susannah Harwood, and George Ward, default likely led to imprisonment and a period of servile labor.[70]

In 1704 Queen Anne attempted to put an end to colonists' monetary licentiousness by issuing a proclamation forbidding American subjects from inflating the value of their currency by more than one-third of its sterling equivalent.[71] The revaluation would have dramatically lowered the value of colonial money, particularly the crucial Spanish American piece of eight. While all colonists would be impacted by the reform, debtors' obligations would be greatly increased if they were forced to repay debts in the new "proclamation money."

When news of the proclamation reached Pennsylvania, a number of Philadelphians immediately petitioned the assembly, stating great "Inconveniences" would fall upon the people if debts made before the queen's proclamation were not payable "in the same Species and Value as our own Law directs."[72] After much debate, in January 1706 assemblymen passed a statute stating debts contracted prior to the proclamation could be paid at rates in force prior to the act, an apparent victory for debtors.[73]

Parliament gave Queen Anne's proclamation force of law in 1708. While the Pennsylvania legislature ratified the act the following year, it was ignored by other colonial governments. (New York in fact printed its first £5,000 in bills of credit in 1709, which was followed by many thousands more over the next decade, a development Pennsylvanians were undoubtedly aware of.)[74] Considerable monetary confusion ensued in Philadelphia. A number of townspeople complained to the assembly that creditors engaged in usurious lending practices, noting lenders demanded new rates despite the statute of 1706 stating local debts could be repaid in preproclamation currency.[75] Legislators acknowledged that many creditors had forced borrowers to discharge debts in proclamation money in order to "take advantage" of the queen's act, and stipulated that a ten-pound fine would be given to lenders who demanded repayment in currency's new value for debts contracted before the Pennsylvania's ratification of the law.[76] Philadelphia landlords continued to demand payment in the new rates, however, leading to renter protests in 1711, 1715, and 1718. Colonists proposed a number of possible remedies to the city and colony's economic difficulties in these years, including banning the exportation of silver, raising duties on imports, raising the value of local money, and—most importantly—producing a local medium of exchange. Yet unlike other colonies, Pennsylvania authorities resisted calls to print paper money.[77]

Only in early 1723 did the legislature finally agree to print £15,000 in Pennsylvania bills of credit, which was followed by another emission of £30,000 toward the end of the year. Historians have emphasized the deep economic recession in the city and colony beginning in 1720 and the formation of a populist alliance in and out of doors behind Governor William Keith in facilitating the paper money emissions.[78] Yet the clashes between creditors and debtors, and landlords and renters, in previous decades provided the social background for the much-studied pamphlet war of the 1720s. The publication of anti–and pro–paper money tracts in this decade expressed longstanding grievances in town and country, giving important ideological support to the belief private individuals monopolized money to the detriment of the commonalty. The establishment of a loan office to distribute bills of credit to landed inhabitants put needed money into circulation, as even critics later acknowledged. Yet this very success encouraged demands for more money to facilitate debt repayment and development, maintaining currency as a political flashpoint throughout the eighteenth century.

The first published work calling for Pennsylvania bills of credit was Francis Rawle's *Some Remedies Proposed for the Restoring the Sunk Credit of the Province of Pennsylvania*, anonymously published by Andrew Bradford in 1721. Rawle's pamphlet argued that a lack of money, a trade imbalance with England, and the lapsing of bolting regulations—which, according to Rawle, benefited New York since West Indian buyers preferred New York's better regulated, and therefore higher quality, flour—had all contributed to Pennsylvania's economic woes. Deploying a conventional commonwealth rhetoric, Rawle emphasized that it was the "common People" who were most damaged by currency scarcity, since their labor was not fairly rewarded and it was primarily their estates that were confiscated and sold after default.[79] Though Rawle argued in scholarly and measured prose for the temporary issuing of a strictly regulated paper money, the following year the provincial council charged Bradford with libeling the government of Pennsylvania by publishing the tract.[80]

Other pamphlets published in the early 1720s by longtime political opponents David Lloyd and James Logan were learned arguments centered on issues of law and sovereignty, specifically the extent of the proprietary's and the assembly's legislative power.[81] Beginning in 1725, however, a series of anonymous satirical dialogues and allegories articulated a populist view of social relations in town and country. Published by the recently arrived Samuel Keimer, the *Dialogue between Mr. Robert Rich and Roger Plowman* (1725) adapted to the colonial mid-Atlantic environment a medieval literary tradition that contrasted the simple farmer with the grasping lord (or in this case the urban merchant).[82] Rich informed Plowman that paper money had nearly destroyed the country, lessening money's value and driving gold and silver from the province. Paper, in contrast to specie, was "good for nothing in itself," and its use would inevitably end in financial ruin. Plowman disagreed, responding in part with the simple assertion: paper money "will purchase Land or the Country Produce as cheap as ever it was sold: And is that good for nothing?" For Plowman, paper money's ability to stimulate the economy and facilitate the purchase of necessities—importantly without a rise in prices—provided a practical material justification for its use.[83]

Plowman also pointed to a fundamental contradiction in colonial society certain to resonate with local debtors: creditors frequently insisted on repayment in cash when "money is not to be got, neither here nor at the *West-Indies.*" In fact, the primary reason city merchants like Rich opposed paper money was because if debtors were able to repay loans, they would not have to surrender their properties for half their worth. Thus, in addition to a popular sense of paper money's utility was the accusation that city grandees designed to engross the province's land and reduce inhabitants to a state of servility. The example of colonies that had printed bills of exchange like New York and Massachusetts belied merchant predictions of economic collapse should paper bills be issued, according to Plowman, and the balance-of-trade problem with England could be remedied by more domestic production and consumption in the future. Linking the interests of local farmers with Philadelphia smiths, shoemakers, tanners, tailors, weavers, and shopkeepers, Plowman attempted to maintain a popular urban-rural alliance established in the early 1720s in opposition to fearmongering elites like Rich.[84]

Indicative of the growing relationship between monetary policy and popular politics was a short satire published in the same year, *The Triumvirate of Pennsylvania, In a Letter to a Friend in the Country.* The author pretended to overhear a secret discussion among the Pennsylvania "Triumvirate" (proprietary men and land bank trustees readers would have identified as Logan, Isaac Norris, and Richard Hill) in a conference room in the House of Representatives. Assembly promoters of a new bill for another currency emission had refused to ask for the triumvirate's approval according to "Pedagogus Matematicus" (clearly representing the bibliophile Logan), evidence that confirmed the "Democracy in the People" and a desire to place all on a level. The triumvirate's "Perquisits" and their expropriation of all the province's "running Cash" were now at risk because of a money bill put forth by a "mobb Assembly." It was therefore essential to smother the "Monster" of paper currency lest the colony's "Rich Men and Merchants" be "reduced to the same Condition of that we had reduced all Tradesmen, Handy-crafts and Farmers before this Emition was thought of."[85] Paper money, in this account, freed common people from a state of bondage manufactured by local grandees. The *Triumvirate of Pennsylvania* also satirized elites' fear of political leveling, establishing an explicit link between currency and political participation. The money issue thus functioned on multiple levels, with bills of credit restoring debtors' liberty while also fostering a popular political culture.

Critics of paper money did attempt to articulate a hard-money position in the vernacular dialogic tradition as a counter to populist polemics. James Logan's *A Dialogue Shewing what's therein to be found* presented arguments for paper money as little more than "a Parcel of clever Words" intended to appeal to simple people who "will believe strongly what they are told is for their Interest." Echoing a traditional complaint against paper currency made by proponents of the intrinsic value of rare metals, the *Dialogue* claimed Pennsylvania bills were "imaginary Stuff," and Pennsylvania's currency had not depreciated only because of the financial tricks of pro-paper traders. Some of those who obtained bills after their printing two years previously now lent them out, and with little circulating cash they demanded poor borrowers repay debts: "Was not that Oppression?" Despite this gesture, the *Dialogue* was unsympathetic to the plight of debtors, and Logan failed to notice the contradiction between his use of plain-spoken characters and a deeply condescending attitude toward ordinary colonists. Money, according to Logan, was a commodity like any other, and any debtor who had something to sell could buy money if they so desired. Hard work and thrift, rather than fictitious paper or drunken railing against merchants and rates of interest, were the solutions to colonists' economic difficulties.[86]

Scholars have attributed the disintegration of the popular alliance between urban and rural forces in Pennsylvania in the 1720s to differences between leaders Keith (a former Jacobite and advocate for royal power based in the city) and David Lloyd (an antiproprietary Chester County Quaker).[87] While these differences were important, disparate views on money and the value of labor between urban renters and rural assemblymen also contributed to the alliance's demise. Before modern banking land functioned as the main security for loans, and Pennsylvania's loan office trustees could only lend bills of credit to possessors of estates "free from all encumbrances whatsoever."[88] Land ownership was thus a requirement of obtaining a loan, and demands for more paper were accompanied by suspicions of loan office trustees' use of their position for personal enrichment, as was claimed in the *Triumvirate*. In 1726 a number of Philadelphia tenants petitioned the assembly (where Lloyd served as Speaker of the House) to decree that the properties they had improved through their labor be used as security for another emission of bills of credit. Assemblymen rejected the petition, however, arguing that because the estates were not freeholds they were not "a proper Security to support the Credit of a Paper Currency."[89] Here was a concrete demonstration of tenants' belief that their labor was a socially useful form of property and that they were willing to mortgage their "improvements" in the city for additional paper money. Provincial representatives, by contrast, remained more traditional in their view of securitized property as rooted in the land.

An open break between Keith and Lloyd occurred around the same time, after Keith was replaced as lieutenant governor by Patrick Gordon. Following his removal from the governorship Keith won a seat in the assembly and soon challenged Lloyd for speakership of the House. Keith's support in Philadelphia was shown after the legislature gathered for the election of Speaker, when the former governor paraded into the city trailed by eighty mounted gentlemen and the town's butchers, tailors, blacksmiths, journeymen, apprentices, porters, and carters. Despite this public display of urban support, Keith lost his bid for the speakership when rural freeholders elected Lloyd by a wide margin. Lloyd's fear of popular reaction in the city was indicated when he asked Governor Gordon for someone to be elected in his place, which the new governor refused. Lloyd then asked Gordon for protection on behalf of the House—not, he said, on account of legislators' debts, but because of "the Insults of the rude People of this City, from whom he thought there was some Danger."[90]

The disappearance of the polarizing figure of Keith from the political scene did not result in the elimination of money controversies and popular politics in Philadelphia, demonstrating instead the evolution of the narrative of money-hoarding and dispossession. *A Revisal of the Intreagues of the Triumvirate*, published in 1729, again accused Logan and other loan officers of engrossing all the money in the province in order to bring tradesmen and farmers into their debt. Debtors were left "to the Mercy of their Tyrants," who "under pretence of Charity" purchased their homes and properties at greatly reduced rates only to then let them out at exorbitant rents. The trustees' purpose was purportedly to place fellow subjects in a state of "Vassalage" that could not be done without "first Suppressing the current Cash of the Province."[91] A response from "Philadelphus" claimed that the story of specie's engrossment had been told in Philadelphia as "often to weak People" as "the Tales of the King and Queen of *Fairies* to Children." Also fantastic was an oft-repeated story in which a city lot and eight acres of Liberty Land were purchased for five pounds and then let out for six shillings per foot annually in perpetuity. That such fanciful stories were believed by the credulous made it essential that men of "Abilities and Circumstances"—meaning the colony's traditional Quaker elite—be returned to the assembly at election time.[92]

In the fall of 1729, as an immigration surge coincided with growing numbers of insolvent debtors in the Philadelphia jail, assemblymen gathered to discuss a new currency bill.[93] When Governor Gordon and the provincial council announced they would only support a bill for £25,000 instead the £50,000 initially requested, rumors circulated that large numbers of farmers planned to descend on the city and join with townsfolk to "overawe the Assembly" and "storm the government and council." Gordon quickly read the riot act, and the feared uprising failed to materialize. Gordon's proclamation blamed recent "Heats and Animosities" on growing numbers of immigrants of "necessitous Circumstances" and a smaller number of "restless Persons amongst ourselves" who disturbed the "mutual Love and Benevolence" that had ostensibly characterized Pennsylvania society since the founding.[94] While significant numbers of immigrants did arrive in Philadelphia in the late 1720s, attributing popular disturbances to strangers through public proclamation was a common strategy for reinforcing social order in early modern England and America.[95] The phrase "Necessitous Circumstances" implied a desperate state of dependency among aliens that Gordon implicitly contrasted with local independent freemen, who need not stoop to mob tactics of intimidation. If the proclamation and the preventative actions of Philadelphia magistrates forestalled direct popular action, events of the previous decade belied Gordon's blaming of the tumult on recently arrived strangers.[96]

Change, Continuity, and Economic Culture at Midcentury

Philadelphia's population and commerce grew significantly between the late 1720s and early 1760s. Between 1720 and 1740 the city's external trade nearly tripled, and in the 1750s and 1760s its exports were increasingly oriented toward Europe, though the West Indies remained the main destination of grains from the "bread colonies" of the mid-Atlantic. During the Seven Years' War, in particular, southern European demand for American cereals enriched Philadelphia exporters: the proportion of urban taxpayers identifying as "gentleman" or "esquire" tripled between 1756 and 1772.[97] Yet the trade imbalance complained of by Francis Rawle in the early 1720s persisted in Pennsylvania and throughout British America as colonists' dependence on English manufactures grew dramatically in the middle years of the eighteenth century.[98] The prosperity visitors frequently associated with Philadelphia at the end of the Seven Years' War was accompanied by high prices and rising costs of living.

By the late 1760s only ten percent of laboring families in the city owned their own homes; laborers and artisans were paying between ten and twenty-two pounds in rent per year.[99]

One expression of urban growth and diversity at midcentury was the formation of new urban social and cultural organizations.[100] Unofficial associations, such as the laboring-class Tiff Club and the aristocratic Gentleman's Club (both founded by William Keith in 1724), served members as spaces of sociability and political discussion.[101] The incorporation of the Philadelphia Carpenters' Company, also in 1724, is evidence for the adaptation of traditional forms of artisanal organization in the eighteenth-century Atlantic world. (The company was modeled after the Worshipful Company of Carpenters of London, incorporated in 1477.) In addition to fostering education in the science of architecture and mutual aid, the Carpenters' Company endeavored to regulate prices and wages so that "everyone concerned in building may have the value of his money, and every workman the worth of his labor."[102] The founding of the Junto (or Leather-Apron Club) by Benjamin Franklin in 1727 similarly indicates the fusion of customary forms of mutual aid among tradesmen and new organizations interested in scientific, moral, and social betterment.[103] In succeeding decades cultural and ethnic associations, from an aristocratic dancing assembly to the St. Andrews Society for Scottish immigrants, demonstrate how organizational life provided Philadelphians with key forms of social and economic capital. Distinctions even *within* social groups were evident, indicated by the creation of a second carpenters' company at midcentury, established by journeymen in an effort to improve the conditions of wage earners.[104]

Master and journeymen carpenters benefited from a midcentury urban building boom. The construction of Philadelphia's first workhouse, a number of new churches, a new State House, and genteel coffeehouses and taverns transformed the physical appearance of the town. James Porteus, member of the Carpenters' Company, was the principal builder of the Palladian Christ Church on Second Street. Edmund Woolley, also a Company member and an inheritor of common council membership, oversaw the construction of the new State House on Chestnut Street.[105] After Porteus and Woolley negotiated with Anglican elites and government officials for the lucrative construction contracts, they would have contracted with master craftsmen for building, who then drew on a growing pool of wage-earning journeymen, day laborers, servants, and enslaved townspeople to work on the project.

As colonists consumed ever-greater levels of imported goods on credit, local producers emphasized the high (and typically English) quality of their wares. Shopkeepers like Samuel Park of Water Street and John Lee of Market Street advertised numerous goods imported from London to be sold "for ready Money or the usual Credit."[106] Beginning in the 1730s, mechanics published notices of their services alongside newspaper advertisements for recently imported goods. In 1737 the immigrant staymaker Thomas Mallabe emphasized that he brought London craft standards and methods to the city.[107] Other artisans, such as the blacksmith Joseph Richardson, made silver spoons, gold buttons, shoe buckles, and other goods for powerful Quakers like Isaac Norris, Israel Pemberton, and James Logan.[108]

As the North American colonies became a major market for British goods, and as colonial governments printed growing volumes of bills of credit, the Board of Trade took a growing interest in colonial affairs. In 1726, in response to Pennsylvania's printing of £45,000 in 1723, imperial officials informed Lieutenant Governor Gordon that bills of credit had been "of very ill Consequence" in other colonies—though, as noted above, Gordon would approve £30,000 in 1729.[109] In subsequent years London merchants complained of colonists' protectionist duties on English imports (measures designed to reduce colonies' trade imbalances); the Crown ordered the duties be repealed.[110] By the end of the 1730s metropolitan merchants sent numerous petitions to the British Parliament over colonists' repayment of debts in provincial bills of credit—despite allegedly importing much gold and silver from the West Indies.[111] Royal officials also ordered Gordon not to allow any new Pennsylvania statutes laying duties on imported slaves and felons, which had contravened the interests of West African traders and Parliament, respectively.[112]

Around the same time, colonial officials worried that information from England concerning metropolitan legal reforms would have disruptive consequences in Pennsylvania. Provincial councilmen carefully discussed a new law for insolvent debtors in 1730, because the Philadelphia "publick Prints" had informed colonists of recent English legislation for the prevention of abuses in prisons. This was a reference to an inquiry into English prisons in 1729–30 led by James Oglethorpe, a Tory reformer who would soon found the colony of Georgia—notably as a refuge for debtors.[113] Councilmen acknowledged officers should avoid excessive cruelty, but they also claimed that since colonial circumstances differed so greatly from those of England, care should be taken not to make the execution of justice too difficult. Though debtors should not be "oppressed with Severities," whether punishments were excessive or not depended in the last instance on whether they helped creditors obtain debts. The delicate nature of the problem was accentuated in Philadelphia by the "odd humours & Tempers" so frequently displayed by those most likely to be jailed for debt.[114]

Also worrisome for councilmen and creditors was Parliament's potential reaction to the longstanding practice of debt repayment through labor. A key problem in legislators' view was that English authorities were unfamiliar with American social relations. In Britain "they are wholly Strangers to Servitude as practised amongst us, or of binding of Persons otherwise than as Apprentices." But in countries where most labor was performed by unfree or wage workers and where "Husbandmen & others" regularly laid out money for "Purchases of this Sort," it was "highly reasonable that People fitt for Labour" should "by the same Method make Satisfaction for their just Debts."[115] While ostensibly beneficial to debtor and creditor alike, some debtors used the new law to claim insolvency rather than labor in servitude. The assembly therefore revised that statute again the following year, after numerous unmarried residents owing small sums "which they easily could have paid by their labor" claimed bankruptcy instead.[116]

Ordinary colonists continued to link customary ideas involving the exercise of power and the social function of money to the instrumentalization of credit. In 1735 "Constant Truman" castigated freemen for being intimidated at the polls by magistrates and loan office trustees—not out of deference and a respect for social hierarchy but because legal and economic authorities made possible the seizure of land and its alienation to "a set of devouring Harpies." In addition to expressing the familiar theme of officials colluding with creditors to defraud honest producers of their properties, the accusation spoke to popular conceptions of money hoarding by claiming such "Harpies" kept "a stock of Money by them, and are always upon the Watch to catch at a lucky Bargain."[117] Truman's claim would have resonated in an early modern context in which piling up money in an environment of scarcity suggested "an unsociable miserliness" that ran counter to the public interest.[118] Moreover, the notion that such hoarding was not simply for social display but rather was designed to buy up the properties of defaulters exacerbated the apparent perniciousness of the practice. According to Truman, it was especially offensive considering it was the farmer and mechanic who "supplies the Merchant, and fits out the Gentleman with all his fine Cloaths, his gay Houses and Furniture, and his Train of Servants and Attendants."[119]

Truman's pamphlet was addressed to freemen: men able to vote, some of whom were eligible borrow paper money from the loan office. Pennsylvania bills of credit were denominated in amounts from three pence to twenty-shilling paper notes, the latter amount the most common in the colonial era. While lower-denominated bills facilitated exchange, small coins remained essential for the purchase of necessities. In the early eighteenth century, the English copper halfpence began to supplement Spanish pieces of eight and Boston shillings in the colonies.[120] By the 1730s Philadelphia merchants believed the local overvaluation of the halfpence attracted the coin from neighboring colonies and threatened to drive silver and gold from Pennsylvania. In the midst of a frigid winter in 1740–41, in which overseers of the poor were unable to provide adequate food and fuel to their charges, a "General Meeting of the Merchants" decided to set the price of the halfpence at eighteen per shilling rather than the customary twelve.[121] While traders hoped a lower value would diminish its quantity in town and country, devaluation would also reduce wages and make goods more expensive. After the meeting, the city's "considerable Dealers" refused to accept the halfpence except at the reduced rate. Shopkeepers followed merchants' example, and soon bakers refused to bake bread until the confusion over the coin was settled. On a freezing Friday in January a crowd gathered and proceeded to march across town, breaking the windows of traders who refused to accept the copper halfpence at the customary rate. The following day large numbers of townspeople gathered for further demonstrations, "but by the Vigilance and Resolution of some of the Magistrates, they were timely surpress'd, and the City has since remained quiet."[122]

Though magistrates subdued the winter demonstrations, popular hostility to devaluation persisted. While both Philadelphia newspapers were silent on the crowd action and the halfpence controversy, a broadside penned by "Dick Farmer" appeared that provides a view of the monetary alteration that Farmer claimed was shared by most colonists. According to Farmer, it was city merchants themselves who imported the copper halfpence in order to pay them out to farmers, millers, and artisans. After distributing the coins to local producers in wages or credit, merchants then refused to accept the halfpence as payment for goods or debts at the same rate. Great "Confusion" arose among "all Sorts" when the coin's value was lowered, but the revaluation was particularly hard on the "poorer Sort of *Labourers*," whose wages were reduced and whose ability to purchase basic necessities were dependent on the pennies. Farmer recommended that the assembly order the loan office to receive the halfpence at the rate of "One Penny each our Currency," which would, in addition to restoring the coin's value, "rescue the People out of the Merchants Power." Appropriating the *vox populi*, the author claimed his proposals were supported by nineteen of twenty persons in the province, and he signed the broadside "in behalf of *Thousands*."[123]

The assembly did not enact Farmer's recommendation, however, and urban tensions over the halfpence simmered into the summer. In June the common council acknowledged the protracted "Disquiet" among townspeople as a result of some traders' continuing refusal to accept the halfpence, and the council decided to implement a compromise. Instead of eighteen to the shilling, the board proclaimed the halfpence would thereafter be accepted at fifteen to the shilling, which would ideally avoid the importation of the change while also preventing the pennies from being entirely driven from the province.[124]

Mayor Samuel Hassell's proclamation regarding the compromise indicates a desire among urban officials to address popular discontent while maintaining and reinforcing merchant economic and political authority. As Hassell's declaration was reported in the *Mercury*, "some uneasy and ill-disposed Persons, without any Authority or Consent of the trading Part of the Province," were attempting to lessen the value of the halfpence. Until the value of the coin was definitively settled by legal authority, "or general Agreement among the trading Persons and Inhabitants of the Province," anyone who refused to accept the currency at the stated rate was to be considered a disturber of the public peace.[125] While the initial winter plan to devalue the halfpence was devised at an unofficial meeting of city merchants, the common council's summer proclamation oddly claimed that devaluation was being practiced without law or the consent of the "trading Part" of the colony. Hassell's disavowal of the devaluation attempted to appease the populace while portraying those who accepted the coin at the reduced rate as a minority of "ill-disposed Persons."[126]

In the two decades following the halfpence controversy, Philadelphia became North America's largest city and the continent's urban center of Atlantic commerce and industry. While the consumption of imported English goods became important sources of British identity, local economic development contributed to the formation of an artisanal civic consciousness among Philadelphians. Near the waterfront and close to the city's twelve shipyards, smaller industries—blacksmith shops, foundries, ropewalks, tanneries, distilleries, breweries, carriage shops, cooperies, fulling mills—catered to the needs of the urban population.[127] By this time Philadelphia artisans had gained a reputation as the finest craftsmen in British America. Between the 1750s and 1770s, many artisans in New York stressed in newspaper advertisements that they were either from Philadelphia or made "Philadelphia Earthen-Ware," "Philadelphia Brass Buttons," and "Philadelphia Buttons and Shoe Buckles."[128]

No individual better exemplifies this artisanal civic consciousness in early Philadelphia than Benjamin Franklin. And for Franklin, as for many Philadelphians, the issues of currency, class, and improvement were intertwined. In his autobiography, first published in 1791, Franklin claimed his 1729 pamphlet *A Modest Inquiry into the Nature and Necessity of a Paper-Currency* supporting bills of credit was "well receiv'd by the common People" of Philadelphia, while the "Rich Men dislik'd it."[129] The pamphlet followed William Petty and other Restoration-era improvers in arguing that the laboring classes were "the chief Strength and Support of a People," but a dearth of money would discourage laboring people from settling in new colonies like Pennsylvania. Yet Franklin also cautioned readers against a prevalent hostility toward gentlemen in the city. Those opposed to bills of credit were not primarily the rich but rather lawyers and others who made their money from "Court Business," since an abundant supply of cash meant fewer lawsuits for debt. The problem was therefore not elite creditors or politicians but those in the legal profession—an easy target in the early modern world.[130]

Between winning the government contract to print Pennsylvania bills of credit in 1730 to his retirement from printing in 1764, Franklin printed fifteen issues of Pennsylvania paper money totaling almost two million pieces, in addition to printing hundreds of thousands of pieces for Delaware and New Jersey.[131] Curiously, however, in his influential essay "The Way to Wealth," which first appeared in the 1758 edition of *Poor Richard's Almanac* and addressed the chronic issue of indebtedness, no mention of currency is made.[132] In the essay the plain-speaking Father Abraham addresses visitors to a merchant auction and cautions them against a dangerous spirit of luxury among colonists that often leads to debt and the loss of freedom. Abraham's representation of debt bondage would have been familiar to many in Philadelphia: "Your Creditor has Authority at his Pleasure to deprive you of your Liberty, by confining you in Gaol for Life, or to sell you for a Servant, if you should not be able to pay him!" Yet according to Abraham, debtors' loss of liberty resulted from a lack of thrift and a love of superfluous trifles, not a scarcity of cash or the machinations of creditors. "Way to Wealth" individualized and depoliticized what was historically a highly contentious issue in Philadelphia and the mid-Atlantic region.[133]

Franklin's essay was a popular example of a growing literature advocating liberal economic principles and policies. Currency retained its political salience in Philadelphia and the colonies through the mid-eighteenth century and beyond, however. One of the most radical midcentury views regarding paper money was articulated by the Philadelphia writer, editor, and lawyer John Webbe.[134] Unlike most of his contemporaries (including many supporters of bills of credit), Webbe claimed law and public acceptance had made provincial bills of credit *actual* money. Since Pennsylvania's paper bills did not promise specie or anything else at a future date, the notes had themselves become money. Silver was actually inferior to paper as a form of currency, and true value was embodied in the goods and land improved through human labor, not in precious metals. Labor and people, rather than silver and gold, were the true sources of "intrinsic value." Landholders and manual laborers alike benefited from an abundant supply of money; merchants—"as well as usurers or money-jobbers, land-jobbers and super-numerary officers, with their tribe of retainers and dependents"—were the ones who profited from scarcity.[135]

Webbe, though addressing an "intricate" and "abstruse" subject, tried to make a "plain" argument about the function of money in an attempt to reach a broad audience. Yet he spoke primarily for the interests of propertied freemen, craftsmen like the brewer Timothy Mattack, who in 1751 was indebted to no less than sixty-one people. If unable to repay his numerous debts by 1754, Mattack's real and personal property was to be seized and divided among creditors.[136] For those without property, debt default still meant incarceration and forced labor. In the early 1750s the German visitor Gottlieb Mittelberger marveled at the annual increase in homes, ships, and churches in Philadelphia and emphasized workers were well-rewarded for their labor. Yet Mittelberger's astonishment at the city's prosperity was matched by his shock at the extreme penalties for failure to repay debts. A propertyless debtor was sent to prison "till someone vouches for him, or till he is sold," and service for a year or longer was normal for a debt of five pounds. Borrowers' children, regardless of age, were sold into servitude until age twenty-one.[137] Mittelberger's characterization of debt servitude was remarkably similar to that of Philadelphia debtors half a century earlier. If for many townspeople John Webbe's thoughts on paper money spoke to their experience and affirmed the virtues of paper money, Mittelberger's criticism also reflected longstanding practices that, for those lower down the social scale, typified the difficulties of economic life in the early modern city.

Pennsylvania legislators began to discuss a new paper money emission in the early 1750s. As a member of a legislative committee tasked with looking into more bills of credit, Franklin noted that while the striking of paper bills in earlier years was beneficial to the public, the making of loans (and by implication land) widely available to the industrious poor also made labor dear.[138] By 1755 the province's bills of credit had become "so torn and defaced that the currency thereof is almost stopped," so the assembly agreed to issue £10,000 to remedy the "inconveniency."[139] Between 1756 and 1759 Pennsylvania issued an astonishing £285,000, though these emissions were for the Crown's use in the context of the Seven Years' War. In 1764, after the war's conclusion, the assembly agreed to another £55,000, though this too was reserved for frontier defense.[140] Yet the bills furthered colonists' changing experience with money, providing additional evidence that money was something social and political rather than transhistorical and intrinsic. Like corporate governance and laws regulating crafts and debt, monetary policy could serve either public or private interests.

Conclusion

Pennsylvania legislators borrowed from English law and the statutes of other colonies to shape their colony's debt and labor laws. Their reluctance to issue provincial bills of credit, together with the colony's system of debt repayment, fostered the creation of a unique theory of dispossession according to which creditors lent money with the intention of appropriating borrowers' land and labor. This belief evolved after the assembly's emissions of bills of credit in the 1720s, as popular hostility was directed toward land bank trustees and those who opposed further additions of paper money. For many townspeople, the prosperity celebrated by midcentury visitors to Philadelphia remained contingent on customary political practices like petitioning and protest, as well as on a provincial government willing to use its power to make money and enforce its acceptance in contracts.

Historians have emphasized that social relations in Philadelphia and Pennsylvania were profoundly altered between the 1760s and 1790s as urban workers undertook modern trade union activity and engaged in strikes for the first time.[141] Before wages and working conditions became fundamental economic issues for laboring people in the city, social tensions centered on relations between creditors and debtors. The centrality of currency to early Philadelphia social relations demonstrates how, in the early modern Atlantic world, conventional ideas concerning credit and the function of money evolved in a new context of currency and labor scarcity. Land seizure and forced labor as forms of debt repayment were, from debtors' perspective, forms of bondage whose roots lay in the disproportionate power of economic and political elites.

Philadelphians like Benjamin Franklin were pioneers of policies of improvement and increasingly articulated classical liberal economic ideas. Yet a linear narrative of economic modernization is complicated by the histories articulated by Chester petitioners in 1764. Addressed to "the people" as well as legislators, Chester colonists framed Pennsylvania's history in terms of money supply, debt, and the common good. If for self-made artisans like Franklin Philadelphia was a place of individual and civic improvement, for many the instrumentalization of credit portended a damaging loss of freedom. Some, like Franklin's contemporary John Woolman, used the press to argue for a society that eschewed excessive labor and the perpetual striving for wealth. High rents and interest rates continued to act as "snares to tenants" in the 1760s, as wealthy men too often abused their economic power. Woolman believed that "True wisdom" and harmony lay in a balance between physical labor and the cultivation of the mind.[142]

If money (or its absence) could function as an instrument of power as well as provide a distinct use-value and embody freedom, the connection made by many city inhabitants between credit relations and bondage was accentuated by the existence of unfree forms of labor unique to the urban mid-Atlantic context. The denial of liberty—a kind of slavery—that many associated with an inability to repay debts would not have had the force it did in Philadelphia culture if unfree labor was not a crucial component of urban society.

2

"A GREAT NUMBER OF HANDS"

Property, Empire, and Unfree Labor

The same conditions of currency and labor scarcity that fostered frequent arguments over debt and monetary policy also led Philadelphians to invest heavily, often on credit, in unfree labor. Bound workers in Pennsylvania, both indentured servants and the enslaved, were concentrated in Philadelphia from the founding through the American Revolution. While in the town's first two decades indentured servants outnumbered enslaved people, between the 1720s and 1760s there were more slaves than servants in the city. Philadelphia's relatively late origins in the 1680s and arriving merchants' trading experience in Barbados, Jamaica, Massachusetts, New York, and New Jersey meant that many settlers were familiar with bound labor. While less important to the local economy than in the West Indies, Chesapeake, or Lowcountry, at the peak of the practice in the 1730s and 1740s, bound workers constituted close to a quarter of the Philadelphia population and an even higher percentage of the urban labor force.[1] The labor of servants and the enslaved was crucial to the city's economic and social development, as provincial law and urban culture testify.

Scholarship reflects the abundant evidence that exists for the formation of new social, legal, and racialist theories justifying coerced labor in the seventeenth and eighteenth centuries. Documentation of the beliefs and experiences of unfree workers is by contrast extremely rare. One notable exception to this paucity is the autobiography of William Moraley, an English watchmaker and indentured servant in Philadelphia and the mid-Atlantic in the late 1720s and early 1730s. Possessing a level of literacy unusual among eighteenth-century working people, Moraley's ambivalent, ironic, and picaresque portrayal of life in the middle colonies is one of the most thorough accounts of servant life in the early modern Americas.[2] Like the early promoters of immigration to Pennsylvania, Moraley marveled at the wages commanded by free workers in the colony. He also celebrated colonists' spirit of neighborliness and generosity, as well as the fact that "delectable Fruits" grew in abundance throughout Philadelphia (the "*Athens* of Mankind") and were common to all, ordinary traveler as well as rich citizen.[3]

Moraley also emphasized for his English audience that colonists' prosperity and generosity were built on a foundation of unfree labor. In the early period of colonization, "there was a Necessity of employing a great Number of Hands" for the clearing of hundreds of miles of woodland. The few early settlers were insufficient for the huge task of bringing the land under cultivation, however; they were therefore obliged to purchase English servants as well as "Multitudes of Negro slaves from *Africa.*" Servants were initially granted "great Immunities" as well as land at the expiration of their terms of service, in contrast to enslaved Africans. At present Americans were "the richest Farmers in the World," largely because colonists neither paid rent to landlords nor gave "Wages either to purchased Servants or Negro Slaves"—the implication being that relatively wide land ownership and minimal labor expenses were a critical foundation of American wealth. Instead of finding rack-rented farmers, visitors to America "will taste of their [planters'] Liberality, they living in Affluence and Plenty."[4] How Moraley acquired this theory of historical development is a fascinating, if unanswerable, question. It seems probable, however, that the narrative was part of an oral tradition according to which unpaid labor produced a New World society of abundance and wealth.

This historical development corresponded to Moraley's assertion that while considerable wages and relative material comfort were available to mid-Atlantic artisans and journeymen, the experience of those who labored in bondage was equally exceptional. That Moraley found it remarkable that those who worked in both servitude and slavery received no monetary remuneration testifies to the importance of understanding working life and the concept of wages in their historical and cultural contexts. Servants typically earned wages, and in seventeenth- and eighteenth-century England they not infrequently sued delinquent masters for unpaid earnings. By the time Moraley decided to "sell himself" into service in the American plantations in the 1720s, it was common for English servants to live outside the master's home.[5] In addition to receiving no monetary compensation for their labor, servants in America had little recourse to law; colonial magistrates almost never ruled in favor of servants in disputes over masters' noncompliance with indentures. Moraley found through experience that protests against masters produced for the servant only "Licks for his Pains." Servants in America also frequently ran away, despite the near certainty of capture and being forced to work an extended period of time as a punishment for flight.[6]

Servants' pains were however small compared to those of the enslaved. Moraley noted that slaves were brutally punished for the "least Trespass"; for flight (which, as with servants, regularly occurred despite the near certainty of capture) the punishment of whipping not infrequently resulted in death, and masters went unpunished for killing the enslaved. While rural slaveholders allowed slaves to marry and cultivate a small plot of land, according to Moraley these were practical strategies designed to pacify the enslaved population and discourage flight. Permitting the enslaved to procreate reproduced the labor force cost-free, for "all their Posterity are Slaves without Redemption." The "very hard" and "very bad" conditions of servants and slaves, respectively, contrasted markedly with Moraley's famous depiction of Pennsylvania as "the best poor Man's Country in the World."[7]

Moraley's remarks on slavery were not specific to Philadelphia or Pennsylvania; they were designed instead to provide an English audience with a general picture of life in British America. What Moraley's account provides is a unique perspective on the process of labor commodification and the resulting disempowerment of servants in British America generally and in the mid-Atlantic specifically. The treatment of labor power as a saleable commodity was not a colonial innovation; the development of a money economy and the growing prominence of wages in England in the fourteenth and fifteenth centuries encouraged some writers to represent labor as an alienable species of property.[8] By the second half of the seventeenth century, a belief in the individual's freedom to sell their labor as a good like any other was well entrenched among political, legal, and economic thinkers. After the Restoration, and especially in the decades after the Revolution of 1688, political writers applied liberal theories of individual property rights to the Atlantic slave trade and to human captives themselves.[9] Yet according to Moraley, bound workers' lack of rights and recourse to law greatly distinguished America from England.

Like other colonists, Pennsylvanians espoused an English ideology of liberty and property and applied their belief in the sanctity of property to bound workers.[10] Labor in Philadelphia was distinguished by its diversity of forms (slavery, servitude, apprenticeship, wage labor) and workers' disparate origins (England,

Ireland, Scotland, Germany, West Africa, the Americas) in a densely populated urban environment. Significant public oversight of bound labor, together with the gradual formation of antislavery sentiment, also distinguished the urban environment of Philadelphia from rural colonies where masters had wide discretionary powers over unfree laborers.[11] At the same time, the legal edifice constructed by Pennsylvania lawmakers reflected the interests and beliefs of propertied freemen, leading to the social and legal marginalization of servants and slaves noted by Moraley. Midcentury wartime contexts most dramatically revealed the contradictions of bound labor in the city. The British enlistment of servants in the 1740s and 1750s into the army produced bitter recriminations from assemblymen, who argued that servant labor was as sacrosanct as any other. Enlistment also revealed the extent to which indentured servants believed local masters lacked humanity. The emergence of new antislavery voices during the Seven Years' War coincided with mass servant enlistment, the cutting off of servant imports from Europe, and a subsequent surge in the importation of enslaved Africans. The decline of bound labor in Philadelphia and Pennsylvania after the 1760s was a product of long-term economic processes as well as local struggles.

Making an Urban Labor Regime

The initial institutional framework for labor in Pennsylvania was a mixture of customary forms of service, Quaker idealism, and agrarian organization borrowed from other colonies. Christopher Tomlins has noted that Penn's 1682 charter for the Free Society of Traders, a group of Quaker investors in London, resembled quasi-feudal Elizabethan and early Stuart schemes in Ireland and Virginia.[12] In its first year the Society of Traders planned to import two hundred laborers to work its twenty thousand acres of Pennsylvania land. Enslaved Africans held by the society would be freed after fourteen years, after which they were to turn over two-thirds of their produce to the traders.[13] Indicative of the inchoate status of race and the institution of slavery in the early 1680s, the society's charter did not assume the condition of slavery would be permanent.[14] The plan to make African-descended workers proprietary serfs after a very long period of service may have been intended primarily for appearances, however. Society member and coauthor of the charter's preface, James Claypoole, noted in 1682 (the same year the charter was issued) that a major benefit of enslaved workers was that they were held for life.[15] Three years later

Penn, a slaveholder himself, commented favorably on the holding of "blacks" in perpetuity.[16]

More numerous than enslaved Africans were the thousands of servants (approximately one-third of all immigrants to the colony) who arrived in Philadelphia between 1682 and 1686.[17] The Laws Agreed Upon in England fused customary English master-servant relations rooted in paternalistic notions of reciprocity with colonial practices regarding freedom dues and the "custom of the country." Between the 1620s and 1650s Virginia, Barbados, and Maryland established customary practices regulating the goods provided bound workers after the end of service, known as freedom dues.[18] The Carolina Concessions of 1665 granted servants forty acres of land at the expiration of their terms; the following year Robert Horne claimed in a promotional pamphlet that male servants obtained a hundred acres of Carolina land in perpetuity and paid only a halfpence annually per acre in rent. Female servants received fifty acres on the same conditions; both men and women were additionally given two suits of clothing and necessary tools "according to the Custom of the Countrey."[19] Pennsylvania offered servants a fifty-acre headright and, after paying taxes to the colonial government and cultivating twenty acres, they were awarded freemanship status and even the right to stand for provincial office. That the statute used the feudal designation of "scot and lot" to describe taxes while also making it possible for former servants to be elected to the assembly is indicative of the fusion of old and new in early Pennsylvania.[20]

Though colonial governments enacted policies for freedom dues in a discourse of custom, actual practices were subject to significant alteration over the course of the seventeenth century. Changes most often involved the withdrawal of rights to land. After 1626 Virginia's custom of the country no longer provided former servants with land; in Maryland fifty acres on the expiration of service was no longer obligatory after 1663. After 1687 servants in South Carolina received one suit, one barrel of Indian corn, one axe, and one hoe—but no land.[21] In the flurry of legislation in 1683 (and just one year after Penn and investors agreed to the founding laws), Pennsylvania assemblymen revised the colony's terms of service and freedom dues. Servants arriving in the colony without indentures would serve for five years if over seventeen years of age; those underage would work until twenty-two. At the expiration of service, masters were to provide a suit of apparel, ten bushels of wheat or fourteen bushels of Indian corn, an axe, and two hoes. While considerably more generous than South Carolina's revised custom of the country, similar was the absence of any mention of land.[22]

Servants in Philadelphia's first decades were generally successful in establishing an independent competence after the expiration of indentures, however. Many servants who arrived in Philadelphia in the 1680s were already skilled in carpentry, smithing, masonry, and other trades.[23] While technically servants, these laborers were generally older and worked in very different conditions from traditional apprentices and journeymen in the comparatively urbanized British Isles. Despite a continuing demand for labor in Philadelphia, on the expiration of terms servants were more likely to settle in nearby Bucks, Chester, and Philadelphia Counties than remain in the city.[24] This preference testifies to the cultural importance of independence from having to labor for wages in the early modern Anglo-American world. While wages were relatively high in the town, the prospect of obtaining a rural competence remained more appealing for most. Indeed, the Welsh Quaker Gabriel Thomas's use of the term "servant" to describe workers of "all sorts" who commanded high wages in Philadelphia and Pennsylvania at the end of the seventeenth century indicates the state of dependence implied in the wage relationship.[25] While historically connoting those who lived with masters and were unmarried (as distinct from wage-working artificers and laborers), by the early eighteenth century the term "servant" was often used in a broader sense that included those who labored for wages.[26] If former indentured servants preferred to relocate to neighboring counties rather than remain in Philadelphia, they likely practiced by-employments in Bucks and Chester, working the land at planting and harvest time while engaging in crafts when time allowed.[27] However, possession of land made temporary and seasonal wage work supplemental rather than central—a key distinction.

In addition to servants who completed their contracts and left the town were those who ran away. Bound laborers had fled the Chesapeake as early as the 1620s, and by Philadelphia's founding the mid-Atlantic region and New England had become destination points for fugitives from tobacco plantations to the south.[28] The first law passed in 1683 regarding servitude concerned banning the sale of servants outside the province, while the second, as noted in chapter 1, disallowed the seizure of unfree workers for masters' debts.[29] A law regarding runaways passed at the same legislative session at Penn's suggestion significantly differentiated Pennsylvania labor policy from that of other colonies. In contrast to Virginia and New York, where runaway servants were punished with two days of service for every day missed (punishments far more punitive than in England, where runaway apprentices were simply required to serve out their terms), in Pennsylvania absent laborers were to serve five extra days for every day missed. Servants also had to compensate masters for all charges incurred in their capture, a stipulation extending terms of service still more.[30] Moraley portrayed this difference five decades later when he dramatized the "hot Pursuit" that followed servants' flight as well as the substantial rewards offered for capture; the latter was followed by a justice's settling of expenses, resulting in a significant extension of service.[31]

In the 1680s and 1690s, however, evidence suggests more fugitives ran *to* Pennsylvania than from it. During the Nine Years' War (King William's War in the colonies, 1688–97), soldiers stationed in New York abandoned the colony bordering French Canada and fled to Pennsylvania. New York governor Benjamin Fletcher complained that Pennsylvanians harbored and employed soldiers absconding from New York. According to Fletcher, Friends' ostensible desire to protect fugitive soldiers (who would be subject to the death penalty for desertion) was a humanitarian cover for hiring runaways as workers. Not for the last time, imperial officials found Pennsylvania Quakers' professed opposition to arms be little more than a pretense for worldly gain.[32]

The next interimperial conflict, the War of Spanish Succession (Queen Anne's War in the colonies, 1702–13), produced more frictions between Pennsylvania colonists and the Crown. As Pennsylvania assemblymen and royal officials argued over whether the colony was required to supply support for the conflict's American theater, a number of servants enlisted in the army in an effort to obtain liberty. Compensation for masters whose servants crossed the Delaware to volunteer in New Jersey was a key component of the Pennsylvania assembly's decision to provide £2,000 for Queen Anne in 1711, after years of resistance to England's repeated demands for support. Although the act required all freemen to contribute twenty shillings to support the Crown, regardless of wealth or rank, the "great inequalities and hardships" that fell on masters whose servants volunteered made them eligible for ten shillings per month of workers' time absent, or up to twenty pounds total, if they could produce indentures.[33] A pattern was set that would recur with more force later in the century: demands from London during an interimperial war caused tension between provincial and metropolitan authorities, and hostilities were exacerbated by servants' usage of the wartime environment to attain freedom.

The colonial demand for labor meant that few Philadelphians hesitated pur-
chasing slaves if they could afford them. Colonists quickly purchased the first
shipment of 150 enslaved Africans to arrive in Philadelphia aboard a Bristol ship
in 1684, for example.[34] Though evidence in these early years is sparse, Gary Nash
and Jean Soderlund have estimated that by the first decade of the eighteenth century enslaved people comprised more than 10 percent of the urban population,
and before 1706 nearly three-fourths of the leaders of the Philadelphia Yearly
Meeting owned slaves.[35] At this time only the wealthiest urban residents could
afford to purchase captive Africans, and in contrast to rural Pennsylvania, where
enslaved males predominated, in the city sex ratios among enslaved persons
were more balanced, with slavery primarily a domestic institution.[36] While William Moraley and other visitors noted rural slaveholders often allowed enslaved
people to marry, for those in the urban context of Philadelphia, family and communal formation was extremely difficult. As with the rest of the urban population, growth would come through immigration rather than natural reproduction.

Despite significant obstacles, by the 1690s Philadelphia's African-descended
population had established a distinct community.[37] Philadelphia's urban setting, in which news circulated quickly, made it likely that the town's enslaved
population was aware that some local Quakers were opposed to slavery; some
Friends publicly condemned the institution before the turn of the eighteenth
century. Enslaved Philadelphians certainly knew of the public dispute created
by the Scottish Friend George Keith and his supporters, who attacked the
slave trade and the Quaker slaveholding establishment in the 1690s.[38] Enslaved
inhabitants probably also heard of the case of "a certain mulatto" taken from
the Spanish by an English privateer in the West Indies who arrived in Philadelphia in 1703. Like many "Spanish Negroes" captured by the English in colonial
wars, the prisoner petitioned Pennsylvania authorities and claimed that he was
"born free, of free parents, had ever lived so, and could not be now made a
slave by his capture, but a prisoner of war." After a reading of the petition, the
provincial council found the man's application and evidence for his freedom
unconvincing, and he likely remained in slavery.[39] In the years surrounding
1700, in Philadelphia as in New York City, African-descended sailors from
Spanish ships were apprehended and forced into bondage. These discontents
were viewed in both cities as a potential fifth column during Britain's midcentury wars with continental Europe's Catholic powers.[40]

Native Americans in the Delaware Valley protested Pennsylvanians' importation of enslaved Indians from the southern colonies around the same time,

leading the assembly to prohibit the practice in 1706.[41] (The act was careful to stress, however, that Native slaves fleeing to Pennsylvania would not be covered by the act.) In the same year a tax of six shillings per slave was placed on the importation of captive Africans; the duty was raised to forty shillings in 1711.[42] A decade later a number of Friends petitioned the assembly to ban the African slave trade in Pennsylvania, and Robert Southeby took the radical step of calling for the total abolition of slavery in the colony. The House responded that it was "neither just nor convenient to set them at liberty." Representatives argued that slaveholders would be unjustly deprived of their human property if slaves were freed, while also emphasizing the importance of slave labor to the "publick"—reasoning identical to that used two years later in response to day laborers' petition against hiring out the enslaved.[43]

Reform did occur in 1712, though not as a result of local Quakers' agitation. In April of that year a group of Coromantee and Pawpaw rebels from the Gold Coast of Africa, in league with "Spanish Negros" John, Hosea, and Ambrose, killed nine people in New York City in an attempt to foment a slave uprising. News of the rising quickly reached Philadelphia, as did descriptions of the brutal executions of twenty-one insurgents.[44] Pennsylvania lawmakers addressed rebellions not only in the West Indies but on the mainland of North America and specifically in New York by passing a law placing a prohibitive duty of twenty pounds on "every negro or Indian" imported to the colony. Violent action on the part of the enslaved in a neighboring colony, rather than Quaker petitions, first moved Pennsylvania authorities to limit the presence of African slaves in the colony. As with other provincial legislation with the potential to negatively impact metropolitan economic interests, however, the act was repealed by the Crown the following year.[45]

The importance of domestic labor to the institution of slavery in Philadelphia before the 1720s is indicated in part by the ways in which the actions of enslaved people were incorporated into an existing English discourse regarding children and servants. When Philadelphia magistrates complained in 1693 that slaves frequently traveled at night without permission and were often found "gadding abroad," they applied a conventional English discourse of servant recalcitrance and the overindulgence of masters and mistresses.[46] In 1695, when the Philadelphia grand jury ordered the drawing of a warrant for use by the night watch, it lumped "Negroes" together with other "loose people" found "playing about" on the streets on Sundays. Similarly, in the early eighteenth century, youths and servants whose festive practices disrupted the

Sabbath were associated with the "great multitudes" of slaves who congregated at the end of the work week.[47] In the early eighteenth century, on the tobacco plantations of the Chesapeake, masters began to imagine enslaved Africans as members of an extended family under the dominion of a benevolent patriarch; in contrast, in cities like Philadelphia unruly enslaved people were grouped by town officials with women, children, and others allegedly lacking self-control and therefore needing restraint. While the legal system in Pennsylvania came to reflect the commodification of labor occurring throughout the Atlantic world, for some Philadelphians the activities of bound workers and efforts to stop them formed one part of a perennial struggle against lower-sort disorder. A crucial difference, of course, was that over the course of the late seventeenth and early eighteenth centuries Philadelphia and Pennsylvania laws stripped Black people of all legal rights, in stark contrast to English servants.[48]

New Populations, New Representations: Strangers, Servants, Slaves

In contrast to slow population and economic growth in Pennsylvania occasioned by war in the early eighteenth century, the period between 1714 and 1739 was a time of increased immigration to the colony and the first period in which large numbers of Irish and German migrants landed in Philadelphia.[49] In the late 1710s drought combined with British restrictions on Irish trade, high food prices, and rising rents facilitated the immigration of thousands of Irish Protestants to the Americas, with a majority landing at the port of Philadelphia. After a brief lull immigration resumed after 1724, and in the famine years of 1728 and 1729 thousands of Irish migrants disembarked at Philadelphia.[50] German immigrants also arrived in Pennsylvania in significant numbers beginning in the 1710s, with the largest groups arriving in 1732, 1733, 1738, and 1741.[51] This was also the period in which the redemption system, in which immigrants could find someone to pay their passage and "redeem" their person or enter into contracts of service, came into widespread use in Philadelphia.[52]

The influx of non-English immigrants after Queen Anne's War produced mixed reactions in Philadelphia. While employers welcomed the arrival of more labor power, as early as 1713 James Logan expressed worries to Penn over foreigners in the colony. Logan emphasized most new arrivals were property-less servants, appealing to the proprietor's financial interests by emphasizing they were too poor to pay quitrents.[53] In 1715 Jonathan Dickinson commented that local merchants profited handsomely from the growing servant trade in Philadelphia, while two years later the new governor, William Keith, expressed fears that the aliens invading the colony threatened British hegemony.[54] Toward the end of the 1720s, Logan wrote to James Penn that thousands of German and Irish newcomers illegally squatted in the province every year. The Penns nevertheless remained liberal in allowing immigrants to Pennsylvania, largely because they hoped income from new rents would help settle their father's debts.[55] As the city and colony grew more ethnically diverse, officials and lawmakers expressed fears of foreigners by borrowing from sixteenth- and seventeenth-century English poor laws to exclude strangers and vagabonds.[56]

An important feature of servitude in colonial cities like Philadelphia was its relative fluidity and, at times, the lack of a clear separation between freedom and unfreedom. A 1713 petition from a servant by the name of Williams suggests practices that may have been common. The joiner Stephen Armit gave Williams to the carpenter Edward Annelly for the remainder of the servant's time for fourteen pounds. Although laboring for a carpenter and joiner led Williams to obtain valuable woodworking skills, his legal status was that of a bound servant and not an apprentice. For missing four days of work before the expiration of his term, Annelly allegedly forced Williams to labor twenty-four extra days, a punishment evidently based on—though exceeding—the law's requirement of five days' service for each missed. Annelly also seized goods worth ten pounds from the laborer while Williams was imprisoned in the city jail, most likely for debt. Williams's current inability to pay outstanding debts, exacerbated by incarceration, was particularly damaging because he had a "Chargeable family to Maintain." Though exactly what he was requesting is uncertain (the document is torn and often illegible), it appears Williams desired a release from debtor's prison as a result of unfair treatment from Annelly, and because his continued confinement would lead to an additional burden on public relief.[57] Williams's case shows that adult men with families who went into debt also entered contracts to work for a period of years as servants.

Records do not indicate whether Williams's petition was granted, but despite Moraley's claim to the contrary, servants in Philadelphia were on occasion successful against masters in court. Elizabeth Starkey was released from the service of Francis Philipps in 1715, though for unknown reasons. The case also indicates the extent to which masters like Philipps had come to see servants as an inviolable form of property by the early eighteenth century. Philipps was indicted by the city grand jury for contempt after he claimed Mayor Richard

Hall and recorder Robert Appleton were "no better than Rouges Villains & Scoundrells," because in releasing Starkey they had "not done me Justice & might as soon as had one a Man to pick my Pocket or Rob my house as to have taken away my Servt."[58]

The flexible and commodified nature of labor in the mid-Atlantic was enhanced with the arrival of growing numbers of non-English servants in the 1710s, whose foreign legal and cultural status made it easier for townspeople to tolerate disciplinary measures far more brutal than those meted to disobedient servants in England. In 1717 the assembly legalized the sending of insubordinate servants to the Philadelphia workhouse; by this time people on their way to the large market in the center of town could witness the whipping of runaway servants as well as unwed mothers. Servants receiving the treatment were even charged six shillings for the privilege.[59] Public auctions of arriving servants and slaves, together with the public whippings of the unfree for flight and other forms of insubordination, normalized distinctively colonial forms of "correction" among the urban population. Such spectacles also likely alienated a substantial segment of the urban population from traditional norms of community membership.

No local institution shaped urban policies and attitudes toward servants and slaves in early Philadelphia more than the grand jury.[60] In 1726 the jury played a key role in the assembly's passage of An Act for the Better Regulating of Negros in this Province, a law that solidified race as the determining factor in the status of free as well as enslaved Black people. While legal scholars have examined the law's provisions, they have not explored how it originated in part as a response to grand jury complaints of the interracial social practices of Philadelphia's lower sort. In 1722 the assembly established a committee to examine a remonstrance from the city's grand inquest concerning interracial marriage. Grand jurymen argued marriages between Blacks and whites were an "Indecency" that should be prohibited by law. They further claimed that the freeing of slaves was "Pernicious" and that any new law should contain a clause to prevent Black people from gathering in groups.[61] Jurymen bundled a host of disparate complaints concerning inhabitants of African descent into a single petition.

The petition was almost certainly a response to the secret marriage in 1722 of Katherine Williams and an enslaved man held by a Mr. Tuthill, the details of which were revealed to city authorities by one Hannah Cherry. According to a petition from Cherry, Philadelphia magistrates had caused her "utter Ruin" because of Cherry's alleged collusion in concealing the marriage. Cherry's daughter, Rebecca Scott, had been imprisoned along with Williams (though the latter seems to have escaped from the town jail), suggesting the grand jury conducted an investigation of the affair and apprehended the accused.[62] While authorities granted Cherry's request for the release of her daughter, the grand jury found Williams's marriage to be an immoral act requiring legal remedy. Though Virginia and Maryland had passed antimiscegenation laws in the 1690s, in Pennsylvania the impetus for criminalizing interracial relations came not from slaveholders or assemblymen but from Quaker magistrates in Philadelphia. Moreover, in protesting the disparate practices of interracial marriage, manumission, and slave gatherings in one petition, grand jurymen sought blanket legal reform based on race.

The law began with a discussion of crime among the enslaved, demonstrating the complex colonial relationship between property, law, and new forms of racial categorization. The statute's preface claimed slaves in Pennsylvania regularly committed crimes punishable by death. Because the prosecution of enslaved offenders resulted in injury for masters, however, slaveholders frequently concealed slave crimes or sold alleged offenders out of the colony to avoid the economic loss resulting from the trial and punishment of lawbreakers. Slaveholders' desire to protect their property allowed the accused to escape justice, knowledge of which led the enslaved to believe they could commit crimes with impunity. The professed origins of the statute lay in the House's desire to deliver justice while also protecting property, an effort requiring a balance between the needs of civil society and the individual. The first section of the act therefore stipulated that condemned slaves were to be appraised by the court, which would compensate masters of executed offenders out of a fund from the duty on slave imports. While legislators attempted to secure masters' investment in the enslaved, they also required that compensation for lost human property would come from the slaveholding class itself.[63]

The grand jury's complaints were addressed in the act's lengthy regulations concerning the status of free Blacks and the legality of interracial marriage. Masters and mistresses who wished to manumit slaves were required to provide a surety of thirty pounds to local authorities, a stipulation borrowed from Massachusetts that made freeing slaves extremely prohibitive. The apprehension and binding out of free people of African descent was made the prerogative of local magistrates, and the ban against sheltering and trading with the enslaved was reiterated. Clergy who oversaw interracial marriages were to be fined a hundred pounds; for cohabitation whites would pay thirty pounds or be sold into servitude for up to seven years. Free Blacks marrying whites could be enslaved for life; those who engaged in sexual relations with whites would be punished by seven years of servitude. The children of such relationships would be forced to work in servile labor until age thirty-one.[64]

Over the course of the 1730s and 1740s, as bound labor reached its zenith in the city, enslaved Philadelphians continued to work for wages and socialize with city servants. In the decade after the 1726 act, grand jurymen and members of the common council consistently called for a municipal ordinance for "the Regulation of Negroes and White Servants within this City."[65] That bound laborers continued to congregate after the 1726 race statute suggests a refusal to surrender rights established through custom as well as many townspeople's willingness to ignore the law. Indeed, the grand jury argued that masters' and mistresses' disinclination to sufficiently discipline unfree workers was largely why official action was required. And in grand jury complaints, as in the statute of 1726, offences were as much about a morality increasingly defined by racial difference as they were about property crime, with the freedoms that masters, tavernkeepers, and others accorded bound laborers portending the dissolution of society.

The language of the 1726 act borrowed from other colonial precedents, and the statute used a common expression in describing people of African descent as a naturally "idle, slothful people." The notion that common people were naturally slothful had roots in medieval Europe, when among elites it was axiomatic that the peasantry willingly labored just enough to meet basic subsistence needs.[66] The distinction in sixteenth-century England between the deserving and undeserving poor, codified in poor laws, reinforced a notion of natural idleness among a section of the populace.[67] Though in the early seventeenth century European writers often represented Native Americans as unsettled and therefore slothful, William Bullock wrote in 1649 that the new English workforce in the Americas largely comprised "idle, lazie, simple people."[68] The expression was also applied to the Irish. In the 1680s English pamphleteers stated that it was "generally knowne" that the Irish were a "slothfull and Idle people."[69] Around the same time, Barbadian planters disparaged Irish laborers on sugar plantations. In 1676 Jonathan Atkins wrote to the Lords of Trade that Irish workers in Barbados were "commonly very idle" and that enslaved Africans worked more productively—at one-third the cost. In the following decade John Oldmixon claimed that enslaved Africans were as "ingenious and apt to learn as any people." Like Atkins, Oldmixon also stressed that Africans workers were considerably cheaper than Europeans.[70]

In the late seventeenth and early eighteenth centuries the application of the "slothful and idle" refrain to people of African descent was therefore an ideological development meant to justify slavery as well as the strict regulation of free people of African descent in the mid-Atlantic.[71] Its continuing usefulness in England is indicated by the evolution of the theory of the "utility of poverty" (or "leisure preference") in the early eighteenth century, according to which the laboring classes had to be kept in poverty and hunger to be motivated to work. Though a few writers in the seventeenth century began to argue for nonpoverty wages for working people, it was only after 1750 that economic thinkers widely questioned the utility of poverty theory.[72] The racialized conception of inherent Black indolence took far longer to dispel, an indication of the ideological uses and adaptability of early modern social theory.

While people of African descent valued labor and leisure differently than did many colonists, enslaved people's actions belied the notion of natural laziness.[73] This was implicitly suggested by the Pennsylvania statute's acknowledgment of the economic initiative of the enslaved. While earlier laws recognized bound workers' involvement in trade, section 11 of the new statute explicitly forbade masters from allowing slaves to "ramble about under pretense of getting work." Though the phrase "under pretense of" suggests that the enslaved claimed to be working while engaging in unproductive leisure activities, legislators admitted the enslaved did frequently "seek their own employ and so go to work at their own wills."[74] While the assembly's response to the 1723 petitions of day laborers (discussed in chapter 1) found proposals to ban the hiring out of slaves to violate individual property rights and the public good, this position was reversed with the passage of the race code in 1726. Grand jury complaints of interracial socializing likely played a role in this reversal. The act also implied that the excessive liberty in asserting economic independence encouraged a surplus of "willfulness" among bound workers, a complaint regarding insubordinate servants so prominent in early eighteenth-century England that Daniel Defoe wrote a book about it.[75]

By the mid-eighteenth century, unfree labor had become an essential feature of urban life. Ownership of enslaved people was no longer confined to Philadelphia's wealthiest inhabitants, as British dominance in an expanding Atlantic slave trade resulted in lower prices in the colonies, making it possible for American craftsmen to purchase captive Africans.[76] By this time unfree Philadelphians labored in occupations encompassing the whole of urban society, from domestic household work to large construction projects. Although the

social reality of large numbers of bound workers operated with changing policies to shape perceptions of labor in the city, a burgeoning print culture also
played a key role in transmitting images of laboring peoples to local readers.
It is impossible to measure the extent to which publications simply reflected,
or actively shaped, attitudes toward bound laborers in the city. In any case, by
the middle of the eighteenth century, runaway bound workers and their representation had become normative features of Philadelphia society and culture.

Advertisements for Africans fleeing slavery appeared in the *London Gazette*
as early as the 1680s, and slave and servant flight had become a feature of
everyday life in the colonies by the time of Pennsylvania's founding.[77] Yet the
formation of a local print culture in Philadelphia in the 1720s and 1730s significantly impacted the business of bound labor in the city and colony, while
also working to shape readers' views of unfree workers. From *American Weekly
Mercury's* founding in 1719, notices for the sale of newly arrived laborers and
runaway advertisements both provided an important source of revenue for
the publication, as well as providing important information for buyers in the
local labor market. The same would be true for the more popular *Pennsylvania
Gazette* after 1728.[78] Newspaper advertisements for the return of fugitives cast
a far wider net than posters, handbills, or word-of-mouth messages and functioned as important instruments of surveillance and control. At a time when
the face-to-face, small-town environment was giving way to a more impersonal, cosmopolitan urban context, newspapers provided a crucial means of
information and communication.

Runaway ads also served to strengthen a sense of collective interest among
employers while contributing to racial and ethnic identifications among the
general populace. Non-English runaway servants were often described in
terms of their Welsh, Scottish, or Irish backgrounds and accents, a practice that
distinguished proper-speaking British subjects from laboring-class newcomers.[79] If newspapers fostered a group identity among masters, advertisements
also revealed the importance of racial and ethnic solidarities among runaways.
Late in 1733 three slaves (two men and one woman) from Whitemarsh Township, held by two different slaveholders, joined with three other enslaved men
of Philadelphia (belonging to three different owners) in an attempt to obtain
freedom.[80] The coordination required for such a large operation demonstrates
the ability of the urban enslaved to establish relationships and communication networks in the city. Irish servants Terence Toole, Thomas Wildeer, and
Michael Berry were each held by different artisans but were able to use the

urban environment to organize along ethnonational lines and flee servitude in 1740. Their masters (a butcher, a shipwright, and a carpenter) likewise forged new identifications through a mutual loss of labor and the shared cost of newspaper advertisements.[81]

While common cultures and origins contributed to the formation of laboring-class identities in Philadelphia, representations of conditions across the Atlantic also influenced colonial perceptions of new arrivals. In 1729, when approximately four thousand Irish newcomers arrived in ports along the Delaware River, the *Gazette* described famine conditions in Ireland. A report from London referred to the "miserable Condition which the lower Sort of People" were in, which included starvation among the poor. There were riots against engrossers in Dublin, and the tyranny of rack-renting landlords caused "swarms" of Irish to leave for America.[82] News of hardship in Ireland did not greatly soften attitudes in Philadelphia, however. In the same year that the *Gazette* reported on the famine, the assembly for the first time singled out the Irish as a particularly dangerous group of immigrants.[83] The British government contributed significantly to the association between unfree labor and crime with the Transportation Act of 1717 (examined in chapter 4); Pennsylvania legislators responded by characterizing Irish immigrants as probable felons.[84] The visual layout of newspapers, moreover, contributed to a mental linkage between immigrant workers, transported felons, and runaway servants and slaves by placing advertisements for the sale of newly arrived laborers alongside ads for the apprehension of fugitives and convicted felons.

Philadelphia was unique in the 1730s in publishing the antislavery works of activists like Ralph Sandiford and Benjamin Lay.[85] Newspaper portrayals of disorderly and fugitive enslaved people were far more numerous, however, while reports of the brutal repression of the risings of captive Africans normalized punishments unknown in early modern Europe.[86] In October 1729 the *Gazette* contained an account of a slave rising on the English ship *Industry* on its way from the Guinea Coast to Barbados. During the insurrection a female rebel was seized by the captain, who gave her a number of cuts with his cutlass as they struggled. The woman was apprehended as the uprising was suppressed. Though her wounds were not fatal, their severity meant "she would not be fit for the Market." The ship master called a council, at which it was unanimously decided to make the woman an example to the other insurrectionists. "Accordingly they hoisted her up to the Fore-Yard-Arm, in view of the other Slaves, whom they had disarmed, and fired half a Dozen Balls thro' her

Body; the last Shot that was fired cut the Rope which she was flung by, so that she tumbled amain into the Sea at once; which terrified the rest so, that they brought them into Barbadoes safe, without the least Disturbance the rest of the Voyage."[87] In contrast to published accounts of sailors' mutinies, which could on occasion be sympathetic to the plight of ill-treated mariners, Philadelphia newspapers delivered reports of slave rebellions—Antigua in 1736, South Carolina in 1739, New York in 1741, and Jamaica in 1761—in gruesome and pitiless detail.[88] Amidst rapid urban growth and a growing unfree population, readers consumed regular stories that portrayed Blacks as a dangerously subversive race whose importance was woven into the fabric of colonial society.

War, Enlistment, and Antislavery

Just over a year after reading of the planned slave revolt on Antigua in 1736, Philadelphians welcomed the Antiguan sugar planter George Thomas as Pennsylvania's new lieutenant governor. As a West Indian planter Thomas was no stranger to American slavery, yet the new governor found labor relations in Philadelphia and Pennsylvania worthy of note. Writing to John Penn, Thomas expressed surprise at seeing skilled tradesmen labor in servitude. Around the time of his arrival city newspapers advertised for the purchase of newly arrived craftsmen. Thomas may also have referred to defaulters forced into servitude to repay debts in the city and region.[89]

Thomas's initial surprise at the institution of servitude in Philadelphia foreshadowed a two-year clash with assemblymen that highlights competing conceptions of subjects' rights and the status of labor in eighteenth-century America. After his arrival the lieutenant governor first clashed with representatives over the perennial issue of paper money. In 1738 the Pennsylvania legislature agreed to an emission of £11,120 in new bills of credit. After presenting assemblymen with a letter from the Penns ordering no paper money emissions unless proprietary quitrents and exchange rates between Philadelphia and London were secured, Thomas and legislators engaged in a lengthy argument over the terms of the bill.[90] A more rancorous dispute arose the following year. The seizure of British ships by Spanish *guardacostas* in Caribbean waters throughout the 1730s had fomented an increasingly bellicose environment in England, and merchants in British ports throughout the Americas bombarded Parliament and the Board of Trade with petitions demanding redress. When England declared war against Spain in late 1739, celebrations broke out across England;

in large towns subscriptions were opened to pay for the defense of British merchant ships.[91] While British nationalism also suffused Anglo-American culture, the Pennsylvania government refused to support the war effort, to Thomas's extreme frustration. Sounding much like other governors who met with resistance from assemblymen, Thomas wrote to Thomas Penn in the fall of the 1740 that representatives were "a low, sordid & hypocritical sett of people."[92]

Though precedents from the 1690s and early 1700s existed for Quaker assemblymen's resistance to providing support for interimperial conflicts, the context of the late 1730s and early 1740s was different. In addition to a growing sense of British nationalism throughout the colonies, Friends were no longer a majority in Pennsylvania, and popular support for defensive measures was pronounced, especially in Philadelphia. In contrast to earlier governors, Thomas appealed to ordinary colonists' English and Protestant identities while also hinting at the potential sacking of the city by licentious Catholic invaders.[93] The assembly continued to refuse to take action, however, arguing that forcing Quakers to bear arms was a violation of the provincial constitution and a form of persecution. Yet unlike previous decades, Friends were divided on the issue of defense, demonstrated most prominently by the influential Quaker jurist Samuel Chew's legal treatise justifying self-defense.[94]

The dispute between Thomas and the assembly escalated dramatically in the spring of 1740, when indentured servants fled masters in large numbers and enlisted in the British navy. In April, after receiving a letter from the Duke of Newcastle inviting English subjects to volunteer for service in the West Indies, Thomas discussed with members of the provincial council the possibility of issuing a proclamation encouraging enlistment. Though Newcastle instructed Thomas to use his "utmost Zeal and Diligence" in encouraging Pennsylvanians to enlist, the governor creatively interpreted his directions. The duke's proclamation stated colonial enlistees would be placed on an equal footing with British soldiers; uniforms, wages, and access to Spanish booty were to provide material encouragement to volunteers. Colonial soldiers would also be free to return to their places of habitation when the expedition was over, unless they chose to remain in newly conquered territories. This was intended as an assurance that common soldiers would not be forced to remain in service, an important guarantee in an age of widespread popular hostility to impressment.[95]

Thomas dutifully repeated in his own proclamation that the Crown was offering arms, clothing, and an equal share of plunder to American enlistees. Yet he also stated soldiers would be "sent back to their respective Habitations

when the Service shall be over, unless any of them shall desire to settle themselves elsewhere," a slight, though significant, alteration of Newcastle's directions. Whereas Newcastle's emphasis was on the right of soldiers to return
home after service, Thomas stressed enlistees would be free to go wherever
they wished—implying freedom from servitude. In case the suggestion was not
completely clear, the governor repeated the statement verbatim in the following paragraph of the proclamation.[96]

After the meeting Thomas and a group of allied officials walked to the State
House and read the declaration of war "to a very numerous Auditory." Observers expressed joy at the news; a cannon was fired on Society Hill and the governor had barrels of beer provided to the populace.[97] The theatrical display
was a direct challenge to leading assembly resisters and opponents of Thomas
like Israel Pemberton and John Kinsey. Thomas and his allies framed the public declaration as acquiescing to popular demands for defense from Spanish
aggression. Bound laborers in the audience also received the governor's message: immediately after the proclamation large numbers of servants enlisted in
the king's service. By the summer of 1741 incensed legislators claimed more than
three hundred had abandoned Pennsylvania masters. At least 188 of them (valued at £1,580) fled from the city and county of Philadelphia—approximately
one in three of the town's servant population.[98] Thomas's attempt to raise bodies
for the war effort and antagonize representatives set off a mass servant exodus.

In addition to providing further evidence of a colonial absolutist conception
of property, the assembly protests demonstrated representatives' presentation
of themselves as champions of middling freemen. House addresses to Thomas,
authored by the powerful House Speaker John Kinsey, pointed out that
"bought Servants" belonged "to the Inhabitants of this Province"; the governor could not lawfully recruit private property for public service. (Kinsey had
previously worked with Israel Pemberton Sr. to have the Philadelphia Meeting expel the abolitionist Benjamin Lay. After his death in 1750 it was discovered Kinsey had embezzled £3,600 as a loan office trustee.)[99] While the loss of
workers in the labor-scarce colony damaged the public in general, representatives also stressed that it was ordinary farmers and tradesmen who suffered
most from the policy. Colonists had indeed petitioned provincial officials over
servant enlistments earlier in the summer in terms that suggested a significant
level of resentment among middling freemen. A petition from Chester County
claimed that some people's entire estates consisted of servants, while others,
"more wealthy," held "no other Servants but *Negroes*." Enlistment therefore

constituted "a very hard and unequal Tax," since it was nonelite freemen who bore the economic burden of the war.[100]

Some Philadelphia craftsmen also complained of the hardships wrought by enlistment. Masters were unable to carry on trades without their workers; other colonists had mortgaged their estates at the loan office solely in order to purchase laborers.[101] Members of the House sympathized with freemen's difficulties when they informed Thomas that it was "a very melancholy Prospect" to find the families of local farmers and mechanics deprived of a bare subsistence because of the loss of servants.[102] Representatives' defense of middling producers paid off politically: in August a "great Number" of Philadelphia freeholders went before the assembly to deliver a paper expressing their thanks to the House for "endeavouring to preserve their Rights and Properties, particularly with Regard to Servants."[103]

In their public argument with the governor assemblymen articulated a propertarian, rights-based discourse that equated servant enlistment with tyrannical and arbitrary rule. If the masters of servants were correct in their belief that their properties had been violated, then it was clear that "any Goods in which they have the most absolute Property may not with equal reason be taken from them as their Servants." If property in Pennsylvania was so "precarious" as to be subject to the "Will" and "Caprice" of servants and minor officers, those needing labor power would be forced to import African slaves.[104] The notion that servants, as dependents, were divested of individual wills was prominent in early modern England; while in service, laborers were legally and theoretically mere extensions of the master. As Cotton Mather informed Massachusetts bound workers from the pulpit in 1696: "You are the *Animate, Separate, Active Instruments* of other men"; servants' tongues, hands, and feet belonged to "your *Masters,* and they should move according to the Will of your *Masters.*"[105] In the early eighteenth century, as noted above, "willful" servants and slaves were synonymous with disobedience and disorder. In characterizing servants as excessively willful and capricious, Pennsylvania legislators reinforced an ideology of patriarchal authority while also confirming an inviolable right in human property.[106]

Assemblymen also deployed imagery similar to that directed against William Keith in the 1720s in casting Thomas as a manipulator who seduced the credulous with flattery and "extravagant" promises. Thomas's demagoguery was arguably even more subversive, however, since his appeal was not to free commoners but rather to a group of servants who were the property of others.

When large numbers of servants in Philadelphia indicated their desire to enlist, Thomas allegedly took some of them by the hand and informed them that they were no longer bound to their masters. The governor told the servants there was no difference between them and himself, except for his fine clothes and the money in his pocket—differences, it was implied, likely to change after plundering the Spanish enemy. According to Speaker Kinsey and other representatives, servants grew "tumultuous and disorderly" at this information, evidence of dependents' susceptibility to the blandishments of their social betters.[107]

Thomas denied allegations he encouraged servants to abandon their masters. Yet he also disputed the colonists' claim that servants were a property like any other; he asserted that by law English subjects had the right to enlist in the king's service, regardless of their status. In answer to assemblymen's argument that human property was legally the same "as a man's Property in any other Goods or Chattels whatsoever," Thomas argued it did not seem "reasonable" that a contract between subjects gave one a proprietary claim over another that destroyed the king's right to take the latter into his service. The governor also echoed the refrain of worldly Quaker hypocrisy when he noted Philadelphia judges and juries had recently acted "to convict and condemn such little Rogues to Death as break into your Houses, and of acting in other Offices, where Force must necessarily be used for the Preservation of the Publick Peace."[108] Quaker authorities felt no compunction in condemning property offenders to death for private trespasses while refusing to defend the people against a far more dangerous Catholic invasion.[109] If legislators viewed the governor's actions as violations of the provincial constitution, Thomas claimed assemblymen defied their duty as subjects to defend the British Protestant world.

Although Thomas had sought to irritate assemblymen with his proclamation as much as raise bodies for the war, he was unprepared for the enthusiasm with which servants embraced the Crown's cause. The fact that hundreds of bound workers fled service after the proclamation was read suggests the extent of hostility among servants to the colonial labor regime. However much representatives attempted to portray the mass enlistment as a product of an unthinking servant impulse or deceptive flattery from the governor, it was clear that large numbers of laborers were not optimistic about their future economic prospects and felt no obligation to masters. After the assembly first protested the governor's proclamation, Thomas quickly stated that employer applications for the discharge of servants would be granted, and officers were instructed to return those volunteering without masters' permission to their legal owners.

The governor doubted representatives' property-based legal arguments, but he did not want to appear to endorse servants abandoning masters. Enlistees could not be persuaded to return, however. According to military officers, and in a reversal of the flow of soldiers to Pennsylvania from the north during the 1690s, considerable numbers of bound laborers abandoned masters in an effort to reach New York, where it was said supporters of the Crown were welcomed. Though he professed a desire to return servants to masters, Thomas cautioned against discharging volunteers all at once. This would not only thin the ranks of soldiers and therefore injure the king's cause; it could provoke insurrection among an already turbulent population.[110]

Some volunteers may have genuinely shared in a sense of Protestant British patriotism, but evidence suggests the desire to escape bondage was paramount. Some used the proclamation to simply flee both masters' and the Crown's service, and assemblymen were quick to note it was Pennsylvania freemen and not the English state who bore the financial burden when that happened.[111] The threat of a return to servitude also spurred common soldiers to collective action. When, in the early summer of 1740, a Captain Thinn attempted to apprehend and return a group of servants to masters, "Freemen as well as Servants laid down their Arms, and declared that they would go into other Governments where the King's Soldiers were better used."[112] Soldiers quickly became aware of the argument between the governor and legislators as rumors began to circulate that servant volunteers were to be sent back into bondage. In August Thomas received a letter signed by twenty-five officers stating troops under their command had grown "exceedingly uneasy" on hearing news of the return of servant enlistees. Some of them declared they would never "suffer themselves to be separated, and rather than be exposed to the inhumane usage of the Masters of some of them, and the Creditors of others for small Debts, they will go into some other Government where they hope to be better used and protected in His Majesty's Service." Officers added that the controversy had created serious tensions within the companies; in their view only regiment colonels could legally discharge volunteers, whether servants, apprentices, or freemen.[113]

Both Thomas and the officers had an interest in not discharging enlistees, yet the language of inhumanity and oppression repeated by the governor and officers suggests real grievances among volunteers. "Inhumanity" had long been an important keyword in popular criticisms of oppression—within England and in critical treatments of servitude in Virginia and Barbados.[114]

If, as Joyce Chaplin has argued, the concept of a common humanity provided slaveholders with a useful ideological justification for inequality in the late eighteenth-century South, allegations of inhumanity among the powerful also served as a crucial rhetorical weapon of the oppressed.[115] In the dispute between Thomas and the assembly, the accusation of masters' inhumanity offered a telling rejoinder to representations of bound workers as reducible to a species of property. Suggestive also is that servants were joined by debt laborers, who were also allegedly subject to creditors' "inhumane usage."

The enlistees' threats of mutiny and desertion were successful, for most did not return to masters. After considering the officers' letter, the provincial council decided the discharge of soldiers—"whether Freemen or Servants"— portended "Mutinies, Tumults, and Disorders" in the defenseless colony. To try to return volunteers to their former condition of servitude would create a large group of men likely to sympathize with the enemy. The council also sided with the governor in confirming subjects' right to enlist in the king's service, a decision that rejected assembly arguments over the sanctity of property. The council claimed, moreover, that servant enlistments were not as economically damaging as assemblymen alleged, since many had only a short time left to serve, and a recently passed statute allowed masters to retain enlisted servants' freedom dues.[116] In a settlement resembling that of 1711, assembly demands for compensation for lost human property were agreed to as part of a deal to provide £3,000 for the king's use. A committee of grievances was formed to investigate complaints delivered to the House, and servants and apprentices were rated according to the amount paid for indentures and time left to serve.[117]

A repeat of the enlistment controversy occurred fourteen years later, during the Seven Years' War. Beginning in the fall of 1755, British commanders recruited Pennsylvania servants to serve not in the West Indies but on the western frontier, where British forces were then being battered by the French and their Indian allies. Philadelphia lawyer William Peters exaggerated when he estimated that two thousand Pennsylvania servants had enlisted by the end of the year, but as had happened in the early 1740s, the assembly received numerous petitions complaining of the "Inconveniences and Hardships" endured by freemen because of enlistment.[118] Assemblymen again asserted the "incontestable Right of Masters and Owners" to their "Apprentices and Servants" and warned Governor Robert Hunter Morris that if their property in servants was so "precarious," they would purchase "Negro Slaves, as the property in them and their

Service seems at present more secure."[119] Apparently unacquainted with Pennsylvania's recent past (though a native of New Jersey), Morris expressed amazement at representatives' refusal to support the war and their bitter hostility to servants' military service. The people of Massachusetts, by contrast, "chearfully consented" to servant enlistment.[120]

One reason the conflict over servant enlistment was less rancorous the second time around was perhaps because Pennsylvanians made good on their threat to import enslaved workers to replace servants. Benjamin Franklin warned the British government in 1756 that enlisting servants would destroy the important servant trade from England and Germany. The merchant Thomas Willing wrote in the same year that the importation of white workers was ruined by enlistment and that "we must make more general use of Slaves."[121] Gary Nash notes that Philadelphians' importation of enslaved captives picked up in the late 1750s and likely peaked in 1762 when as many as five hundred enslaved people arrived in the city, most directly from Africa.[122] Sharon Salinger documents an enslaved population of 2,366 in Philadelphia in 1763, more than double the 952 recorded in 1754.[123]

Though their opportunities were far more circumscribed than those of European servants, enslaved people also attempted to use midcentury wars to obtain freedom. Advertisements for runaway slaves as well as servants increased in the *Gazette,* appearing alongside advertisements for their sale in the 1740s and 1750s.[124] In 1745 an enslaved man named Jo (who had labored as a cook for Maryland governor Samuel Ogle) ran away from Philip Key in Annapolis, "and has since been out [on] a Voyage in one of the Privateers belonging to Philadelphia, and is returned there."[125] In July 1747 James Logan informed the provincial council of a plan "by some Spanish Prisoners, Negroes, & others to run away with a Ship's Boat in this Harbour"; fears of slaves joining French privateers in the Delaware Bay persisted through the year.[126] In 1761 a "cunning Fellow" named Peter of West New Jersey escaped from John Wood and was seen close to Philadelphia, where he enquired "whether there were any Privateers fitting out."[127]

Successful flight required support from other townspeople, and aid networks in Philadelphia occasionally crossed racial lines. In 1747 the apprentice Charles Badmin and an enslaved blockmaker named Cicero fled the city together; owner William Hasleton offered twenty shillings for the return of Badmin and thirty for Cicero.[128] Judas Hays suspected an enslaved runaway named Sarah was harbored and concealed "by some white person in this

FIGURE 2. William Bradford's London Coffeehouse, at the southwest corner of Front and Market Streets. A center of Philadelphia's economic and cultural life, the coffeehouse was the site of slave auctions, held outside on Front Street, seen here on the right. In the foreground, a woman of African descent carries a basket on her head. (London Coffee House; plate published in John F. Watson's *Annals of Philadelphia*, 1830; courtesy of the Library Company of Philadelphia)

town" and offered five pounds for the return of the woman and ten pounds for information on who was sheltering her.[129] As in other cities with large populations of enslaved people, Philadelphia's small free Black population harbored runaways despite the severe fines for the crime outlined in the race statute of 1726. John Poole of Philadelphia County believed "Molattoe Jack" would remain in the area since he had "several negroes about the city of Philadelphia, and the county also."[130]

Even as the enslaved population spiked in the late 1750s and early 1760s, Philadelphia became a center of antislavery criticism in the Atlantic world. Franklin published John Woolman's *Some Considerations on the Keeping of Negroes* in 1754; Woolman published a second part in 1762. Originally from Burlington County, New Jersey (less than twenty miles from Philadelphia), Woolman argued like other antislavery Friends that enslavement violated the Christian golden rule as well as slaves' "natural right of freedom." Woolman's argument that a dependence on slave labor bred idleness and luxury among slaveholders was not original, but his Christian mysticism was informed by a deeply egalitarian belief in the necessity of simple living.[131] Woolman's anti-slavery activism (in the late 1750s he traveled through the southern colonies and, in addition to socializing with enslaved people, attempted to convince individual slaveholders to manumit slaves) was part of a broader critique of British Atlantic society.[132]

While Woolman and his writings were well known in Philadelphia, it was Anthony Benezet's abolitionism that had the greatest impact in the city between the 1750s and 1770s. Born in 1713 to a Huguenot family in Saint-Quentin, France, Benezet arrived in Philadelphia in 1731 after fleeing France for Holland. In 1750 Benezet began instructing Black Philadelphians in the evenings at his home; four years later he started the city's first secondary school for girls; and in 1770 he built Philadelphia's first free day school for people of African descent. More than other eighteenth-century writers and activists, Benezet worked to dismantle dominant cultural beliefs in Africans' alleged idleness and inferiority. His frequent interactions with enslaved people on Philadelphia's streets and in the markets confirmed Benezet's belief in Africans' intellectual capacities and added to his general commitment to human equality.[133] In his written works Benezet drew on firsthand accounts of European visitors to Africa to prove that Africans practiced agriculture and had complex societies, primarily to refute contemporary justifications for the Atlantic slave trade.[134]

After midcentury the proportion of servants, and especially slaves, in the Philadelphia population declined precipitously.[135] While structural changes in the Atlantic economy contributed to the growing prominence of wage labor in colonial port cities, slavery and servitude in Philadelphia developed distinctive characteristics between the 1740s and 1760s. The advocacy of Woolman and Benezet undoubtedly contributed to the Philadelphia Yearly Meeting's warning to Friends against slaveholding in 1755, the prohibition against members importing or buying slaves in 1758, the Meeting's banning of slave ownership in 1776, and Pennsylvania's Act for the Gradual Abolition of Slavery in 1780.[136] War and enlistment shaped the experience of indentured service in Philadelphia in the 1740s and 1750s, and by this time arriving servants were a mix of Irish, German, English, and Scottish newcomers. The possibility of social mobility available to servants in the city's early years largely evaporated after the 1740s, and by the 1770s wage labor had effectively replaced indentured service in Philadelphia.[137]

Conclusion

Benezet, Woolman, and other antislavery Quakers in Philadelphia pioneered a fusion of seventeenth-century Christian radicalism and eighteenth-century natural rights discourse that would define abolitionist ideology in subsequent decades. Yet their calls for self-denial and renunciation of the world were at odds with a dominant culture that increasingly celebrated a British Atlantic conception of property. Few enslaved people were freed in the city before the American Revolution; just fifty-two Philadelphians manumitted ninety enslaved people in the sixty-five years before 1763.[138] And despite the decades of the 1750s and 1760s marking the beginning of slavery's end in Philadelphia, the city's liberal reputation paradoxically contributed to writers' romanticization of master-slave relations in the city and colony well into the nineteenth century.[139]

Arguably the system of servitude best demonstrates the contradictions of unfree labor in early modern Philadelphia. Though in the decades after the founding masters adopted an evolving American conception of property in human labor, they continued to deploy moralistic language touting master-servant obligation into the 1760s when they complained runaways and disobedient servants "wronged" them.[140] Employers were required to pay for the maintenance of servants when they were arrested and placed in jail—even when masters and mistresses were themselves the victims of servant theft.[141] The continuing dominance of a propertarian ideology in labor is perhaps best illustrated in an extended 1759 pamphlet titled *A True and Impartial State of the Province of Pennsylvania*. Responding to the Reverend William Smith's criticisms of the assembly's treatment of Governor Thomas during the enlistment controversy of the early 1740s, the author claimed servants were "our *Property*," sanctioned by parliamentary and provincial law. They were "personal Chattels," given to the executors of the deceased and as payment for debts, just like other goods. Upon them "the Cultivation of our Lands, our Trade, and Commerce principally depend."[142]

Some Philadelphians may have been benevolent masters and mistresses. Yet a revolutionary and early republican view of paternalistic relations between bound laborers and masters in the city is belied by abundant evidence. Some masters believed autonomous slave and servant cultural practices encouraged disobedience and flight, which in turn contributed to a view of the unfree as an idle and dangerous underclass. Philadelphia authorities' anxieties concerning bound laborers' mobility and leisure pursuits in the city and throughout the colonies in some ways resembled contemporary English worries over laboring-class idleness. The different ways in which propertied freemen in Philadelphia came to view bound laborers are suggested by Andrew Mackraby, who wrote to Sir Philip Francis in 1769 that servants brought to the colonies from England were "spoilt in a month." Those born in America were "insolent and extravagant"; the Dutch (meaning German) were "ignorant and awkward"; the Irish were "generally thieves, and particularly drunkards"; and "the negroes stupid and sulky."[143]

The formation of ethnic and racial stereotypes in the early modern Americas were inextricable from the development of novel forms of unfree labor. Though evidence is scattered and fragmentary, it is clear that many bound workers in the Americas found working life oppressive and masters "inhumane." There is, moreover, considerable continuity between the complaints of servants between the mid-seventeenth and late eighteenth centuries. William Moraley claimed that on many days in Philadelphia and the mid-Atlantic, he became "Drunk for Joy that my Work was ended" and that when he finally obtained his freedom it was "impossible to express the Satisfaction I found at being releas'd from the precarious Humour and Dependence of my Master."[144] For servants like Moraley and Peter Williamson of Scotland, Philadelphia was a place of wealth and wonder. It was also a place where workers were sold for as much as sixteen pounds per head at auction and where traditional English rights afforded to individuals were denied.[145]

PART II

LAW AND DISORDER

3

"UNINTELLIGIBLE STUFF CALLED LAW"

Cultural Legalism and Authority in the City

A recurring theme in William Moraley's *The Infortunate: The Voyage and Adventures of William Moraley, an Indentured Servant* is the extent to which bound laborers were deprived of legal rights in early eighteenth-century America. Though in his verse tribute to Philadelphia Moraley appropriated the voice of a free citizen in proclaiming "No unjust Sentence we have cause to fear," a striking absence of legal protections defined the existence of unfree workers— especially those enslaved. Conditions for slaves were miserable largely because of the "Severity of the Laws" in the colony; Moraley also found it notable that there were "no Laws made in Favour of these unhappy Wretches." Masters who killed enslaved people faced no punishment, there being "no Law against murdering them." Moraley referred to the recent 1726 race code when he noted a provincial statute effectively prohibited manumission since a large security and plot of land had to be provided by slaveowners to guarantee freed slaves would not become a public burden. If enslaved people were most deprived of recourse to law, servants were also at a severe legal disadvantage. Though theoretically servants of European descent had legal rights, judges generally favored masters, and bound laborers therefore rarely resorted to the courts to redress grievances.[1]

Moraley's many comments on the Pennsylvania legal system are testimony to his coming from a culture in which the rights of the subject and the rule of law were fundamental components of English identity. By the time Moraley migrated to America, an exceptionalist conception of British rights and the ancient constitution had long existed in England, and settlers brought this cultural legalism to the colonies.[2] Like other colonists, Philadelphians cherished their rights and privileges as British subjects, and the notion of subjects' equality before the law was arguably the most important component of colonists' self-identification as free Britons.

Yet like money and property, law was a freighted concept that strongly informed political and cultural differences in early Philadelphia. As proprietor, William Penn was allowed to establish any laws in Pennsylvania not in contravention of those of England. Pennsylvania law enshrined representative government, religious freedom, accessible courts, the absence of corporal punishments, and a system of public education, all of which recalled radical political demands first articulated in the upheavals of the 1640s and 1650s, as well as the views of reformist Friends after the Restoration.[3] At the same time, in Pennsylvania's founding constitution, the Frame of Government, Penn recognized man's sinful nature and the divine right of monarchs as a tribute to Charles II as well as an assertion of proprietary authority.[4] As John Smolenski has argued, Pennsylvania's famed tolerance and diversity were balanced in the colony's early years by elite Quakers' desire to maintain order and control.[5] Over time Philadelphians from disparate political persuasions would come to see Pennsylvania's distinctive legal system as a dangerous deviation from English law and, paradoxically, as less just than that of the metropole.[6]

The differences that emerged between William Penn and settlers after the founding were expressed in a constitutionalist language of right, contract, and law. In disputes with proprietary factions and imperial authorities, Quaker assemblymen belonging to an emerging antiproprietary elite cited the sacrifices they made in emigrating as well as legal agreements. Constitutional disagreements that culminated with the 1701 Charter of Privileges, which gave the assembly the right to initiate legislation (and therefore cemented the colony's reputation as having a "popular" form of government), led some in the proprietary faction to believe Pennsylvania would be better off under royal rule.[7] In the view of William Penn and his supporters, colonists' disputatiousness—evident in litigation, petitions, and the press—signaled the failure of a Quaker vision of civic harmony. For those of the antiproprietary party, by contrast, the Pennsylvania charter confirmed the British notion that laws should conform to the unique conditions of the people living under them.

If debates and arguments involving law demonstrate how Anglo-American constitutional norms were established in early Pennsylvania, other evidence shows how customary attitudes toward legal authorities were also manifested in Philadelphia. A general belief in the special role of English liberty among free colonists was not inimical to a traditional popular distrust of law and legal professionals. According to this tradition, "crafty" lawyers learned in the intricacies of law used their specialized knowledge for personal gain, a subversion of law's function as neutral guarantor of subjects' formal equality. Law, like money, was a source of liberation as well as oppression: it could secure justice and the liberty of a freeborn people, but it could also function as a tool of tyranny and a weapon of the powerful. Accordingly, a notion of local rights that drew on an established tradition of English constitutionalism was celebrated in a culture in which refusal to sit on juries or pay fees, assaults on law enforcement officials, jailbreaks, and expressions of antipathy toward lawyers and magistrates occurred regularly.[8]

As the center of the Pennsylvania government, Philadelphia especially embodied the contradictions of early modern Anglo-American legal culture. The governing authority of the city was physically represented by the building of two new state houses (and jails) in the first half of the eighteenth century. Factional political tensions were most pronounced in the city, and in addition to assembly meetings quarterly court sessions were important cultural events throughout the region.[9] As the provincial metropolis, Philadelphia was also the place where public expressions of defiance toward constables and magistrates were most pronounced, and therefore challenging to institutional authority. And as the center of the regional press, the publication of statutes and legislative developments in the city was accompanied by representations of longstanding popular suspicions of laws, lawyers, and even lawmakers.

Crises of authority involving urban, provincial, and imperial relations were expressed in disparate attitudes toward law and justice in early modern Philadelphia. Petitions critical of William Penn implicitly questioned proprietary authority, while freemen's assertions of local legislative supremacy challenged imperial dominion. Constitutional and legal questions remained prominent in the city and colony's political culture through the Seven Years' War. While provincial law evolved to accommodate the city's incorporation into a larger Atlantic world, a traditional popular suspicion of the power of law continued to inform everyday life. The slogan of "rights and liberties" was a "clamor" regularly heard in the legalistic culture of the early modern Americas. Its articulation in Philadelphia spoke to contrasting visions of the colony's founding, the supremacy of British laws, and the nature and function of legal power.

English Legalism and the Roots of Quaker Justice

In the twelfth century the bishop and philosopher John of Salisbury claimed that good princes obeyed laws and acted in the service of the people. Failure to avenge enemies of the commonwealth—specifically tyrants who defied law—was a transgression against "the whole body of the earthly republic."[10] The agreement between King John and a group of barons in 1215 codified in the Magna Carta became an essential symbol of rights and liberties that, in the view of English people, distinguished England from continental European and Eastern despotisms. The belief in the supremacy of law over arbitrary rule that emerged in medieval England was not limited to legal and political theorists. In the late Middle Ages, as slavery was eliminated and replaced by serfdom and villeinage, English peasants frequently used manorial, and especially royal, courts to obtain freedom from servile status. By the fourteenth century a popular valuation of the distinctive rights of freeborn Englishmen made possible legalistic critiques of lordly oppression by bondmen and their defenders.[11]

Over the course of the late medieval and early modern periods, an exceptionalist conception of liberty and the rule of law sank deep roots in English culture. In the fifteenth century John Fortescue made a fundamental distinction between "royal" and "political" kingship, emphasizing the subject's right to consent to rule in the latter form of government, a right that would pervade English legal thought for centuries.[12] Supporters of the Reformation forged an association between English freedom and Protestantism in the second half of the sixteenth century. According to Thomas Smith, "The nature of our nation is free," and the people were "stout-hearted, courageous and soldiers, not villeins and slaves."[13] Patrick Collinson has characterized England under Queen Elizabeth as a "monarchical republic" characterized by Protestantism, local autonomy, and the rule of law.[14] Disagreements over England's "fundamental laws" shaped political arguments during the mid-seventeenth-century civil wars, while radical writers increasingly wrote of natural law and right in a language that stressed legal equality and freedom of conscience. Whig political theorists after the Restoration never reached the democratic conclusions of revolutionary-era groups like the Levellers, but legal equality played a similarly important role in the thought of writers like Algernon Sidney and John Locke.[15] As in other areas, the presence of Locke loomed large in eighteenth-century English legal theory; Locke and William Blackstone (in his *Commentaries on* the Laws of England [1765–70]), were the authoritative voices in British legal thought in the eighteenth century.

Yet while early modern jurists, philosophers, and politicians celebrated England's system of justice, commoner attitudes toward law were ambivalent. Many people believed the subtleties and confusions of law provided lawyers and magistrates with privileged access to knowledge that could be used to oppress those excluded from the fortress of law. Lawyers, often associated with usurers, used their expert knowledge to obtain money from honest, though unlettered, people. As early as the fourteenth century poets Geoffrey Chaucer and William Langland satirized lawyers in an emerging commercial society; rebels in the Great Uprising of 1381 targeted legal professionals and others connected to the judicial system.[16] Criticisms of the enclosure movement and capital punishments joined antilawyer sentiments in the early sixteenth century, most famously in Thomas More's Utopia, where there was no private property and simple laws in plain language made lawyers superfluous.[17] A popular tradition of English justice legitimated extralegal direct actions such as the destruction of enclosures, while Protestant social critics decried the widespread abuse of law in the 1540s and 1550s. In the view of Commonwealthmen like Henry Brinkow, lawyers used "innumerable wiles, crafts, subtilties and delayes that be in the lawe" to dispossess the poor, making lawyers almost as bad as representatives of the Antichrist like bishops and priests.[18] During the reign of Elizabeth I radical Protestant criticisms—some of them termed by critics "antinomian," meaning released by grace from the moral law—emerged to challenge institutions and statutes instituted by authorities who allegedly monopolized knowledge and power.[19]

During the cultural and intellectual ferment of the 1650s, few groups were more critical of institutional authority than Quakers. Friends emphasized the Inner Light—the light of God within each individual—and rejected predestination; taken with their opposition to traditional markers of status and their opposition to tithes, these stances placed them on England's religious extreme in the 1650s. Quakers also shared with other radicals hopes for a more accessible legal system that, if put into practice, would have deprofessionalized law. Their critics argued such beliefs could only undermine the authority of church and state; this was one reason why their opponents associated Quakers with anarchistic Ranters and Roman Catholics.[20] The first statute targeting Friends in England was the Vagrancy Act of 1656, whose threat to apprehend and punish "wandering persons" was intended to stop Quakers' itinerant proselytizing.

...ıe Restoration, however, that the English government attempted to
-ƒ eradicate dissent through a series of acts (the Clarendon Code) intended
to reestablish the supremacy of the Anglican Church.[21] Scholars have estimated
that more than ten thousand Friends were jailed for their beliefs, and hundreds
died between 1660 and the early 1680s.[22]

Like their attitudes toward political authority, Quaker writers moderated
their legal views after the Restoration while retaining a traditional suspicion
of the legal profession. The common association of Quakers with Ranters and
other antinomian groups in the 1650s was repudiated by George Fox and other
Friends during the Restoration. The acceptance of human sinfulness and the
resulting need for traditional forms of order in church and society were cor-
nerstones of Robert Barclay's defenses of the Society of Friends in the 1670s.
Proper government required good laws and worthy judges; discipline and obedience were divinely ordained. Shepherds were needed to guide the sheep, for
when everyone followed their own conscience, a rejection of submission to
rightful authorities was the inevitable outcome.[23] Yet even advocates of order
like Barclay expressed customary suspicions of lawyers and legal machinations.
Were truth and righteousness to prevail in the world, he wrote, priests as well
as that "deceitful Tribe of Lawyers" could be dispensed with. Both professions,
through their numerous "Tricks" and "endless Intricacies," were burdensome to
"honest Men."[24]

Law, Justice, and "Governmentish" Colonists

Colonial governments subjected Quakers to legal repression and state violence
after their arrival in the Americas, not dissimilar to what they experienced
in England. Massachusetts and Virginia banned Friends in the late 1650s;
between 1659 and 1661 the colony of Massachusetts infamously executed the
Quakers Marmaduke Stephenson, William Robinson, Mary Dyer, and William Leddra. Though the death penalty was suspended in 1661, proselytizing
Friends in the Bay Colony were to be stripped from the waist upwards, tied
to a cart's tail, and whipped through town.[25] Quakers challenged the authority
of the Dutch West India Company in New Netherland as early as 1657: after
landing in New Amsterdam on a ship flying no flags, Friends refused to show
deference to WIC officials. New Amsterdam dominies Johannes Megapo-
lensis and Samuel Drisius characterized the group as fanatics tolerated only
in Rhode Island, the "latrina" of New England dissenters. In 1663 the Dutch

colony borrowed from English law and banned "Vagabonds, Quakers and other Fugitives" from New Netherland.[26]

The creation of Pennsylvania made possible the establishment of a legal system influenced by Quakers' experience of persecution as well as their Commonwealth-era commitment to legal reform. Criticisms of law in early modern Europe included its general inaccessibility arising from prohibitive costs and highly specialized language. William Penn, trained in law at Lincoln's Inn in London, quipped in 1670 that the complexity of English common law made it "far from being common."[27] This did not lead Penn to formulate a legal system based on popular demands, however. According to the political theorist Algernon Sidney, an early draft of the Pennsylvania constitution contained "the basest laws in the world, not to be endured or lived under, and the Turk was not more absolute" than his friend Penn.[28] Republican influences like those of Sidney prevailed, as Penn's Laws Agreed Upon in England (also known as the Frame of Government) mandated that all court proceedings would be "short, and in English, and in ordinary and plain character." Those accused of crimes would be tried by a jury, and court fees would be "moderate."[29]

Yet Penn's preface to the Laws Agreed Upon also expressed a conventional view of law's essential function. Penn traced the necessity of law to the biblical Fall and the rule of man by passion rather than reason. Law as a method of restraining man's corrupt nature was ordained by God. Alluding to the civil wars, the Restoration, and his own power as proprietor, Penn claimed the supremacy of divine rule had been settled beyond dispute—though adherence to the rule of law would prevent any degeneration of colonial government. Moreover, however good laws in any commonwealth may be, men of special "wisdom and virtue" were necessary for their proper administration. While requiring that Pennsylvania law be comprehensible and accessible, Penn's interpretation of the founding laws was premised on a traditional view of human sinfulness and the need for specially trained authorities to administer justice.[30] If "reasonable" court fees and proceedings in plain English were in keeping with radicals' hopes in the 1650s, Penn's argument concerning the need for legal hierarchy to protect society from man's innate lusts departed from the perfectionist views of early Quakers.[31]

Founding Philadelphians welcomed the privileges granted to freemen in the Pennsylvania charter and utilized customary methods of legal protest when they felt their rights were violated. A 1684 remonstrance from First Purchasers complained that Penn altered the design of Philadelphia, giving them less land than promised in 1681. They accused the proprietor of charging settlers excessive quitrents, denying them access to the town's natural resources, and reserving the best lots along the Delaware waterfront for personal favorites. In addition to citing their possession of deeds of conveyance guaranteeing their purchases, petitioners emphasized the risks taken by themselves and their families in emigrating, as well as the many improvements they had made to the town in a short time. Petitioners' sense of betrayal was accentuated by the fact that Penn had encouraged First Purchasers to emigrate in promotional pamphlets.[32]

After the Crown's reconfirmation of Penn's proprietary charter in 1694, Lieutenant Governor William Markham's attempt to revise the Frame of Government met with a similar protest. In March 1697 more than a hundred freemen of Philadelphia County sent a remonstrance to Markham after the introduction of the new constitution. The new charter required possession of an estate of fifty pounds, free of debt, to vote in the city, while it also reduced the number of representatives per county.[33] Although the new Frame was an attempt to reduce the political power of non-Quaker immigrants, petitioners cited their rights and privileges as founding settlers and the reconfirmation of Penn's charter by William and Mary in 1694. Like the 1684 remonstrance, petitioners evoked the hazards and hardships of migration and emphasized the "great Liberties franchises & Imunities" promised by Penn "in divers papers published" prior to their departure from England. Laws related to settlement were confirmed by the assembly at the founding, and petitioners believed that with the restoration of the proprietary charter, the people's liberties did "of right" return to them. Revisions to the initial Frame could only be made through procedures outlined in the original charter; the new methods introduced for passing bills in the legislature and the reduction of representatives were thus violations of the constitution.[34]

For Penn's supporters, the vigorous manner in which some Philadelphians proclaimed their rights and privileges indicated not a commitment to English constitutional norms but rather a failure to live up to Quakers' professed ideals. As early as 1685, not long after receiving the first remonstrance from First Purchasers, Penn wrote to Thomas Lloyd and the provincial council: "For the love of god, me, and the poor country, be not so Governmentish, so Noisy and open in your dissatisfactions."[35] Two decades later James Logan complained of the "Knaves & fools" in the legislature who blindly followed the "Rattle of Rights & Privileges." In reference to what Logan viewed as the excessively democratic charter of 1701, he suggested to Penn that colonists would not be brought to order until ruled directly by the Crown.[36] In 1710 Isaac Norris complained that

the "Popular & Plausible Cry" of supporting "*Liberties & Privileges*" had produced legislative paralysis.[37] For Penn, Logan, Norris, and others of the proprietary faction, "governmentish" representatives had poisoned a founding vision
of Quaker peace and harmony.

In contrast to some colonists' politicking, Philadelphians' regular disregard of
laws indicated rather different attitudes toward legal authority. In seventeenth-
century England utterances like oath-taking, while technically illegal, were seen
by some as evidence of "stout courage."[38] Pennsylvania's Frame made "swearing, cursing, lying, prophane talking," and other moral offenses illegal.[39] Speech
acts were unusually prominent in early Pennsylvania legislation, however, and
in Philadelphia blasphemous and scandalous language was vigorously prosecuted.[40] In 1685, for example, Peter Cook was fined five shillings for "swearing
in the open fase of the Court"; some years later George Tomson and George
Robinson were indicted for "Swearing profane." Robinson, a butcher, was a regular disturber of the peace; in 1702 he was again presented by the grand jury as
a "comon swarer and a comon drinker," having cursed and uttered "very bad"
oaths in the marketplace.[41] Many marketgoers likely found Robinson's drunken
swearing offensive; some however may have found his irreverence evidence
of "stout courage." Refusals to pay licenses and fees for market stalls were also
regular sources of frustration for a municipal government dependent on such
charges for revenue.[42]

Demonstrations of disrespect for law enforcement officials, especially
officers of the night watch, were common in early modern Europe. Whether
because of their relatively low social status, perceived corruption, or as a result
of their enforcement of unpopular laws, constables and watchmen were often
objects of ridicule and abuse. Many watchmen wisely chose not to enforce
unpopular laws.[43] As in Europe, intoxicated Philadelphia tavern goers angry
with orders to disperse after the nine o'clock curfew assaulted watchmen and
constables. In 1695 Samuel Holt was fined ten shillings for abusing constable
James Coate; shortly thereafter the grand jury indicted Francis Jones, Samuel Perry, Samuel Stacy, James Metcalf, and Thomas Merriot for assaulting
the watch after they were confronted by authorities during nighttime revelries
in the tavern of "widdow Cox." Revelers called watchman Thomas Morris a
"Rascall Curr, Beast, Impudent Dog etc."[44]

Yet there were also complex personal and political dynamics surrounding
attitudes toward the law and the city watch, and watchmen on occasion used
their position as a source of power. After his arrival in Philadelphia in 1704,

new lieutenant governor John Evans objected to the Pennsylvania manslaughter act, noting that a "Ruffian" convicted of manslaughter would serve only a year of imprisonment, while a rich man could be ruined by being forced to pay restitution.[45] The new governor's youthful arrogance did not endear him to many townspeople. But it was Evans's attempt to establish a local militia, membership of which was a key marker of status in England and Anglo-America, that led to violence between his supporters and watchmen. After Evans offered to exempt militia volunteers from the low-status watch, a confrontation in the tavern of Enoch Story erupted into a brawl. City watchmen fought with supporters of the new governor—one of whom was William Penn Jr. Two months later watchman Solomon Cresson arrived at Story's bar well after midnight to disperse a group of drinkers. Cresson beat patrons slow to leave; one of the revelers turned out to be Governor Evans. In the ensuing melee town officials hostile to the young governor came to the watchman's aid, and a fight between Evans and his supporters and Cresson and town authorities followed.[46] In a remonstrance against Evans's actions in the aftermath of the affair, the Philadelphia commonalty cited the city's new legal status as a corporate entity and complained that the governor's disrespect for urban rights and privileges would render the municipality's authority "contemptible" to townspeople.[47]

The commonalty's form of complaint against Evans—the remonstrance, or petition—was the most common method of legal protest in Europe by the later Middle Ages. Historians have noted the ambivalent nature of petitioning as a political practice between the fifteenth and eighteenth centuries. While the petition's conventional form required a language of deference and subordination, it could also challenge or even threaten authorities.[48] In mid-seventeenth-century England the published petition became a shaper of public opinion and a crucial source of politicization. Groups like the Levellers used petitions to Parliament for propaganda purposes as well as to mobilize massive street demonstrations. After the Restoration, Parliament passed an act against tumultuous petitioning that prohibited the collection of more than twenty signatures in any document that challenged the policies of church or state. Far from reinforcing a culture of deference, recent "sad experience" had shown that petitions could lead to revolutionary disorders.[49]

The remonstrances delivered by Philadelphia freemen to Penn in the 1680s and 1690s were not revolutionary, but their use of contractual language and references to English rights seriously challenged instituted authority in the new colony. A commonwealth and Leveller belief in popular sovereignty was evident in a 1692 antitax petition to the assembly signed by 161 freemen. Petitioners reminded legislators that they were merely the people's "Delegates"; it was by electors' "Choice you are, by whose Power you act, and with whose Liberties you are Intrusted."[50] The notion that elected representatives were subordinate to the people and served primarily to protect the people's liberties was a radical one whose origins lay in the ferment of the 1640s. The document's implicit warning, that should representatives ratify the bill they would be replaced by others more attuned to the will of the people, was far from deferential.

Most petitions reflected everyday disagreements among individuals within the urban community. Those from larger collectivities could reinforce a sense of community, on the one hand, or internal political differences on the other. The sending of remonstrances signed by hundreds of freemen to the proprietor would have been widely discussed in town in the 1680s and 1690s, for example. In 1704 Philadelphians still unhappy with quitrents petitioned the assembly to have their complaint added to a different remonstrance in the process of being sent to Penn. While grand juries and the corporation of Philadelphia petitioned representatives over vice and licentiousness in the port, townspeople requested internal improvements and protectionist trade regulations. Some lodged complaints against landlords and creditors; others brought disputes with fellow craftsmen to the attention of provincial authorities.[51]

An equally important colonial expression of English cultural legalism was the custom of court days. Court hearings were open to the public in Pennsylvania, and in Philadelphia, as in England and other colonies, a festive cultural component accompanied the events' serious legal functions. According to Gottlieb Mittelberger, on court days young and old alike entered chambers and listened to witness examinations and judgments, "which often cause[d] the listeners to burst into uproarious laughter."[52] As sites for the administration of justice *and* as places of local theater, the courts served crucial, if potentially contradictory, social functions. The court dispensed legal rulings and ideally bound settlers together through the authority of law; it was also a space of entertainment and revelry in which the follies of high and low were exposed to public view. Courts were also spaces in which English legal forms contrasted with distinctive Quaker beliefs—most obviously in the display of Friends taking affirmations rather oaths. Few events more publicly demonstrated how Quaker practices departed from traditional English norms than court proceedings.

Friends' departures from metropolitan legal practices in Pennsylvania were also politicized by opponents of the proprietary elite. Not long after his arrival as lieutenant governor in 1717, William Keith used the provincial courts' alleged shortcomings to wage a battle against his political opponents. In February 1718 the new governor evoked the royal prerogative in calling for a court of oyer and terminer and general gaol delivery in order to try two men accused of murder in Chester County. Disagreement between Keith and the provincial council over commissions for the court developed into a debate over royal and proprietary legal jurisdiction, with Keith delivering an extended argument in defense of the royal prerogative. According to Keith, and despite the views of "several Gentlemen" with great "Experience and Knowledge" of proprietorial privileges, commissions for judges and justices of the peace ought to be issued in the king's name.[53] Though at this time the governor observed formal niceties to his council opponents, this was a founding moment in a dispute between Keith and Pennsylvania authorities that persisted through the 1720s.

Oathtaking constituted a crucial display of individual honor and honesty in eighteenth-century Anglo-America, and the taking of oaths was intimately bound up with public rituals of office holding and legal testimony. Oaths bound their takers to tell the truth or to perform that which was promised on pain of otherworldly and earthly punishment.[54] While the colony's non-Quaker minority had from the founding likely been suspicious of Friends' refusal to take oaths, it was the accused murderers mentioned by Keith who first claimed the taking of affirmations rather than oaths in Pennsylvania violated the rights of British subjects.[55] In May 1718 the court of oyer and terminer established by Keith in Chester convicted millwright Hugh Pugh and laborer Thomas Lazarus of murder. On being informed of their death sentence, Pugh and Lazarus sent a petition to provincial authorities in Philadelphia professing, in addition to their innocence, a desire to appeal their case to the king on procedural grounds, which was their "undoubted Right." Pugh and Lazarus claimed that seventeen members of the grand inquest who found the indictment against them a true bill, and eight members of the jury that found them guilty, had not taken oaths. Affirmations or declarations as substitutes for oaths were contrary to English law, and the provincial act for qualifying judges, jurors, and witnesses was passed after the crime took place.[56]

Pennsylvania authorities unsurprisingly rejected Pugh and Lazarus's plea. All but one member of the provincial council agreed that the convicted men were "notorious" leaders of a "Lawless Gang of Loose fellows, Common Disturbers of the public peace." Yet the fact that the men had boasted that the government of Pennsylvania had no power to try capital crimes according to the common and statute laws of England, which they planned to claim as their right, suggests a general awareness of the novelties of the colony's legal system.[57] Such accusations of criminals' knowledge of ostensibly lenient Pennsylvania law, whether true or simply useful propaganda for critics of proprietary government, made possible the introduction of English common law punishments in 1718 (discussed in chapter 4).

Justice, Grand Juries, and Authority

The creation of a national identity in early modern England was closely related to the expansion of commoner participation in local government, which bound local officeholders to the central state. Common people's involvement in the machinery of local government was noted by Thomas Smith as early as the 1560s, when he claimed that in incorporated towns with no middling yeomen those of the "fourth sort"—day laborers, poor farmers and merchants, copyholders, and mechanics—occasionally served on inquests and juries or as churchwardens, ale runners, and constables.[58] A legal body that played an instrumental role in local government, the grand jury was "the body of the country." Composed largely of an expanding middling sort, grand juries heard petitions and presentments that provided a means whereby new, national conceptions of order were expressed at the local level.[59]

Grand juries were also key institutions of order in the colonies. Jury membership, particularly for grand juries, became increasingly restrictive in the middle colonies in the early eighteenth century, however, and in Philadelphia and the Delaware Valley grand jurymen were invariably Friends. As emphasized in chapter 2, the Philadelphia grand jury was active in attempting to maintain labor discipline and public morality in the city.[60] While many colonists saw the grand jury as representing "the body of the people," some in Philadelphia saw it as a deeply partisan, pro-proprietary institution.[61] In 1723 James Logan used his position as Pennsylvania's chief justice to publish *A Charge Delivered from the Bench to the Grand-Jury*, a customary formal legal proclamation that served in Philadelphia as a polemic against popular politics. In contrast to other British territories, whose administrations resembled the superior English system of mixed government, according to Logan there was a lack of submission to instituted authority in the mid-Atlantic. Logan's repeated emphasis on justice primarily concerned issues of a "*Private* or *Commutative*" nature, a reference in support of creditors at a time when many were calling for debt relief and paper money. In Logan's view, legal justice—a concept so important that it "in some measure Comprehends all other Virtues within it"— secured to all what was rightfully theirs. Logan also claimed he published the *Charge* "at the Desire of the said *Grand-Jury*," suggesting an overt political role for the body during a period of unprecedented social conflict.[62]

For colonists experiencing economic difficulties in the early 1720s, law often appeared as an instrument of power unjustly wielded by urban grandees. The publication of speeches to the grand jury demonstrated how partisan politics had corrupted what was ideally an impartial dispenser of justice. Anonymous pamphlets characterized legal officials as "Villains" who used their authority to oppress and expropriate the property of honest producers. At the founding William Penn created a court system to be administered in English and affordable to all. By the 1720s, however, court costs had become prohibitive for common people: "What shall a Poor Man do, that has not where-withal to go either to Law or Equity?" This tract, published anonymously by Governor Keith, emphasized that it was individuals and not the system that were oppressive. England's laws remained superior to all others, and "all that an Honest Man, in any Condition of Life, can demand" was an equal distribution of law.[63]

One writer used an ideal of English legal equality and impartiality to attack Isaac Norris's partisan address to the court of common pleas in 1727.[64] According to "Jotham," Norris used his power as a judge to harangue the public from the bench with the aim of turning the people against Norris's personal enemies. Such factionalism was unbecoming the office and station of a magistrate, Jotham argued, and it was a particular abuse of authority to use the address to encourage the election of only wealthy men to the House of Representatives. Norris's public promotion of the election of the "*Rich* and *Parcimonious*" was an obstruction of the "natural Freedom of Elections" and an abuse of judicial power. Referring to elite criticisms of popular participation at recent elections, Jotham claimed elections in England were far more "mobbish" than in Philadelphia. In the home country common people believed all to be on a level at the polls; during elections the law made no distinction between a cobbler with a forty-shilling freehold (the traditional minimum requirement for the franchise) and the "greatest *Knight*, who may be worth as many Thousands of Pounds."[65] Pairing this idealized conception of popular participation in elections in England with an accusation that Norris abused his authority as a judge in advocating the election of the "best men" contributed to an image of local oppressors who disregarded the rights of Englishmen.

Critics of provincial government continued to stress the importance of wide political participation and legal power after the decline of the factionalism of the 1720s. On the eve of assembly elections in 1735, "Constant Truman" wrote that the ability to speak freely was a privilege denied those living under arbitrary governments and this right was to be cherished as much as life itself. For arbitrary rule signified bondage and slavery, as those afraid to *speak* freely inevitably soon found themselves unable to *act* freely. Without the rule of law the people were reduced to "Beasts of Burden" who were forced to "quietly submit your Necks to the Yoke, receive the Lash patiently let it be ever so Smart, and carry all the Loads they think proper to clap on your Backs, without kicking or wincing." Formal legal equality between the many and the few prevented the powerful from enslaving the populace. Not voting, or voting against conscience out of fear of reprisals from provincial grandees, was a betrayal of the rights and duties enshrined in the English constitution as well as the Pennsylvania charter.[66]

According to Truman, Anglo-Pennsylvanian liberties needed to be defended against the very men who were entrusted with the preservation and application of justice. Too often the "honest plain Man" failed to vote because he was afraid that a magistrate standing for assembly election would use his legal authority to rule against the citizen in court. Similarly, loan office trustees intimidated voters by using the threat of land dispossession to coerce freeholders into selecting certain trustees for office. Truman's longest reproach was reserved for attorneys, however—specifically the "crafty popular Lawyer." This figure often used the wiles and tricks of his profession "together with abundance of unintelligible Stuff that he calls Law" to dupe the credulous, influence a judge or jury, or carry an unjust cause. Not all lawyers were corrupt, of course; some were honest men who served virtuously in public or private capacities. Many, however, used their special training ("long Habits to Contradiction") to pervert the "true Sense" of things.[67]

Though Truman's plea for popular political engagement was a pamphlet published at election time, antilawyer sentiment was evident in everyday print culture. In 1723 the newly arrived printer Samuel Keimer reproduced a longstanding bias against university-educated professionals in a one-sheet doggerel that ridiculed the occupations of law, medicine, and the priesthood.[68] Seven years later, Ralph Sandiford's antislavery tract *The Mystery of Iniquity* similarly railed against "Priests, Physicians and Lawyers, the one making a Trade of the Soul, the other of the Body, and the other of the Property of the People."[69] According to this longstanding belief, the exchange of money for spiritual, medical, and legal favors signified the corruption of practitioners and the exploitation of those in need. The addition of medicine and law to religion in university education began in the Middle Ages. A popular early modern view that painted physicians and lawyers as secular versions of a clergy whose languages were similarly unintelligible was expressed in early Philadelphia humorously in verse and seriously in antislavery tracts.[70]

The notion that disputatious relations between neighbors benefited lawyers to the detriment of community harmony was also present in Philadelphia. In the first edition of *Poor Richard's Almanack*, published two years after Sandiford's *Mystery of Iniquity*, Benjamin Franklin satirized the frequency of lawsuits in the region by representing two beggars going to court over an oyster found in the road. The lawyer who took on the case "knew his Business" and was therefore not interested in true justice, choosing instead to make "the best o'th' Cause." "Lawyer-like," he determined to give each beggar an equal share with the *"Friendly Law's impartial Care"*: each received a shell while *"The Middle is the Lawyer's Fee."*[71] Courts were essential institutions that ideally provided the impartial administration of justice in a litigious commercial society. Yet according to popular wisdom as reflected in almanacs and other cheap prints, they should be used only when absolutely necessary, for those who profited most from legal action were lawyers, a "throng" of greedy professionals with little or no allegiance to truth, justice, or the common good.[72]

In addition to a distrust of legal professionals, colonial cultural legalism associated the notions of participatory government and equal justice with knowledge of distinctive local conditions.[73] In Philadelphia, however, there was little consensus regarding local needs and circumstances; this became especially clear in the 1720s and 1730s. In large part, this lack of consensus stemmed from the ways in which colonial law departed from metropolitan norms. Supporters of the Pennsylvania constitution, such as a 1738 *Pennsylvania Gazette* author, defended the provincial legal system as uniquely suited to local needs. In contrast to most eighteenth-century legal and political writers, however, the *Gazette* writer was highly critical of the English constitution, whose mixed system of government and titles, honors, and distinctions were represented as the fruits of the Saxons' martial conquest rather than a unique expression of freedom. Pennsylvania, by contrast, was founded by compact and was based on principles of civil and religious liberty. The Charter of Liberties of 1701 placed legislative power in the hands of the people, who were free to choose their own representatives. The laws of the colony, like those of all free nations, conformed to "the circumstances, the genius and humours" of the people from whom they came.[74]

Yet the Pennsylvania constitution was also—wisely, in the author's view— far from democratic. Quaker founders had experienced despotism in England and therefore knew the true value of liberty. But the colony's first settlers were also of "*sober disposition and independent circumstances,*" meaning they were propertied men with moderate political views. While the "chimerical schemes" of speculative writers who never studied human nature except in books were usually harmless, in Philadelphia there were some who dangerously argued for changing the colonial system of government.[75] Since at least the time of Thomas More's *Utopia* in the early sixteenth century, authors often charac- terized equalitarian ideas as "chimerical" and "fantastical." In this case, how- ever, utopian schemes were curiously associated with the mixed British form of government. The link was made explicit with the writer's claim that such designs as were circulating in Pennsylvania were "almost as wicked, as was the attempt to change the *English Constitution* into a *Democracy*" during the English Revolution. The civil wars had shown, the *Gazette* suggested, that democratic experiments invariably descend into anarchy.[76]

Distinctions between British and Pennsylvanian legal and political systems in Philadelphia were always highly contextual. In 1687 William Penn pub- lished a long pamphlet in the town titled *The Excellent Priviledge of Liberty & Property, Being the Birth-Right of the Free-born Subjects of England* that situ- ated the Pennsylvania charter in a lineage beginning with the Magna Carta.[77] Penn consistently argued for the superiority of English law, and ruling Quak- ers in Philadelphia would long remember Charles II granting the proprietary charter and Penn's friendship with Charles and his brother, the Duke of York (later King James II). Critics of the Pennsylvania constitution and legal system were careful not to explicitly attack the Society of Friends, never condemning Quakers or their religious beliefs as such. Leading Friends also notably did not oppose the legislature's introduction of English common law in 1718, which vastly expanded capital offenses and was justified in a language of the "birth- right of English subjects."[78] Legal convergence, particularly regarding criminal law, is one demonstration of Philadelphia and Pennsylvania's incorporation into a larger British Atlantic world. At the same time, law continued to be a key object of division in the city and colony.

Law's importance to partisan hostilities in Philadelphia extended to events occurring in neighboring New York. In 1734 the German immigrant John Peter

Zenger was hired by Lewis Morris, an opponent of Governor William Cosby of New York, to print the *New-York Weekly Journal*, the city's second newspaper.[79] The *Journal* articles of lawyers James Alexander and William Smith lambasted Cosby and his supporters in a republican political language. Appropriating an artisanal voice, contributions emphasized legal inequities in New York: "Suppose any great Man should draw his Indignation, and whip you through the Lungs; or with a Stone, or Brick-Batt knock your Brains out, and he should be presented by the Grand Jury, pray what Notice would be taken of it? If we may guess at what will be, from what has been; I believe very little."[80] Zenger was arrested and put on trial for libeling Cosby. The Morris faction enlisted Andrew Hamilton, a Scottish attorney resident in Philadelphia since 1717, to defend the printer. Hamilton's defense elevated the power of the jury as representative of the people, arguing that juries could decide both fact and law—an argument that relegated the judge to a simple presiding role. Drawing on John Milton's free-speech pamphlet *Areopagitica* and John Trenchard and Thomas Gordon's *Cato's Letters,* Hamilton also made a case for press freedom, claiming the suppression of criticisms of magistrates was permissible only if such criticism could be proven false. Zenger's acquittal was met with riotous celebration in New York; Hamilton was given the freedom of the city and was presented with "an elegant golden snuff-box with many classical allusions."[81]

People throughout the Atlantic world followed the trial, and editions of Alexander's *A Brief Narrative of the Case and Trial of John Peter Zenger* were published in New York, Boston, Philadelphia, Barbados, and London.[82] An extended criticism of Hamilton's argument as portrayed in the *Narrative* was printed in Philadelphia in 1737. Written by "Anglo Americanus," a Bridgetown Barbadian, the critique was originally published by Samuel Keimer of the *Barbados Gazette.*[83] (Keimer had formerly been a printer in Philadelphia.) Shortly thereafter a letter signed by "Cato Jr." appeared in Philadelphia's *Mercury* that, while acknowledging the right of the people to judge their magistrates, cautioned against following men "of profligate Lives and Manners." The author claimed some men of "mean circumstances" who had been forced to flee their homes for crimes committed had then courted popularity through seduction and delusion. The former claim alluded to the murkiness of Hamilton's Scottish childhood before his 1697 arrival in Virginia. Born in the 1670s, Hamilton's parentage was unknown, though he had clearly obtained a genteel education. One story held that he was forced to flee Scotland after killing a man in a duel, and for a time he discarded Hamilton for the surname Trent. Nineteenth-century historians speculated he was a

Jacobite during the reign of William and Mary.[84] Any doubt that the object of the letter was Hamilton was eliminated when the *Mercury* author quoted Exodus 23:8: "Thou shalt not wrest Judgment nor respect Persons, neither take a Gift, for a Gift doth blind the Eyes of the wise, and pervert the words of the Righteous." This was a clear reference to the golden snuff box given Hamilton by the City of New York. Hamilton was portrayed in the *Mercury* as an unethical, and even criminal, seducer of the multitude whose "powers of Rhetorick" subverted the cause of justice.[85]

Three weeks later a response to Cato Jr. appeared in the *Gazette*. According to "Z" (probably John Webbe, a writer and editor well known in Philadelphia by this time), every "True Lover of Pennsylvania" would receive satisfaction from Hamilton's defense of the "Rights of Mankind" in New York. Hamilton's reputation in England and in the colonies was elevated as a result of his work for Zenger and the assembly of Pennsylvania, which he had served for ten years. His *Mercury* detractors had "spit their poison *in the dark*," and men of sense should ignore "such scribling *Reptiles*." Z claimed Hamilton would be honorably remembered as a defender of press liberty and promoter of the good of humanity.[86] Historians are in general agreement that the Zenger trial had little significance as a legal precedent. Yet the case was symptomatic of a broad English and colonial American legal culture taking shape in the eighteenth century. The New York jury's verdict was seen throughout the British Atlantic world as a vindication of the British system of law; conversely, it was cited as evidence of the dangers of an excessively open press. Within Philadelphia, Hamilton's role in the Zenger case hardened already existing political divisions.[87]

Legal developments less sensationalistic than the Zenger case, though much more consequential for many colonists, occurred closer to home around the same time. Access to water had been a source of contention in England as far back as the Magna Carta, which called for the removal of fishing weirs—obstructions placed in waterways to direct the passage of fish—from the Thames and Medway Rivers. In 1549 opposition emerged to feudal riparian laws that restricted common access to water: protesters in Norfolk, Suffolk, and Norwich demanded "Ryvers may be ffre and comon to all men for fyshyng and passage" during Kett's Rebellion.[88] While sixteenth-century rebels saw limitations on rights to fishing and travel as part of a general process of enclosure, in late Tudor and Stuart England the passage of laws prohibiting fishing weirs demonstrated policy shifts that facilitated commerce and improved communication. Fishing weirs were increasingly characterized as a "publick

nuisance" that hindered economic development. The growth of water transportation in England in the sixteenth and seventeenth centuries lowered transport costs and reduced regional price differences, enabling national economic
integration and expansion.[89]

While in England authorities removed barriers to water transport in the
interest of new conceptions of improvement and the public weal, Charles II
gave William Penn neofeudal fishing rights by granting him title to all the soil
and rivers of Pennsylvania. The 1681 proprietary grant gave Penn control over
all "Seaports, harbours, Creeks, Havens, Keyes and other places, for discharge
and unlading of goods, and merchandize."[90] The assembly addressed the use
of fishing weirs in 1683 when it banned the use of any barriers stretching from
bank to bank in all the colony's rivers and streams on pain of a ten-shilling fine.
In 1700 the act was reconfirmed—though mill-dams and those using weirs on
their own properties were exempted.[91] Penn's monopoly on waterways and fish
had evidently been a source of complaint, for William Markham's new Frame
of Government of 1696 granted inhabitants fishing and hunting rights in all
unenclosed places in the colony.[92]

The second Frame justified common fishing rights in language citing the
people's right to subsistence and access to what "God in his providence hath
freely afforded."[93] Fishing weirs, by contrast, were deemed a public nuisance
that obstructed boat traffic on Pennsylvania waterways. Yet settlers defied the
law and continued to use fish traps on the Schuylkill River despite the potential fine, which at the time amounted to about two days' wages for a Philadelphia journeyman. In 1730 the assembly again mandated the removal of all
river obstructions, while tripling the fine from ten to thirty shillings. Violators
unable to pay could have their goods seized; those with no moveable property
could spend twenty days in jail. The stated purpose of the act was to keep the
river clear for boat passage and trade, specifically for the easy transportation of
wood—a probable reference to the Philadelphia shipbuilding industry's need
for lumber from the colony's interior.[94]

Two years later, in 1732, a number of Philadelphia gentlemen created the
Schuylkill Fishing Company, the colonies' first sporting club, housed on the
river on the western edge of the city limits. Club members excited to hunt
and fish near the picturesque river would not have looked kindly on the large
fish traps and boisterous crowds that continued to gather along the river in
defiance of the recent law. Conversely, fish trappers likely viewed the genteel
new club with suspicion. In 1734 the legislature raised fines for using racks

and weirs to forty shillings, with one part of the proceeds going to the construction of the new Philadelphia workhouse and the other to the informant of the violation. The new act empowered any person in the area to destroy any weirs, dams, or racks on the river; anyone who resisted the obstructions' removal would be punished with a fine of up to ten pounds.[95] The statute was followed by a petition from inhabitants requesting an amendment to allow weirs during April and May, when fish were running. Governor Patrick Gordon cited precedents from seventeenth-century England and Pennsylvania to argue against the petition. Gordon added a moral justification when he noted that in addition to depleting the river's stock of fish, the use of weirs was often accompanied by "riotous Behaviour, Quarrels, Contentions, & even Outrages amongst the young People and others who assemble as to a Merry-making or a publick Diversion."[96]

The threat of increased fines again failed to deter trappers, however. In late April 1738 the provincial council received a report stating "a great Number of Men" armed with clubs, staves, and other weapons had violently attacked several constables and their assistants when they attempted to remove fishing racks from the Schuylkill.[97] Constable William Richards testified that he and Robert Smith, constable of the township of Oley in Philadelphia County, had sailed with assistants down the river in three canoes after receiving warrants to remove river obstructions from the Philadelphia magistrate George Boon. On arriving at Mingo Creek upriver from the city, they found a large number of racks and removed the implements unhindered. Four men fishing on a nearby island watched the removals closely, however. The constables and aides then paddled downriver toward the city, where they found more racks at the mouth of Pickering Creek. The upriver anglers must have sounded an alarm, for as Richards and Smith were removing the Pickering Creek weirs, two hundred men streamed down both sides of the river and threatened Richards and his company. Richards, warrant and constable's staff in hand, ordered the men to leave in the king's name and stated he was there to remove the obstructions as ordered by law. The men replied, "Damn'd the Laws & the Law makers," and proceeded to verbally attack Richards and his helpers. A man named James Starr then knocked the constable into the river with a large club or stake while other assistants were similarly assaulted. Officials fled the scene, allegedly in fear for their lives.[98]

Sailing downriver for the safety of the city, the group came upon a different set of racks guarded by another large group of men. Richards and his company told the crowd that if allowed to pass they would not interfere with any weirs, to which the men responded with abuses and curses. The heat of confrontation gave vent to personal grievances when one of the men called out an offer of five pounds for the head of Timothy Miller, evidently one of the constables' aides. (Another of the rioters, however, "called out to the s'd Timothy to make haste away.") The group pursued Richards and his men further downriver, "Who for fear of being Murthered" abandoned their canoes when they reached the mouth of Perkiomen Creek, where they went ashore and "left their Canoes there with several Cloaths, Which Canoes are since Split in Pieces (as Reported) & several of the Cloaths turn'd adrift on the s'd River."[99] The rioters' message to law enforcement was clear: further attempts to suppress local fish trapping would be met with further, possibly more severe, violence.

The rough justice delivered to constables on the Schuylkill in 1738 involved, in addition to access to the Schuylkill, a fundamental disagreement over the legitimacy of provincial law. Some Philadelphians viewed fishing weirs as obstructions to trade and therefore as impediments to development and the public good. Lawmakers agreed and sanctioned removal of the racks. Fish trappers in Philadelphia County saw the three statutes of the 1730s as attempts to eradicate subsistence practices legitimated through custom, and they defended these practices with real and symbolic violence after failing to sway the legislature with petitions. Governor Gordon claimed earlier Pennsylvania restrictions on fishing weirs were "copied from the Example of our Mother Country," which had long made provision to protect the fish population and promote trade in England.[100] He also disliked festive springtime gatherings on the river, a view likely shared by members of the new fishing club. Local trappers saw attempts to remove weirs and the new club as related demonstrations of the unjust expansion of city power and the erosion of customary rights. From their perspective, threatening and attacking constables (and damning lawmakers and their laws) were valid responses to this expansion.

A statute passed more than two decades later, in 1761, indicates the continuing sensitivity of fishing regulation on the Schuylkill. Legislators stressed that a project to improve the Schuylkill's navigability would be specially "advantageous for the poor," since those living upriver could more easily transport their goods to the Philadelphia market. At the same time, those who obstructed the project to clear the river—including those who used racks and weirs—were to be fined twenty pounds or serve six months in prison, more than doubling the previous fine.[101] Later in the decade, after the river's clearing, it was ordinary inhabitants who demanded laws restraining exporters' use of fish traps and private dams that limited the people's access to nature's bounty.[102] Though the decade-long legal dispute culminated with the "Fish-dam Riot" of 1738, disagreement over what constituted legitimate use of the area's natural resources persisted for decades after.

The ambiguities of cultural legalism continued to inform high politics and everyday differences at midcentury. The enlistment controversy of the early 1740s was expressed in competing languages of legal rights and privileges, with assemblymen citing the Pennsylvania charter and their opponents defending the right and duty of British subjects to defend the kingdom. Similar arguments over the legalities of defense infused wartime polemics during the Seven Years' War. Defenders of the Pennsylvania charter's opposition to arms characterized founder William Penn as a "Lover and zealous Defender of Liberty" who, "by the excellency of his Maxims," had become one of the most admired men of the age. The author, "Philadelphus," also drew on customary suspicions of lawyers to criticize professed patriots who clamored for war. Languishing trade and the lack of money in the city and colony led to an increase in lawsuits, and those who benefited from court fees were lawyers and other court officials. Was it unreasonable to believe that "some, whose Employment and Estates are supported by the Contentions and Misfortunes of their Neighbours, are the Patriots who now so zealously exert themselves with a Shew of Regard to our Liberties?" Rather than being burdened with new and arbitrary "Military Laws," it would be better to send to the House men familiar with the colony's principles and sentiments.[103] Philadelphus's arguments citing Pennsylvania's unique laws and liberties, together with his characterization of critics as unscrupulous lawyers, failed to sway a majority of freemen in the context of the Seven Years' War, however. Townspeople's fears of invasion and anger against the provincial government's inaction led the Philadelphia commonalty to petition the provincial government for money and a militia to protect the city and its people.[104]

Less ideological differences over law enforcement continued to shape urban society through the middle of the eighteenth century. The Philadelphia grand jury had complained of the inadequacies of the city night watch as early as the 1690s, and in early 1743 that body presented the common council with a petition on the need for a paid watch "not to be conducted by the citizens as formerly." The jury claimed a paid watch would be "more diligent & Carefull," providing townspeople with better security than had historically been the case; a managed assessment rather than an annual charge would also be more cost effective.[105] Later in the decade, and despite the growth of war-induced crime and disorder at the end of the War of Spanish Succession, the assembly had yet to enact a law for a professional watch in Philadelphia. A municipal board unanimously decided to apply to the assembly for an act to support a paid watch in the city, "as is done in London and other great Towns in England."[106] In 1751 the Pennsylvania legislature approved an act for a paid watch and for lighting the streets of Philadelphia, modeled on a London act of 1737; it was the first law of its kind in North America.[107]

Yet the creation of a paid night watch did not eradicate a traditional disregard for law enforcement in the city. A year after the law's passage James Logan (not the proprietary leader), Michael Dowlan, and Christopher Harding were convicted of assaulting and beating watchmen, and were each fined twenty pounds for the offense. At its meeting in November the common council heard the men's petition, which claimed they were "utterly unable" to pay the fines. The council agreed to release them in exchange for retaining their bonds.[108] Two years later George Lee and Richard Davis also petitioned the city for the remittance of fines for assaulting the watch. A useful remedy to incarcerated men unable to pay fines throughout the war was to free them on condition of volunteering to serve on privateers or in the navy; after their release Lee and Davis boarded a war sloop then in the Philadelphia harbor.[109]

A celebratory vision of liberty and justice that pervaded British culture on both sides of the Atlantic in the eighteenth century remained compatible with a conventional popular distrust of lawyers, unjust laws, and local law enforcement officials. Law continued to play an ambivalent role as guarantor of equal treatment, as a protector of liberties, and as an institution of power through which lawyers and legal officials benefited from the misfortunes and contentions of others. In Philadelphia humorous proverbs warning against recourse to law and "pocket-rifling" lawyers continued to appear in local publications.[110] A pamphlet written by William Noble called *A Terror to Some Lawyers* suggests the continuing prominence of law to colonial culture at midcentury. Though the pamphlet's contents are lost, the extant title page claims the essay was a "terror" to lawyers because it was a "Light to the People" in providing basic legal information that would allow a "School-Boy" to correct any "Attorney or other Officer" in the service of a friend. The indispensability of legal information, including a commentary on the laws of Pennsylvania, reflected new needs in the eighteenth century as well as ancient wisdom, as suggested by the cover's quote from the Book of Hosea: "For the People perish for want of KNOWLEDGE."[111]

Conclusion

Pennsylvania's Laws Agreed Upon in England established a system of law unprecedentedly reflective of popular legal demands dating to England's mid-seventeenth-century Commonwealth. The Laws guaranteed that courts would be open to the public, persons "of all persuasions may freely appear in their own way," and people were to plead their own cause. Justice additionally required that all proceedings be conducted in English "that they may be understood," the accused were to be tried by a jury, court fees should be "moderate," and "prisons were to be free, as to fees, food, and lodging."[112]

Coming from a culture in which law signified not simply a system of rules for regulating behavior but also the unique liberties and privileges of the English people, Philadelphia's first settlers were highly conscious of their legal rights. As a group that had experienced legal persecution in England, Quaker colonists were especially sensitive to law's power. They also recognized that law would be instrumental in securing their privileges, as early petitions showed. When they perceived Penn's failure to honor his obligations, remonstrances to the proprietor quickly followed in a language of contract and right that emphasized the exceptional challenges immigrants faced. In the late seventeenth and early eighteenth centuries, some of Penn's supporters came to believe that colonists were hopelessly factious and that Philadelphia Friends had abandoned any commitment to the Society's ideal of civic harmony. Factional differences continued to be articulated in arguments over the virtues and vices of the Pennsylvania and English constitutions through the Seven Years' War, as law's signifying power remained embedded in urban political culture.

Yet law's importance in early modern Philadelphia extended beyond the constitutional arguments of proprietary and antiproprietary factions. Blasphemous and seditious language, disorderly taverns defying curfew, and assaults against watchmen and constables provided evidence for the persistence of a libertarian strain in Anglo-American culture. A traditional popular suspicion of the abstruse power of law and, especially, "crafty" lawyers was also brought to the colonies, and was expressed in Philadelphia in almanacs, pamphlets, and other publications. At the same time, townspeople recognized the power and importance of law as petitions, assembly meetings, and court days were important elements of urban life. The legal ambivalence expressed by William Moraley in the late 1720s was therefore not unique to the indentured servant from London. But the punishment of runaways and the enslaved emphasized by Moraley points to another challenge involving law and power in the early modern Atlantic world—that of crime.

4

"A GROWING EVIL IN THE CITY"

Law, Crime, and the Atlantic Diaspora

Pennsylvania's legal system underwent significant alteration between the 1680s and 1760s. Laws regulating debt, currency, and labor shaped the development of the urban and provincial economy, while political disputes were strongly informed by competing views of metropolitan and provincial constitutions and systems of justice. But the most profound legal transformation in early Philadelphia concerned crime. Pennsylvania's founding legal code avoided exemplary corporal punishment, with prisons and workhouses intended to function as places of restitution and reform. In 1718, however, the provincial legislature passed An Act for the Advancement of Justice, which introduced English methods of punishment. Prior to this act only murder and treason were capital offenses in Pennsylvania, a result of Friends' experience with persecution and their opposition to the death penalty for theft in seventeenth-century England.[1] The act expanded the number of capital offenses to twelve and was explicitly modeled on English punishments; legislators justified this by claiming some lawbreakers had been encouraged to "transgress certain statutes against capital crimes" because acts of Parliament did not extend to the colonies.[2]

While the year 1718 marks a major watershed in Pennsylvania legal history, crime was an important social issue in Philadelphia from the founding. The occurrence of crime in the town and its hinterland between the 1680s and 1710s was less a result of offenders' knowledge of a lenient Quaker system of law, as some scholars have suggested, than of the colonial environment generally, and of Pennsylvania's mid-Atlantic geographical location specifically. The most substantial form of property crime in early modern America was the flight of bound workers, and unfree workers from the Chesapeake region fled to the north from the 1640s onward. By the 1690s Philadelphia, like other colonial ports, had become a magnet for fugitive bound laborers, while urban servants and enslaved people frequently absconded from the town. Servant and slave flight and other offenses were therefore early sources of legal change. Port cities had also long been centers of piracy, smuggling, and other illicit practices. Pennsylvania lawmakers introduced corporal punishments for robbery and assault before the colony was two years old, and at the turn of the eighteenth century the legislature instituted a separate court system for enslaved persons accused of felonies that sanctioned public whipping and the death penalty.

The expansion and integration of the British Atlantic world between the 1720s and 1760s had equally profound impacts on crime and punishment in Philadelphia. The Act for the Advancement of Justice coincided with rising immigration rates as well as Parliament's passage of the Transportation Act, which brought an estimated fifty thousand convicts to the American colonies between 1718 and 1775. Though most transports landed in Virginia and Maryland, Pennsylvania was the third largest destination for felons shipped to the Americas.[3] Legislators responded by laying prohibitive duties on imported convicts in the early 1720s; alleged crime among Philadelphia's Black population also justified the assembly's passage of the Act for Better Regulating Negroes in 1726. Although counterfeiters of Spanish-American pieces of eight and Massachusetts shillings were active in the colonies in the seventeenth century, the growing volume and diversity of paper monies in North America in the early eighteenth century stimulated the creation of elaborate counterfeiting rings that spanned the Atlantic. Counterfeit bills landed in and circulated through port towns like Philadelphia, and by the middle of the eighteenth century convicted counterfeiters of Pennsylvania bills stood in stocks and had their ears cropped at the entrance to the city market.[4] The increasing likelihood of offenders being sentenced to death, as well as the practice of expulsion, reflected the adoption in Philadelphia of English displays of state power and forms of punishment.[5]

An important dimension of Atlantic integration involved communication and the press, and crime was a prominent feature of Philadelphia's print culture. After its founding by Andrew Bradford in 1719, the *American Weekly Mercury* contained regular notices of urban and regional runaways and jailbreaks. Beginning in the late 1720s the *Mercury* and the new *Pennsylvania Gazette* reported on the movement of counterfeit bills of credit in the city and region and announced the weekly public punishments given to offenders on market days. Newspapers and chapbooks sold in the city also contained narratives of sailor and slave uprisings as well as stories of piracy. Closer to home, newspapers warned inhabitants to be on the lookout for roaming confidence men and women. Following the conclusion of the War of Austrian Succession, the city's three newspapers portrayed a midcentury crime wave that spanned the British Atlantic world as a veritable epidemic, for which the Transportation Act was allegedly to blame.[6]

The colonial state's application of corporal punishments and periodic public hangings in Philadelphia at midcentury testifies to the city's incorporation into a British American legal regime. The growing circulation of goods that nurtured colonists' commitment to the rights of property included a flow of people, voluntary and involuntary, who were drawn to cities like Philadelphia for a variety of reasons. A. Roger Ekirch has estimated that close to 10 percent of runaways identified as convicts fled to Philadelphia, making the city the main urban attraction in America for fugitive laborers. Though the majority of all runaways (67.4 percent) attempted to board ships leaving the colonies, cities like Philadelphia and, to a lesser extent, New York and Boston, provided opportunities for concealment and employment.[7] Changes in colonial criminal law reflected economic and social transformations that were instrumental in the making of the early modern Atlantic world. The appropriation of popular literary forms like criminal narratives and last dying speeches in cities like Philadelphia was a crucial expression of this transformation.

"Much Robrey in Town and Country": Beginnings

Quakers' turn to nonviolence in the 1660s played a major role in discussions of criminal law at Pennsylvania's founding.[8] In a draft charter for the colony, William Penn echoed George Fox in asserting that "to shed man's blood and take away his life for worldly goods is a very hard thing." He therefore decided there would be no executions for theft in Pennsylvania.[9] The Laws Agreed Upon in England stated felons in Pennsylvania would make satisfaction to their victims through land or goods; those without property were to labor in the local prison or workhouse and compensate the injured party. The Laws Agreed Upon made no mention of traditional corporal punishments like whipping or the pillory; only willful murder was specified as a capital offense.[10] In addition to an open and accessible legal system, Pennsylvania's initial focus on the rehabilitation of offenders reflected Friends' belief in redemption and reformation.

The assembly's ratification of the Fundamental Laws in 1683 meant that Pennsylvania had instituted the most enlightened penal code in the world.[11]

However, legislators quickly amended the colony's laws, and these reforms established an early link between bound laborers' disobedience and crimes like theft and assault. As noted in chapter 2, assemblymen significantly expanded terms of service for runaway servants less than a year after settlement.[12] In 1684 Pennsylvania attorney general Nicholas More wrote to Penn that robbery was rampant in town and country, claiming "Vices creepe in like the old Serpent" in the colony. More also noted that he had purchased 4 of the 150 recently arrived "Negroes" from West Africa; all were quickly "sould for redy money, which has Caused Money to be Very scarce." More's "two best" slaves absconded with another servant, however, and the following year the Philadelphia merchant Samuel Carpenter asked the provincial council to set up a special court to prosecute one of his servants for theft.[13] Men like More and Carpenter immediately recognized the deficiencies of Pennsylvania's legal system. In 1684 the legislature acknowledged the need for corporal punishment but limited the number of stripes (lashes) to twenty-one. In the same year representatives added whipping to restitution for those convicted of the crimes of robbery or assault; repeat offenders would receive thirty-one stripes.[14]

Authorities continued to group runaway workers with thefts and robberies in new bills in the 1690s, though Pennsylvania legislation was interrupted by conflicts with new royal governor Benjamin Fletcher during King William's War.[15] Not long after William and Mary restored Penn's colony in 1695, the proprietor wrote to the provincial council that reports in London had informed him that no place was more overrun with wickedness than was the town of Philadelphia. Inhabitants illegally traded with Scots and Dutch merchants, and colonial officials not only tolerated but actively embraced pirates in the port. Moreover, "Sins so very Scandalous" the proprietor's modesty did not allow him to name were committed in defiance of law and virtue in the town—likely a reference to prostitution. Penn demanded no licenses be henceforth given for public houses unless publicans could provide a "great securitie to keep Civil houses."[16]

A committee assigned to investigate Penn's charges deflected the proprietor's criticisms and blamed the weakness of provincial laws instead of officials' tolerance for vice and criminality in the port. Committeemen informed the proprietor that the town was "the rode where sailors and others doe frequentlie pass and repass between Virginia and New England, that it cannot be avoided but the bad as well as ye good will be entertained in such an intercourse." The committee did not respond to Penn's accusation concerning local merchants' involvement in illegal trade, emphasizing instead large numbers of sailors and other rogue elements passing through the region. It was true that "Loossnes & vice" had emerged in Philadelphia, but officials professed they had diligently administered "deserved & exemplary punishments" to offenders—to the extent legally possible. In addition to the suppression of ordinaries, what was needed were more "wholsome & severer" laws to punish wrongdoers.[17]

Assemblymen duly implemented more punitive laws in subsequent years. A 1698 statute included whipping for the stealing of goods worth more than five shillings and required offenders to wear the letter "T" on their clothes as "a badge or mark of his or her thievery" for six months. Repeat offenders were to receive thirty-nine lashes and banishment from the colony. Two years later legislators enacted new punishments for a variety of offenses, from fornication to, yet again, servant flight.[18] The legislature's justification for the reforms echoed the Philadelphia vice committee's claim that weak laws were responsible for crime. Previous punishments were "so Easy" that they had "not Answered the Good End proposed in making thereof."[19] For lawmakers it was clear that traditional exemplary punishments rather than novel attempts at reform would better deter potential offenders. However well-intentioned founding laws may have been, in the view of assemblymen the facts on the ground necessitated more punitive measures.

Initial laws failed to mention the institution of slavery in the colony, despite the widespread recognition that colonists would purchase and trade in enslaved people. But in 1693 a complaint from the city grand jury concerning "tumultuous" gatherings of enslaved people on the Sabbath led to the creation of Philadelphia County's first race-based ordinance. After receiving complaints of slave gatherings, Governor William Markham and the provincial council gave all free Philadelphians authority to apprehend enslaved men and women found outdoors without a pass from a master or mistress and deliver them to jail. Following a night in the town jail with no food or drink, offenders were to be given thirty-nine lashes on the back, for which owners would pay fifteen pence to the town whipper.[20]

Seven years later, amidst a host of legal reforms, the colonial government established special courts for the prosecution of enslaved offenders in Pennsylvania. Though the Act for the Trial of Negroes borrowed from Carolina and East Jersey laws in creating a separate court system for slaves, it preceded and influenced other proprietary colonies with larger slave populations, such as New York and New Jersey.[21] The statute stipulated two justices of the peace and six of the wealthiest freeholders of the neighborhood would try enslaved people accused of crimes, and the courts were given absolute power to condemn offenders. The law extended beyond trials to include the policing of slave gatherings and the carrying of weapons but, as Christopher Tomlins has noted, the slave courts were the act's centerpiece. The courts' powers were absolute, and as elsewhere their creation marked a key moment in the institutionalization of slavery as a distinct legal regime.[22]

The English Crown did not object to the creation of special courts to prosecute slaves in new proprietary colonies, though ironically, some metropolitan officials viewed Pennsylvania statutes as excessively severe. One of the reforms of 1700 included castration for men convicted of sodomy or bestiality; the act for the trial of enslaved inhabitants mandated castration for men convicted of attempting to rape any "white woman or maid."[23] Attorney General Edward Northey argued there was no precedent for such an act in Britain, and the Privy Council repealed the statute. Northey also found Pennsylvania punishments for robbery excessive, specifically the selling of unpropertied offenders into servitude, as "selling a man is not a punishment allowed by the laws of England."[24] If restitution through labor rather than whipping made humanitarian as well as economic sense to Quaker legislators, English legal experts believed forcing poor offenders into servitude contradicted the common law. Though the initial slave trials act was repealed, legislators quickly passed a revised statute that simply omitted castration. Pennsylvania's slave courts remained in place until the new state of Pennsylvania enacted the gradual emancipation statute in 1780.[25]

Despite the longevity of the courts, problems with the slave trials act became evident not long after its passage. In 1707 two enslaved men, Toney and Quashy, were sentenced to death in Philadelphia for burglary under the act. Slaveholders William Righton and Robert Grace petitioned the provincial council, complaining that they would be greatly damaged if their property was destroyed without compensation. In contrast to other colonies, Righton and Grace noted, Pennsylvania had no legal provision requiring the public to recompense masters whose slaves were executed by the government. The petitioners therefore requested Toney and Quashy be sold out of the colony rather than put to death—though they also assured authorities that if they were allowed to administer corporal punishment to the offenders as "a Terror to others of their

Colour," they would certainly do so. The provincial council granted their petition and demanded a detailed punishment, worth quoting at length: "They shall
be led from the Market place, up ye Second Street, & down thro' the front street
to ye Bridge, with their arms extended & tied to a pole across their Necks, a
Cart going before them, and that they shall be severely Whipt all the way as they
pass, upon the bare back and shoulders; this punishmt. shall be repeated for 3
market days successively; in the meantime they shall lie in Irons, in the prison,
at the Owners Charge, untill they have such an Opportunity as shall best please
them for transportation."[26] The brutality of the punishment is not the only point
of interest. The spectacle was also an improvised response to the alleged shortcomings of the Pennsylvania legal system regarding slave crime, despite the creation of special courts for accused offenders seven years earlier. In Righton and
Grace's view, the destruction of property required restitution from the public—
as, they stressed, was the case in other colonies. Slaveholders' articulation of
an absolutist conception of property, to which officials acquiesced, fused with
medieval and exemplary punishments as a deterrent to others.

In contrast to offenses committed by enslaved persons, there existed abundant
English precedent for the punishing of counterfeiters and coiners. The "clipping"
of coins—the cutting or shaving of silver off the edge of coins to be used to illegally mint new coins—was a common practice in early modern England. Though
a treasonable offense since 1553, the chronic shortage of specie in the country
led to the general acceptance of coin-clipping among the populace. As long as
diminished coin did not lead to inflation, many saw it as a legitimate medium
of exchange. Since coining was not a mortal sin, it was difficult for authorities
to justify the death penalty for the offense. Some historians have argued counterfeiting in early modern England was a social crime similar to other popularly
sanctioned offenses like poaching, wrecking, smuggling, and rioting. A number
of skilled craftsmen who engaged in counterfeiting and were represented in popular criminal narratives even obtained folk-hero status.[27]

It is therefore unsurprising that the manufacture of unofficial currency was
widespread in the cash-poor American colonies in the seventeenth century.[28]
The first prosecution for counterfeiting in Philadelphia occurred in August
1683, after "bad money" had been found in the town. On being apprehended,
Robert Felton, a silversmith, admitted to receiving twenty-four pounds of sil-
ver from the merchant Samuel Pickering, after which Felton made seals for
New England shillings (minted in Massachusetts since 1652) and Spanish-
American pieces of eight. Felton admitted the silver was alloyed with copper,

though he claimed he did not know exactly how much copper had been used. When Samuel Buckley, another confederate, was asked if it was he who had mixed the silver with copper, he wryly confessed that he was "guilty of somewhat of that." Pickering, the merchant leader of the counterfeiting ring who put the coins in circulation, was given a forty-pound fine and was required to make restitution to those to whom the coins had been given. Buckley was fined ten pounds, while Felton was sentenced to stand one hour in the newly constructed Philadelphia stocks.[29]

This episode provides suggestive evidence for how evolving perceptions of money and crime were manifested in the colonies in novel ways. Pickering and Buckley freely admitted before William Penn and his council that they manufactured the coins, but they justified their actions by claiming that "their money was as good Silver as any Spanish money" and noting that others in the city did the same. The merchant Pickering defended his honor and his coin, asserting, "[N]oe man should Loose anything by him."[30] The *quality* of the coins produced was of paramount importance in the view of the accused, rather than any violation of the law. The state's monopoly over the production of money had not yet achieved widespread acceptance in an environment of currency scarcity. Officials' interest in the amount of silver in the New England and Spanish-American coins indicate the problems such practices posed to authorities in the absence of a specific statute, as well as the council's concern with money's value within the colony. Pickering's reputation seems not to have been seriously damaged by his conviction; he remained a prominent Philadelphia trader and provincial assemblyman. Following his prosecution the silversmith Felton put his coining skills to use in a number of places, including Boston, Northampton, Long Island, and Connecticut.[31]

A popular acceptance of counterfeiting was one of many irritants experienced by Capt. John Blackwell after his arrival in Philadelphia as Pennsylvania's lieutenant governor in 1688. Blackwell encouraged Philadelphia merchants to issue private bills of exchange in lieu of a land bank (which he favored), but he warned them to be cautious if they did so since those who "usually Clipp'd or Coyn'd money, would be apt to Counterfeitt their bills."[32] The new governor also noted in a letter to Penn that counterfeiters had recently surfaced in the city, but inhabitants failed to realize the seriousness of the offense. On the contrary: according to Blackwell, the "poorer sort" were under the "erroneous apprehension" that as long as money was not debased "below its currency, they wrong nobody!"[33] As with Pickering, Buckley, and Felton, townspeople's interpretation of coining—that it was legitimate as long as no one was "wronged"—indicates a pragmatic and moralistic approach to counterfeiting in the early modern period. The gulf between Blackwell's view that coiners were "vile persons" and the populace's belief in the relative harmlessness of passing unofficial currency further suggests the disjuncture between official and popular attitudes.

Women were prominent in unofficial exchange in early Philadelphia. Elizabeth White and Mary Jerome admitted at a 1695 court of quarter sessions to having received stolen money from John Maclebray. Both women failed to appear at the next session as required by the court, however.[34] In 1702 John Sable was indicted for passing counterfeited money to a woman named Ann, listed as the wife of a city laborer. Sable's indictment was quashed by the city grand jury for lack of evidence, however, a frequent result of difficult-to-prove accusations of knowingly passing counterfeit money.[35] In the spring of 1714 Mary Perkins petitioned the common council for the return of her goods—the "Wine, Beer, Cyder, Rum & other Liquers"—that the sheriff had recently seized. Perkins's tavern had been raided after her husband, George, broke out of the Philadelphia jail following his arrest on suspicion of having manufactured pieces of eight. Perkins emphasized the "great Hardships" she had labored under since the confiscation, noting she and her three children had "not a Bed to Lie on or any household Goods or Stock to carry on her trade to Support herself & children." Acknowledging that Perkins and her children were likely to become a public charge and that the goods seized were "Generally Lumber & of Small value," the council granted her petition.[36] If George Perkins used the weakness of Philadelphia law enforcement to escape from the city jail (and apparently abandon his family), Mary Perkins utilized the petition and the municipality's worries over public relief to reclaim her goods and trade.

Pennsylvania lawmakers' revisions of the colony's penal code in the decades after the founding were responses to social problems inherent in the Atlantic economy. The American labor regime led to worker flight and theft, while currency scarcity in a commercial environment contributed to counterfeiting and other illicit forms of exchange. Between the late 1710s and the mid-eighteenth century, however, the adoption of English criminal punishments, immigration, and the establishment of an urban print culture combined to create a whole new culture of crime in the city.

"Practices of very dangerous Consequence":
Legal Change and Threats from Without and Within

In November 1717 new lieutenant governor William Keith solicited the Pennsylvania provincial council's opinion concerning his desire to publish a proclamation for information concerning pirates or their confederates in the colony. Keith also wanted to include an order for local magistrates to be on the lookout for "Vagabonds & Suspected persons, more Especially seafaring men, who can give no accot. of themselves." According to the governor, pirates had "infested" the Lower Counties' (Delaware) coast and disrupted legitimate trade. Keith complained of the large numbers of German immigrants who illegally dispersed after landing and took up residence in the colony; he also criticized provincial courts' inability to adequately prosecute offenders like accused murderers Hugh Pugh and Lazarus Thomas in Chester County, and he moved the accused and their trials to Philadelphia.[37] In early 1718 the assembly cited the founding legal system's emphasis on restitution, fines, and incarceration in an act for the construction of houses of correction in Philadelphia and elsewhere. Just three months later, however, it ratified An Act for the Advancement of Justice, which vastly expanded capital punishments and effectively eradicated any vestiges of the humanitarian legal code established at Pennsylvania's founding.[38]

For a statute that so profoundly transformed the provincial legal system, there was little discussion of the bill in the assembly.[39] The limited extent of official concern over the implementation of the new act was demonstrated in 1720 after a court of oyer and terminer condemned Edward Hunt for manufacturing coins and Anne Huson for burglary. In early November, Attorney General Andrew Hamilton informed the provincial council that Hunt and Huson languished in the Philadelphia jail, as no date of execution had been scheduled. Hamilton was informed that judges had delayed setting an execution date to give the accused time to appeal for mercy to Governor Keith, who had been away during the trials. After his return Keith deferred to the judges and councilmen, who were divided over whether to recommend pardons for the condemned. Some urged compassion for Hunt since the punishment of death for counterfeiting would be the first of its kind in the colony. Those opposed to a reprieve argued that the serious nature of the crime justified execution. In all civil governments it was necessary to "make some public Examples" of offenders, and a pardon "to so miserable a Life" as Hunt's would be of no service to the public. The council was also divided over Huson. According to her defenders Huson's behavior showed her to be a "weak ignorant Woman," and the evidence that resulted in her conviction was questionable. Those in favor of execution again took a wider societal view in arguing that Huson's crime "was a growing Evil in the City of Philadelphia." As with the case of coining, burglary had only recently been made punishable by death, so it was necessary "to make a proper Example of the force of that Law." Unable to come to an agreement, councilmen again deferred to Keith, who pardoned Huson but let Hunt's sentence stand.[40]

The idea that the public execution of a local coiner might deter others proved misguided in the environment of the 1720s and 1730s. As colonial governments printed larger amounts of bills of credit, counterfeiters attempted to pass fake bills in different colonies, and counterfeiting networks spanned the Atlantic.[41] Shortly after his arrival in 1727, Governor Patrick Gordon informed the assembly that he had discovered a "horrid attempt" to adulterate neighboring colonies' bills of credit in Pennsylvania. After their arrest in New York City for the manufacture of New Jersey bills, David Wallace and David Wilson told officials that the large quantity of counterfeit bills flooding the mid-Atlantic had been produced in Ireland. Though according to Gordon counterfeiting was the "blackest and most detestable Practice" known, he urged the gentlemen of the House to be on the lookout for counterfeit bills, since it would take "more Skill to distinguish them than is to be expected amongst the common, and especially amongst the Country People."[42]

While some representatives may have taken to heart Gordon's exhortation concerning the "detestable Practice" of counterfeiting, questions over the legitimacy of using counterfeit bills remained. In 1732 Richard Brockden, proprietor of the Indian King tavern, suspected a man who requested change for three twenty-shilling notes was attempting to pass false bills in the bar. The man and his sister were soon apprehended, and the man confessed to receiving a large number of bills produced in Ireland. The notes were received from one Watt, who allegedly convinced the siblings that passing the bills "was no sin, for it would make money plentier among poor People."[43] Whether the man's claim to ignorance was feigned or not, the justification of passing counterfeited currency by appealing to a Christian moral code continued to be a plausible defense. Joseph Watt was soon apprehended and convicted of manufacturing Pennsylvania bills. After standing in the pillory and enduring an ear cropping, Watt escaped from the city jail. Authorities captured the counterfeiter the following January, however, and he was again whipped, pilloried, and cropped—presumably on the other ear. Yet according to the *Gazette,* Watt's courageous, or perhaps sufficiently penitent, behavior in the stocks touched "the Compassion of the Mob, and they did not fling (as was expected) neither Snow-balls nor any Thing else" at the pilloried man.[44]

Pennsylvania legislators responded to transatlantic counterfeiting networks with enhanced efforts to stop the practice. When legislators passed a new currency bill in 1739, the House declared counterfeiters could be punished by death without benefit of clergy; informers could receive as much as fifty pounds for information. The clause addressed the practice of sending newly printed bills from the colonies to England, Ireland, the Netherlands, or Germany for copying, stating the crime need not take place in Pennsylvania for prosecution.[45] In the same year a London printer informed authorities that he had received samples of Newcastle and New Jersey bills from a Dorsetshire mariner named Robert Jenkins, who had obtained the notes from his cousin, Peter Long, a Philadelphia weaver. Jenkins was apprehended in the summer of 1740 in New York while working on a vessel as a cook. Authorities found 971 counterfeit bills in a secret compartment in his chest; Jenkins was promptly sent to Philadelphia for questioning. Though denying any knowledge of the money, Jenkins did admit to forging a document in order to avoid the press gang after previously being forced to serve on a man of war.[46] Rachel Brick of Salem County, New Jersey, was also deposed in Philadelphia. During a discussion at her home between William Paulling and Peter Long, Paulling claimed "amongst all the Counterfeiting" no Jersey money had been faked. Not so, said Long, who proceeded to take from his pocketbook what appeared to Brick to be a "large parsale of money." Long then demonstrated the difference between "true Bills" and counterfeit Jersey notes.[47] What happened to Jenkins and his collaborators is unrecorded. Clearly, however, the printing of paper money in the colonies produced legal difficulties with no precedent, and the adoption of English punishments for counterfeiting failed to eliminate the practice.

The experience of incarceration and the growth of the practice of simply banishing offenders also reflected the incorporation of British methods of punishment in Philadelphia. In March 1727 the jailer William Bidle requested money from the common council for the maintenance of prisoners unable to pay jail fees and likely to "perish for want," demonstrating that the founding laws' rejection of forcing prisoners to pay for their incarceration had lapsed.[48] A growing number of offenders jailed for minor theft or keeping unlicensed taverns petitioned authorities for the remittance of fines, which were usually granted on condition they leave the city and not return.[49] On occasion urban law enforcement officials apprehended fugitives wanted in other colonies and obtained compensation from public authorities. In 1739 Philadelphia sheriff Septimus Robinson requested £6 16s 2d from the Pennsylvania assembly for transporting James Lee back to North Carolina, where he was wanted for robbery.[50]

The irony of banishing convicted felons at a time of growing hostility toward English convict transportation (which had surged after the Transportation Act of 1718) was evidently lost on Pennsylvania legislators, who deployed a variety of strategies to keep dangerous foreigners out of the colony.[51] In 1722 representatives first introduced a tax on the importation of transported felons, justified by the assertion that transports often fled service after their arrival and proceeded to commit crimes in town and country.[52] Repealed by the Crown, the act was repassed and amended in 1729 and 1730, with the statute's language indicating a growing association among lawmakers between transportation, crime, and the arrival of impoverished foreigners. In 1729 the assembly had expanded on the earlier act by discouraging the arrival of "lewd, idle and ill-affected persons" in the colony. A duty of forty shillings per convict was intended to reduce the arrival of criminals, while traders importing Irish servants or redemptioners had to pay a tax of twenty shillings per individual. The following year the House raised the duty on imported felons to five pounds each and mandated a prohibitive surety of fifty pounds for the convict's good behavior for a year.[53] At the end of the 1730s a petition delivered from Philadelphia recommended giving the duties collected on imported felons to the overseers of the poor.[54]

A number of public executions for robbery and burglary in the city in 1736 and 1737 reinforced a distinction between upstanding local residents and alien criminals. In April 1736 John Whatnell of England, Michael McDermot of Ireland, and Catherine Connor, an Irish transport initially sent to Virginia, received sentences of death for burglary in the city. Whatnell and McDermot were hanged on May 6, while Connor "pleaded the belly" (claimed to be pregnant) and received a reprieve.[55] The following year Henry Wildman was condemned for robbery, while Isaac Brandford and Catherine Connor were sentenced to death for burglary. Wildman was a nailor from Shropshire in the West Midlands; Connor's status as an Irish transport already pardoned in Philadelphia likely factored into her sentence. Brandford received a reprieve on the day of the hanging in exchange for the macabre job of acting as Wildman's and Connor's executioner. Whereas Wildman delivered a penitent speech before his hanging, Connor, the first woman executed by the government of

Pennsylvania—and found not to be pregnant by a jury of matrons—said "little or nothing" at the gallows.[56]

Governor George Thomas referenced the hanging of Whatnell, McDermot, Connor, and Wildman in his dispute with representatives over servant enlistment in the war against Spain in 1740. In response to Quaker assemblymen's profession of nonviolence, Thomas pointed out that legislators had themselves recently condemned "such little Rogues to Death as break into your Houses," a seeming contradiction.[57] Assemblymen distinguished between "those little Rogues (as the Governor is pleased to call them)" and foreign soldiers, however. There was, they claimed, a great difference between soldiers doing their duty and fighting at the command of a sovereign and burglars "who broke into our Houses, plundered us of our Goods, and perhaps would have murder'd too, if he could not otherwise have accomplished his Ends." The burglar, in contrast to the soldier, knew at the time of the crime that he was violating the laws of God and man and therefore deserved the severest punishment allowed by law. Citing once again the provincial charter and the colony's founding, assemblymen also stressed that William Penn, as a Quaker, wrote at length of his principled opposition to war and violence.[58] They neglected to mention that Penn and other seventeenth-century Friends opposed capital punishment for property crime, a fact that would have greatly undermined their argument.

All authorities could agree on the benefits of war for ridding the city and colony of undesirables, however. Henry Ennals Gollorthur, convicted of counterfeiting bills of exchange in 1745, had his petition for the remittance of his fines rejected by the common council. Instead, he was allowed to enlist in the coming expedition against the French in Canada.[59] Philadelphia laborers Patrick Burne, Michael Burne, and William Ward were condemned for burglary in 1747. While the Burnes (likely brothers) were hanged, Ward received a reprieve and was sent to serve on Cape Breton.[60] As in London and New York, Pennsylvania jurors often resisted condemning offenders to death for theft; thus expulsion and military service offered a convenient way to avoid potentially controversial trials while also purging Philadelphia of dangerous foreigners.[61]

While magistrates favored flogging, branding, fines, and banishment for transient offenders from throughout the Atlantic diaspora, the status of local bound workers as a form of property complicated prosecution and punishment. The confinement of Griffith Jones, a servant of Philadelphia merchant Joshua Emlen, for attempted rape caused Emlen great personal hardship, and he petitioned the common council for the remittance of Jones's fine. The fine was reduced to twenty pounds on condition Emlen pay the costs of Jones's prosecution and provide a security of thirty pounds for the servant's good behavior.[62] Far more common than violent crimes among bound laborers were thefts and illegal gatherings in unlicensed taverns. Though quarter-sessions records for Philadelphia are largely nonextant, in Chester County servants outnumbered all other occupations combined in accusations of theft, burglary, and robbery, while casual and unskilled laborers trailed far behind.[63] It is probable that the county and city of Philadelphia were not substantially different, particularly as the urban context afforded considerably more opportunities for pickpocketing and shoplifting. Whether any masters or officials considered servants' unpaid labor to be one motivation for servant theft (rather than a simple belief in servants' natural propensity to thieving), prosecuting the unfree created considerable problems for masters and mistresses in lost labor and financial liabilities.

Philadelphia's enslaved inhabitants were aware that their status as property conferred certain protections from the laws' severities. The 1726 Act for Better Regulating Negroes claimed as a primary justification that slaveowners concealed slave crimes and sold violators out of the province to protect their economic investment. Knowledge of their economic value ostensibly fostered a belief among the enslaved that they could commit crimes with impunity. Condemned enslaved people would therefore be assigned monetary value by the justices and freeholders who convicted them, and masters would be compensated out of duties and fines collected from those who imported the enslaved. Any money collected from the numerous fines decreed by the statute was to be placed in a fund for the prosecution of slaves accused of felonies.[64] Though the race code extended law's reach into every aspect of life for Black Philadelphians, free and unfree, the statute was ostensibly enacted because slaves, keenly aware of their value to masters and colonial society, knowingly committed capital crimes in the belief they would "escape justice."

The new act did not eliminate problems in punishing enslaved people, however. Arson, as a number of scholars have pointed out, has historically constituted a fundamental "weapon of the weak."[65] In 1737 a "Negroe man" of Philadelphia was convicted of arson in a special slave court and sentenced to death. Despite the "the wicked Disposition of the Criminal" and his previous threats and "bad Character," a number of "assistant Freeholders" sitting at the trial applied on the accused's behalf because of deficiencies in the prosecution. The owner of the slave and torched house, provincial council president James

Logan, admitted that he was put in a difficult situation by the freeholders' petition. To ignore the men's plea and proceed with the execution could be perceived as an act of vengeance for the personal loss sustained by Logan, while
to submit to freeholders' application would set a dangerous example for the
town's enslaved population. The enslaved community's apparent knowledge of
legal developments and trials was a source of concern, and more than a decade
after the 1726 act the "insolent Behaviour among the Negroes" in Philadelphia
had again been "much taken notice of." The board of justices commissioned
to look into the matter therefore decided that while so heinous a crime could
not go unpunished, it would be unwise to ignore the jurymen's application on
behalf of the arsonist. They therefore stayed the execution for three months
out of regard to the freemen's plea.[66]

"The most flagitious Banditti on Earth": Crime and Print Culture in Atlantic Philadelphia

Published reports of crime in mid-eighteenth-century Philadelphia performed
sociocultural work similar to that of runaway advertisements. Local accounts
of thefts and other crimes often emphasized that the offenders were runaways
and transported felons, contributing to a view of bound laborers from overseas
as marginal and dangerous social elements. While local newspaper ads and
crime stories reflected colonial conditions, criminal narratives and last dying
speeches were modeled on popular literary forms developed in late sixteenth-
and seventeenth-century England.[67] Colonists were also familiar with fictional
works that depicted a vast English criminal underworld, such as Daniel Defoe's
Moll Flanders (1722) and John Gay's *Beggar's Opera* (1728). Colonial printers
sold collections of crime narratives like the *Proceedings of the Old Bailey* and
the *Ordinary of Newgate's Account* in the colonies, as well. In 1731 Benjamin
Franklin commented that in his printer's shop numerous copies of *Robin Hood's
Songs* consistently sold well at two shillings, while a small number of *David's
Psalms* sat unsold for more than two years. Seven years later he advertised in
the *Gazette* for the return of the second volume of his copy of *Old Bailey Proceedings*.[68] Though criminal narratives formulaically warned youth against the
slippery slope from minor sins to serious crimes whose end was the gallows or
transportation, representations of outlaws who defied social norms also were
highly entertaining and made such figures celebrities.[69]

Crime reports featured prominently in Philadelphia newspapers from the founding of Andrew Bradford's *American Weekly Mercury* in 1719. In its first year of publication alone colonists read of pirates in the Americas, slaves in revolt off the coast of West Africa, European peasant risings, and, closer to home, of jailbreaks in the Chesapeake Bay and Delaware Valley.[70] The paper also informed townspeople of the disturbing prevalence of property crime in England. Samuel Keimer's *Pennsylvania Gazette* reported shortly after its founding in 1728 that robberies had become so frequent in London that the Crown was offering upward of a hundred pounds for the capture of offenders. The next month the new paper contained an account of official investigations into the growing "Audaciousness" of street robbers in London and noted there were two hundred prisoners in Newgate and other city jails awaiting trial.[71]

Criminal narratives from England had a special significance for readers in Philadelphia and throughout the mid-Atlantic region, as the dangers posed to the colonies by the policy of transportation was implicit in some stories. In January 1722 a man sentenced to death with two others for horse theft at the Stafford assize begged to be transported after declaring it was a hard thing to be "hanged for stealing of Dogs Meat." When asked where he wanted to be sent, the man sardonically replied: "To any Place where there is no Dogs Meat." Four months later the Pennsylvania assembly passed its first law restricting the importation of felons to the colony.[72] Many Philadelphians would have seen in the *Gazette's* account of the two hundred Newgate prisoners awaiting trial the specter of felons invading Maryland, Virginia, and Pennsylvania in coming months.

William Bradford published Philadelphia's first criminal narrative in 1691, an account of the murder of John Clark of Philadelphia by Thomas Lutherland in West Jersey.[73] Colonial criminal narratives like that of Lutherland, which ran between ten and twenty pages and cost two pence, followed the metropolitan form in emphasizing the offender's descent into a life of crime and, crucially, their acceptance of the justice of their execution. The first person executed in Philadelphia after the passage in 1718 of the Act for the Advancement of Justice, the coiner Edward Hunt, did not follow the traditional script in his gallows speech, however. In the account published in the *Mercury*, Andrew Bradford noted in a preface that Hunt had been captured in 1715 at the Battle of Preston in Lancashire during the Jacobite rising against George I and the new House of Hanover and was transported as a bound servant to Antigua.[74] The printer emphasized Hunt was "most justly" condemned for counterfeiting

Spanish silver coin in Philadelphia, a crime of high treason "made current by Act of Parliament within all his Majesties Colonies in *America*."[75]

Bradford's comments were necessary: first, as some on the provincial council noted, Hunt's execution was the first of its kind in Pennsylvania; second, Hunt refused to follow the penitential script of the last-dying-speech genre. While admitting that he had coined Spanish-American silver, Hunt claimed he had never intended to cheat or defraud anyone. He simply "thought I might cut those Impressions as innocently as any other, or the Stamps that the Gentlemen of this place imploy'd me about, to make farthings." If city gentlemen regularly employed Hunt to cut farthings (quarter pennies originating in the medieval era and revived in the early 1700s by Queen Anne), why could the silversmith also not make impressions of Spanish coin? Hunt also claimed in his speech that he had not been tried according to the laws of England, suggesting jury members had not taken oaths. In contrast to the traditional gallows' confession, Hunt's speech was an indictment of the Pennsylvania legal system and a refusal to admit his punishment was deserved. Yet Hunt ultimately did follow custom in making a "good end": the silversmith implored God to help his wife (Martha Hunt was unprecedentedly sentenced to life imprisonment for aiding Edward) and to preserve her from the "Pollutions of the World" in the hope they would meet again where "we shall both be happy to all Eternity."[76]

Bradford's introduction characterized Hunt's unrepentant speech as an attempt to "infuse both ill Principles and Practices into the Minds of the People" and to misrepresent the administration of justice in Pennsylvania. The *Mercury*, rather than the accused, claimed the punishment was just and in keeping with English and provincial law. If the acceptance of death typically reinforced the power and legitimacy of law in early modern criminal narratives, transportation and pardons reduced the likelihood of popular sympathy with the condemned.[77] While execution rates for those convicted of capital crimes rose in Pennsylvania after midcentury, banishment and pardons remained common.[78] As noted above, Ann Huson received a reprieve in 1720 despite her burglary conviction. Four years later a pregnant Ann Mitchel was also pardoned, and the following year Martha Hunt, wife of Edward Hunt, was released after serving five years for aiding her husband's coining operation.[79]

The drama of the criminal narrative and the majesty of the official pardon were conjoined in Philadelphia in Franklin's *Gazette* in late 1729. In December the newspaper reported on the trial of immigrant laborers James Prouse and James Mitchel at a court of oyer and terminer. Prouse was born in Middlesex in

1710 or 1711 and was sent as a servant to America as a rebellious twelve-year-old. The slightly older Mitchel was apprenticed as a bookbinder in Antrim, Ireland, and came to America as an indentured servant after being pressed into naval service in England. In Philadelphia the two young men, who had broken out of the city jail but were apprehended in Amboy, New Jersey, were convicted of the theft of seven pounds in paper money and some copper halfpence from the house of a Mr. Sheed. On being found guilty and sentenced to death, Prouse said nothing in his defense, though he insisted on Mitchel's innocence. The court therefore encouraged Mitchel to appeal to the governor for mercy.[80]

Three weeks later Franklin informed *Gazette* readers of a "remarkable Transaction" in the city and proceeded to narrate Prouse and Mitchel's execution day. Though some "compassionate People" had urged clemency after the trial, authorities deemed it necessary to "make some Examples" for the "common Good," since "several Malefactors" had recently been pardoned in Philadelphia and because of the great increase in "Vagrants and idle Persons" from Europe.[81] As a large crowd gathered around the prison on execution day, Prouse began to weep, though Mitchel displayed great fortitude and comforted his friend: "Do not cry, Jemmy. . . . In an Hour or two it will be over with us, and we shall both be easy." The two men were placed in a cart accompanied by two coffins and were then driven through Philadelphia to the scaffold. While awaiting their hanging, the condemned were unaware of the reprieve being read until they heard the words "PITY and MERCY," after which the formerly courageous Mitchel fainted after blessing Governor Gordon. The collective relief and joy expressed by the city's inhabitants was, according to the *Gazette*, a testimony to the humanity of all city residents, including "our common People."[82]

Much like Bradford's *Mercury* account of the execution of Edward Hunt, Franklin's *Gazette* representation of Prouse and Mitchel's reprieve attempted to shape the public's impression of the spectacle after the fact in a way that entertained while also reinforcing institutional authority and community cohesion. The account's emphasis on the dangers of crime in the city and the justice of the death penalty for the offenders was accompanied by a celebration of the compassion of leaders and the humanity of townspeople when pardons were granted. The representation of the last-minute reprieve reproduced a collective catharsis for an audience far larger than that of the spectacle itself. The *Gazette* narrative also emphasized Mitchel's apparent reversal on the scaffold from courageous youth to obsequious penitent. Mitchel's "manly" countenance on the gallows, gendered evidence of bravery that was an important element in the crime narrative genre, was ultimately belied by his fainting on receiving pardon—an emasculating response to the governor's merciful act that showed the offender's true powerlessness. The *Gazette* account subtly critiqued a convention that emphasized making an honorable end by implying that Mitchel's brave self-presentation was but an act.

The Irish bookbinder, sailor, and indentured servant seems to have been unreformed by his gallows experience, however. The following November a James Mitchel ran away from the cooper John Orr, after which he must have been captured, for he fled service yet again the following June. By this time Mitchel had been branded by Orr; he also had an image of two fish tattooed on his right arm. Readers were informed that, like many servants and enslaved people, Mitchel was multilingual, able to speak Irish, Dutch, and Spanish. A few *Gazette* readers may have recognized this was the same Mitchel pardoned by Governor Gordon the previous year, though no mention was made of his earlier exploits or reprieve.[83]

Historians have examined how runaways and confidence men like James Mitchel exploited the eighteenth-century colonial environment to "counterfeit" identities, in the process subverting elite beliefs in social distinctions based on innate differences.[84] Bustling colonial port cities like Philadelphia provided fertile ground for self-fashioning men and women. In the mid-1730s the *Gazette* warned inhabitants in town and country about a "Vagrant Fellow" named John Mitchel (no relation to James) who claimed to be a Dutch clergyman of "great Estate, and Owner of [an] abundance [of] Money." Mitchel was in fact from the Raritan Valley in New Jersey and was suspected of fraudulent real estate deals (in addition to some "lesser Matters") in the area.[85] About a month after this warning appeared, an advertisement placed by horse dealer William Herbert claimed a John Mitchel had stolen a horse from Herbert a few hours after selling the trader the same horse. Of middling height and wearing a brown coat, a flaxen wig or cap, sharp-toed boots, and bearing a large scar on his neck, Mitchel rode a good horse and traveled with a young Welsh woman who was believed to be riding the pilfered horse.[86]

Mitchel was in fact no stranger to Pennsylvania authorities, having been in the region for years and spending considerable time in Philadelphia. He was probably the same John Mitchel who petitioned the colonial government on behalf of his wife, Ann, in 1724, who was in the Philadelphia jail under sentence of death for burglary in the city. Though because of her pregnancy Ann was pardoned, John also requested she be released from jail on condition she never return to Philadelphia. Whether Ann left the city after her release, or whether she was the woman described by Herbert, cannot be known, but John at least remained in the mid-Atlantic region. Two years after pretending to be a wealthy European investor and stealing a horse from William Herbert, John Mitchel worked for Robert Story in Dutchess County, New York. Mitchel and another laborer, Tobit Gilder, had fled the service of Story with two of his horses. Though Story suspected that the men turned the horses loose after their escape, Mitchel's past involvement in horse theft suggests they tried to sell the valuable creatures. Story offered a fifty-shilling reward (or five pounds for both) for the men in "Pennsylvania money."[87]

While local sharpers like Mitchel used their knowledge of mid-Atlantic law and culture in their exploits, transported English felons also used the anonymity of growing colonial cities to their advantage. The fame of such outlaws was made possible by the expansion of a British Atlantic print culture, as by the mid-eighteenth century the convict returned from America became a popular subject in English newspapers, collections of criminal biographies, dramas, and novels.[88] Autobiographies like those of imposter Bampfylde-Moore Carew and highwayman John Poulter (both of whom commented on life in American cities like Philadelphia), first published in 1745 and 1753, respectively, remained in print in England throughout the eighteenth century. In addition to providing picaresque and often humorous stories for popular consumption, first-person portrayals of the hardships of colonial life tarnished the image of the American colonies and contributed to public opposition to transportation in England.[89]

An example of a celebrity felon who escaped from servitude and later recounted his adventures in America, Pennsylvania included, was Carew. The self-proclaimed "King of the Beggars" of Devonshire and a notorious confidence man, Carew was transported to Maryland (where transported felons were known as "His Majesty's Seven-year Passengers") for vagrancy sometime in the 1730s. After a failed escape shortly after his arrival, Carew was forced to wear an iron collar, a painful and humiliating punishment typically reserved for runaway slaves and servants. Local Indians, evidently familiar with fugitives in the region, aided Carew's second flight attempt, helping remove the collar and providing the runaway with food and drink. After a meeting with George Lillycraft, leader of one the Chesapeake's Algonquian peoples and described by Carew as an Indian king, Carew reflected on his hardships and the capriciousness of fate. Only a few weeks earlier "our hero" had been "treated like a beast of burthen, heavily loaded, cruelly whipped, coarsely fed, and all by the insolence and inhumanity of his own countrymen." Among Native Americans, however, he was "seated in a strange country, with kings and princes, and consulted by a whole nation."[90] Carew's literary inversion was a common device in contemporary social satires, though in this case the reversal was civilizational, as noble and benevolent Indians were contrasted with cruel and "inhuman" English colonists.

More surprising than Carew's account of oppressive conditions in the Chesapeake was his portrayal of Pennsylvania, a place that would have conjured for many English readers a land of Quaker simplicity, benevolence, and prosperity. Carew countered this notion by justifying his appropriation of a Quaker identity by equating the civilized, polished world of Pennsylvania with artifice itself. In contrast to "simple and honest" Native Americans, Pennsylvanians had forgotten the ways of nature and instead "act[ed] everything in disguise." Seven miles outside of Philadelphia, Carew pretended to be a sailor recently redeemed from Havana when he met the noted evangelical George Whitefield, who gave the apparent mariner "three or four pounds of that county['s] paper money" for his troubles. In Philadelphia, one of the largest cities in the British Empire, a thirsty Carew counterfeited a "brogue" and passed a day drinking "very merrily" with an Irish publican in Market Street. During his exploits in Philadelphia Carew also claimed to have fooled the principal merchants of the city as well as proprietor John Penn and Governor George Thomas.[91] An Augustan literary convention in which things were not what they seemed and where criminal rogues exposed the superficial pretenses of elites held a special sting when applied to humanitarian and enlightened Philadelphia.

Carew's picaresque autobiography remained a best-seller in England for the remainder of the eighteenth century. A short account of his adventures appeared in the Boston Post-Boy in 1751, and by the 1770s residents of Philadelphia and New York City could purchase Carew's book in local bookshops.[92] More famous in the colonies was Tom Bell, whose escapades from Barbados to New Hampshire produced more than a hundred newspaper articles in the Americas between 1738 and 1755.[93] Bell made numerous appearances in the mid-Atlantic, and his sightings were covered in detail in Philadelphia and New York newspapers.[94] By the late 1740s Bell was a colonial celebrity, and in September 1749 readers of Philadelphia's Gazette read a report stating that the "noted vagrant" Bell was currently suspected to be lurking somewhere in New York. The paper denied its account contributed to Bell's popularity, claiming that the newspaper's aim in representing the trickster was to warn people about a man who should have long ago taken "the swing his merits deserve." Unfortunately, however, Bell was protected by "some of *Gay's Monkeys,* who flock round him in every Place, *grinning Applause* to his *redundant Chattering."*[95]

While colonial writers rejected the possibility that their reports contributed to local criminals' notoriety, they expected readers to recognize references to English works that popularized metropolitan crime. John Gay's *Beggar's Opera* (first performed in the mid-Atlantic at New York's Nassau Street Theatre in 1750) satirized the corruption of the Walpole government and English society through its representation of a criminal underworld in which beggars and thieves were not very different from courtiers. As in other popular works of the time, transports returned from America are important characters in the play.[96] The Philadelphia press demonstrated the extent of a shared Atlantic popular culture of crime when it compared Tom Bell to the *Opera's* fictional highwayman Macheath, whom Gay modeled on the real-life Jack Sheppard. That works like Gay's and Carew's exposed the alleged insincerity, hypocrisy, and selfishness at the heart of respectable society in England and America indicates the ambiguous function of criminal literature in this culture.

In the summer of 1752 a report from Virginia informed readers of Philadelphia's *Gazette* that Tom Bell, "the famous American traveller," had recently appeared in Williamsburg. For over two years the former confidence man had labored as a schoolmaster in Hanover County, where he behaved with "Justice, Sobriety and good Manners." The "principal Gentlemen" of the county even signed a certificate absolving him of his former misdeeds, and Bell promised to remain a "useful Member of Society"—an increasingly common expression among eighteenth-century social reformers.[97] Bell's alteration, the report concluded, would be a surprise to those fond of the well-known proverb: "Can the Aethiopean change his Skin, or the Leopard his Spots; then also may he do Good that has been accustomed to do Evil."[98]

Many would have indeed been surprised by Bell's respectable turn, for in the middle decades of the eighteenth century the concept of criminal reformation seemed an increasingly unlikely possibility to many colonists—even (perhaps especially) in Pennsylvania, where reform was initially a guiding principle of penal law. Following the Treaty of Aix-la-Chapelle in 1748, which ended the War of Austrian Succession, a postwar outbreak of crime in England and the colonies was portrayed in the colonial press as directly attributable to transportation.[99] The midcentury crime wave consequently exacerbated hostility to transportation throughout the colonies, though postwar demobilization likely played as prominent a role in mid-Atlantic crime. In Philadelphia a series of burglaries and robberies between 1749 and 1752 was presented by the urban press as constituting a major threat to property and social order, a result of a metropolitan policy likened to the unleashing of a plague on loyal American subjects.

In December 1748 William Bradford's *Pennsylvania Journal* warned townspeople to be on alert after a series of thefts and burglaries in the city. Two days after Christmas, Philadelphians were further instructed not be out after dark unless well-armed after four gentlemen were attacked in two separate incidents.[100] Some months later townspeople read of break-ins committed in New York by a group of robbers who traveled up and down the North (Hudson) River by boat. At the end of the summer in 1749, it was rumored that some members of "the Gang" had moved to Philadelphia, for highwaymen had recently robbed three men on their way to the city. One of the victims recognized two of the robbers on the edge of town sometime later, and the sailors Thomas Fielding and James Johnson were arrested and jailed. A number of robberies, attempted break-ins, and thefts involving men and women in the city after Fielding's and Johnson's arrests suggested more of the gang were on the loose in Philadelphia. A strategy of deterrence through public hanging was not working, the *Journal* reported: "It is but a few Weeks since two Men were hanged at *Newcastle* for House-breaking; which it seems has not been sufficient to deter others from the same Practices."[101]

In September 1749 Fielding and Johnson were convicted of highway robbery in the Northern Liberties, and the following month the provincial council unanimously agreed to uphold the death sentence.[102] Though the council claimed the robbery was the first of its kind in Pennsylvania, while the two highwaymen were in the Philadelphia jail a Mr. Patterson was robbed of 120 pieces of eight on a road leading to town. Two weeks later a Mr. Calvert was met by two men with blackened faces between Philadelphia and Chester; they knocked him off his horse, informed him they had been waiting a full three hours for his arrival, and robbed him of fifty-seven pistoles and a few pieces of eight. Before the end of October, and despite a nearly successful escape attempt, Fielding and Johnson were hanged on the Philadelphia commons.[103] The men who robbed Patterson and Calvert appear not to have been found by authorities, however. If, as Robert Shoemaker has argued, in mid-eighteenth-century England the image of the violent urban street robber was contrasted with that of the polite gentleman highwayman, in Philadelphia no such distinction existed.[104] Fielding and Johnson were sailors, and rather than apologetically identify themselves as poor gentlemen in need, Calvert's attackers wore disguises and violently knocked the Marylander off his horse.

A series of burglaries and hangings in 1750 most dramatically demonstrated the importance of the press to representations of crime in Philadelphia at mid-century. A number of house break-ins occurred in the city in the last week of October. Burglars stole a significant amount of women's jewelry and clothes from the house of Benjamin Franklin, and the printer advertised a ten-pound reward in his newspaper for any information concerning the crime. Rumors circulated that a gang of Maryland convicts had passed through Philadelphia and were likely heading to New York; New Yorkers were warned to be on their guard. In early 1751 a published grand jury address linked the Philadelphia housebreakings to disorderly revelries in town, arguing that an insufficient night watch was a cause of recent burglaries as well as tumultuous New Year's festivities. The following week burglars broke into Abigail Pederow's shop on Water Street and made away with shop goods and money to the value of £500, an impressive sum for a night's work.[105]

As housebreakings continued, newspapers reported that a Philadelphia brewer named Edmund Nihil had informed authorities that he suspected a laborer in his employ was in possession of stolen goods. After it was found that the goods belonged to Pederow, the servant John Crow confessed to receiving the items from a group that included Betty Robinson, Francis and Mary McCoy, Joseph Cooper, and John Morrison (alias Morris), the group's suspected leader. Authorities apprehended all the suspects at the McCoys' dwelling except Morrison, who fled out the back door; after a bounty of sixty pounds was quickly raised, Morrison was captured at the tavern of John Stinson on Water Street. After his arrest the *Gazette* reported that Morrison claimed that "when he went upon any Robbery, he chose to take Betty Robinson with him rather than any two Men, as she was (tho' an Englishwoman) a true Heart, and that she could get into a House, and go up or down a Chimney, as well as any Man in America."[106] Following a quick trial Morrison, Robinson, Crow, and Francis McCoy were condemned for the Pederow break-in; for being an accessory after the fact, tavernkeeper John Stinson was to be branded with the letter "T" on his hand, while Mary McCoy received a pardon. City papers reported that in mid-February Morrison, Robinson, and Francis McCoy were hanged on the Philadelphia commons, while Crow received a gallows' reprieve.[107]

The Philadelphia robbers did not fall immediately into obscurity, however. On February 19, a week after the execution, the *Gazette* advertised *An Account of the Robberies Committed by John Morrison,* a fifteen-page chapbook costing four pence.[108] Most of the information provided on the Atlantic criminal underworld in Philadelphia was provided by Joseph Cooper, a young laborer found in the McCoys' house. Cooper had met Betty Robinson in Maryland, where he evidently became infatuated with the English transportee. On hearing she was in the Philadelphia jail, Cooper left Maryland and found Robinson in the Philadelphia workhouse. While laboring in the city for a local turner to earn enough for Robinson's release, Cooper was introduced to Morrison, the McCoys, and Crow and was soon recruited by the gang. Told he could earn enough money "to buy his Time, and make himself free again," Cooper broke into a number of homes with Morrison. After the McCoys plied him with liquor, Robinson and Morrison convinced Cooper to help break into Pederow's house. About two in the morning they broke into the dwelling and by candlelight took the best goods in the shop as well as silver, paper money, and some pennies. From other parts of the house they took silver spoons, silver jacket buttons, a pair of gold buttons, two pistols, and other goods.[109]

Accounts of the capture and confessions of Morrison and Crow, and of the trial and condemnation of the accused, followed. Crow provided testimony concerning a number of Philadelphia thefts and the Morrison-Robinson relationship; though not involved in the Pederow burglary, Crow swore an oath to Morrison to keep his knowledge of the crime secret. Morrison admitted to no less than seventeen thefts in the Philadelphia area, providing detailed accounts of each burglary. Notably, he did not implicate Robinson in any of the crimes, while Robinson either refused to talk or was simply not included in the *Account.* While the accused were awaiting trial, jailers apprehended a boy in the prison carrying metal files intended for an escape; the gang was thereafter watched closely. A short account of the trial and conviction was followed by brief biographies of the condemned. Morrison, aged twenty-four, had emigrated from Ireland as a servant at age fourteen, and as a "bad Boy" his lying and pilfering eventually gave way to housebreaking, a skill honed in Philadelphia as a door-to-door seller of limes and onions. Robinson was an English transport sent to Maryland, where she continued her criminal ways and seduced the young Cooper. After arriving in Philadelphia, she was whipped for shoplifting and stealing cambric (a light linen cloth), but she "would not take warning." The McCoys, who regularly received stolen goods, were also from Ireland but had lived many years in Philadelphia. Morrison and Crow were Irish Catholics; Robinson and McCoy were Protestants.[110]

The narrative concluded with a dramatic portrayal of the hangings. On February 13, 1751, attended by clergymen and "a prodigious Number of People," Morrison, Robinson, McCoy, and Crow were carried from jail on two carts to the place of execution. At the gallows Robinson's rope fell from the tree, and the "flash of Joy" visible on her face indicated she believed she had received a reprieve, but the rope was soon made fast again. Crow, however, obtained a pardon. Morrison had apparently suspected this and, evidently holding no grudge against Crow for breaking his oath of secrecy, lifted his cap to the reprieved man as he left the scaffold. "'Tis said he then spoke a few words to Crow, and the Cart drawing away left them all three Hanging together!" Robinson died immediately, but McCoy struggled "a long Time and died very hard." A formulaic *Lamentation and Confession* was appended to the *Account*, signed by the contrite offenders and admonishing youth to remain on the straight path of obedience, morality, and industry.

Burglaries continued in Philadelphia despite the exemplary hanging of Morrison and his confederates. A number of men and women arrested in New York and Chester County after the executions were suspected of belonging to the gang now known as the "Philadelphia robbers." Elizabeth Herbert of Philadelphia and a male companion were arrested for a number of New York burglaries in New Brunswick; New York and Philadelphia papers reported that the couple were likely the "Chiefs" of a gang operating in the area.[111] The crime wave occurring throughout the Atlantic world led to the publication of different views regarding the merits of capital punishment. In addition to continuing weekly reports of crimes from New York to Virginia, the *Gazette* reprinted an editorial from London's *General Evening-Post* in April 1751. The *Post* criticized hanging for larceny, arguing convicts should instead be put to hard labor for the "Good of the Nation" and in the hopes of saving the souls of these "poor Creatures." As was becoming glaringly evident at public hangings, the threat of death carried little or no terror; "Philanthropos" therefore declared it would be wiser and more becoming of Protestants to exempt those currently condemned for theft from execution.[112]

While some Philadelphians may have agreed with Philanthropos, the bulk of reporting from the midcentury years did not encourage a belief in mercy and reform. Many colonists would have interpreted the *Post*'s recommendations as resulting in more transported felons in the Americas at a time when hostility to transportation was at a peak. The week after the publication of the London editorial there appeared further reports of crime in the Chesapeake along with a jeremiad against the "Villainies perpetrated by Convicts transported from *Europe*."[113] Less than a month later, two letters opposing transportation were published in the *Gazette*. The first, from Maryland, claimed the Chesapeake colony would be overrun with felons if so many did not run away to the north every year—an assertion clearly intended to resonate with Pennsylvanians. The infectious danger of convicts was also emphasized: "Not only our other Servants and Negroes are corrupted and spoilt, but even our Children begin to be vitiated by them." The second letter was Benjamin Franklin's famous satire of the Transportation Act. Using the language of the act itself, "Americanus" ridiculed the act's justification (of "well peopling" the colonies) by proposing to send American rattlesnakes to the mother country as a "publick utility."[114]

Reports of crimes committed by transported felons contained little, if any, information concerning convicts' thoughts or motivations. Yet, as noted above, criminal narratives occasionally afforded a voice—however mediated by clergymen and printers—to those convicted of felonies. In Philadelphia the publication of the words of Edward Hunt, James Prouse, and John Morrison presented them as sympathetic, if flawed, characters whose mistakes may or may not have warranted death. In one case a Chesapeake convict dramatized the complex psychological damage the colonial labor regime could inflict. In April 1751 Philadelphians read that a transported felon in Maryland decided to kill his mistress with an axe. However, after seeing "as he express'd it, *how d—d innocent she look'd*," he instead put his own left hand on a block and chopped it off. Throwing the severed hand at the woman, the man allegedly exclaimed: "Now make me work if you can."[115]

More common after midcentury, however, were quotidian representations of grisly public punishments that had become normalized among the populace. While reports of criminal gangs and robberies diminished in the late 1750s and early 1760s, accounts of counterfeiters and their prosecutions remained common. For coining pieces of eight and counterfeiting Maryland ten-shilling bills, William Kerr and Daniel Jessop were whipped and ordered to stand in the pillory, where each man was cropped.[116] Such punishments were reserved for lower-sort offenders, though in 1751 Thomas Penn complained to Governor James Hamilton that even people "of substance" regularly engaged in counterfeiting in Pennsylvania. A year later he wrote that all the power of government would be needed to suppress the practice, since many inhabitants—Quakers included—often sheltered the "sanctified Villains" from the law.[117] In 1770 the Pennsylvania government brought capital punishment for counterfeiting back, when Herman Rosencrantz was hanged in Philadelphia for counterfeiting pro-vincial bills of credit. His eleven-page *Life and Confession* was printed and sold by James Chattin on the corner of Second and Market Streets.[118]

Of course, not all urban crimes in eighteenth-century Philadelphia involved intricate plans or were punished with spectacular and exemplary demonstra-tions of the law's power. More typical in the 1750s and 1760s were minor thefts that reflected urban life in a growing metropolis of the British Atlantic world. And as in other urban centers, women were frequently among those indicted for theft who received public whippings, fines, and banishment.[119] In the July session of the 1759 mayor's court, for example, of ten presentments for felony theft, nine of the accused were women. There were just five other indictments at the session: three for assault, one for the keeping of a tippling house, and one for forging bills of exchange.[120] By contrast, in more rural Philadelphia County indictments for assault, fornication, and the keeping of tippling houses con-sistently outnumbered those for theft in the late 1750s.[121] Some poor women, particularly in the context of growing inequality that followed the Seven Years' War, found theft to be an irresistible temptation. By the 1760s the jail terms, trials, whippings, fines, and banishments for property crimes that occurred on a weekly basis in Philadelphia demonstrated an Atlantic urban society and sys-tem of punishment profoundly different from that envisioned by seventeenth-century Quakers.

Conclusion

By the middle of the eighteenth century, Pennsylvania's notoriety as a center of culture and knowledge in British America was accompanied by a reputation for severe corporal punishments. In 1748 the Swedish naturalist Peter Kalm noted that the "barbarous appendages of whipping-post, pillory and stocks were placed full in the public eye hard by, on High street directly in front of the market, and on the eastern side of Third street."[122] A few years later Gottlieb Mittelberger was shocked by the punishments he witnessed for larceny and wrote that counterfeiters of Pennsylvania paper money were hanged without possibility of pardon. For the theft of something as small as a handkerchief or a pair of stockings, offenders were tied to a post in the public market, stripped to the waist, and lashed to the point where skin and flesh would hang from the body. Repeat offenders were bound and transferred to the gallows in a cart, where a rope was then placed around the neck of the condemned. "The cart is then driven away and he is left to hang. Many suffer miserably, and die in agony."[123] Though often hyperbolic in his account of Pennsylvania, this last observation probably referred to the suffering of Francis McCoy, which Mittelberger may have witnessed firsthand.

"Barbarity" is of course impossible to quantify, and for many colonists it was England's policy of transportation that explained the need for colonial severity. Historians have noted an increase in capital punishments for property crimes in Boston, New York City, and Charleston as well as Philadelphia in the decades after midcentury, suggesting a process that encompassed all of British North America's major ports.[124] It is indicative of Pennsylvania's legal transformation, however, that at midcentury other colonists could point to Philadelphia as an example of how to deal with transported felons. A 1753 letter in New York's Whiggish *Independent Reflector* claimed the Transportation Act had unleashed "a Herd of the most flagitious Banditti upon Earth" on the colonies. According to the *Reflector*, the Philadelphia newspapers had noted that of the "great Number of Criminals" executed there in recent years, few were "Children of *America*"; publications advertised "the Tryal or Execution of an *English* or *Irishman*."[125] The underappreciated role of transportation and convicts ("inhuman Savages," according to the *Reflector*) in colonial criticism of English policy was pronounced in Philadelphia, where from the 1720s significant numbers of immigrants and transports landed.

At the same time, colonists looked to metropolitan statutes in their responses to crime and adopted an English literary genre as a form of popular entertainment. Following piecemeal reforms in the late seventeenth and early eighteenth centuries—including the creation of a special system of prosecution for the enslaved—lawmakers abandoned the founding penal system for exemplary forms of public punishment. While Pennsylvania would return to its roots as a vanguard of penal reform in the revolutionary context of the 1770s and 1780s, the years between the 1680s and 1760s saw the city's and the colony's integration into a British Atlantic culture of crime, punishment, and representation.

PART III

SPACES OF PLEASURE AND DANGER

5

THE URBAN BATTLE OF IDEAS

Order, the People, and the Press

In February 1741 an essay in the *Pennsylvania Gazette* titled "Common Sense" stated that the preservation of liberty was entirely dependent on the "first Principles" of religion. It argued that when people begin to doubt the existence of a supreme being, and therefore the likelihood of having to answer in a future state for their actions in this one, they "naturally, and even reasonably" focus their desires on the advancement of their fortune in this world. Virtue, morality, and "social Liberty" were sacrificed when "the far greatest Part of the People, I mean those of *mean* or *middling* Circumstances," supported arbitrary governments in the hopes of advancing their material interests. Why did the majority support arbitrary governments when fear of divine retribution was absent? Because under such systems people could rise more quickly than they could in a free and well-regulated society. By the whim or fondness of a prince or prime minister, the lowliest person could "jump at once into the Rank and greatest Fortune," whereas in free states individuals rose only slowly, by degrees. Great fortunes in public service were not easily made in free states, moreover, because "the publick Money is *sparingly* advanced, and must be *strictly* accounted for"—a statement with particular significance for some in midcentury Philadelphia. The overturning of constitutions and the invasion of liberties are therefore to be expected where the first principles of religion are neglected.[1]

"Common Sense" represents a commonplace elite view of human nature in the eighteenth century and of the consequent need for social order—in this case through the instrumental use of religion. Historians have often commented on the perennial early modern obsession with order, a concern that was especially pronounced in large and growing cities.[2] Though by the middle of the eighteenth century new ideas concerning the positive relationship between individual profit and national economic development had become acceptable in mainstream discourse, they had not displaced conventional beliefs in the need for social harmony and mutuality.[3] Social and political writers also continued to describe the ideal commonwealth using organicist bodily metaphors, in which a healthy society was composed of interdependent, if unequal, parts. An unhealthy, or diseased, body politic was by contrast "disordered," a condition that portended chaos and anarchy. As "Common Sense" suggests, a view of most people as driven mainly by selfish material concerns—and therefore as requiring ideological restraints for the maintenance of social order—survived well into the eighteenth century.[4]

Imposing order on the American wilderness through the establishment of towns as well as agricultural settlements was a major objective for colonial English officials in the late seventeenth century.[5] The importance of creating an orderly New World environment was arguably most strongly felt by the founders of Pennsylvania, however. Accusations of licentiousness and anarchism were frequently leveled against Quakers in the 1650s and 1660s. Critics characterized early Friends as the latest iteration of a tradition of religious anarchy that rejected institutional order that began with Anabaptists in the 1520s. Parallels with Anabaptists and other radical Protestants resulted from Quakers' rejection of church hierarchy and a corresponding belief in the individual believer's ability to understand and interpret scripture. The Society of Friends' adherence to Restoration-era norms of order therefore pervaded defenses of Quakerism in the 1670s. In a new colony in which Quakers for the first time constituted the social and political elite, leaders were keenly aware of the need to maintain discipline and control.[6]

The *Gazette*'s "Common Sense" essay reflected a post-1688 consensus among the political classes on both sides of the Atlantic concerning balance, order, and "social Liberty." While historians have long noted the influence of the Whig political thought of John Locke, John Trenchard, and Thomas Gordon on colonial writers and politicians, scholars have more recently explored radical republican beliefs among middling mid-Atlantic farmers and artisans.[7] Seventeenth-century politics loomed particularly large in ideological disputes in Philadelphia. For proprietary supporters, criticisms of institutional authority recalled the chaotic specter of "democracy" that allegedly gripped England in the 1640s. They saw in the upheavals of midcentury England concrete evidence of the social and political problems that inevitably follow from popular politics and cultural permissiveness. Populist pamphleteers, by contrast, drew on revolutionary-era ideas concerning human equality while updating older literary conventions that contrasted the honest, if unlettered, producers with powerful and self-interested grandees. Printed works intended for a mass audience deployed biting humor to attack inequality and oppression.

The axiomatic privileging of the common good in public discourse encompassed a variety of political orientations and modes of expression. Essential to a wide distribution of ideas and beliefs in the eighteenth century was a vibrant print culture. Scholars have associated the notion of a public sphere with eighteenth-century print and coffeehouse cultures, and in the relatively decentralized Americas Philadelphia was a center of publishing and an active public sphere.[8] Yet printers' commitment to open debate and discussion fostered contentions in which disputants invariably looked to history and tradition to legitimize their positions. Like the author of "Common Sense," Philadelphia writers adapted and refined conventions to suit contemporary ideological needs and aims.

Legacies of Dissent

Medieval European society theoretically comprised three orders: the clergy, the nobility, and the peasantry—those who pray, those who fight, and those who work. A major cultural distinction within the tripartite social order was that between the learned and unlearned. According to the dominant clerical vision of a society of orders, laboring people were incapable of abstract thought and were therefore for the most part uneducable.[9] Though some Renaissance authors began to argue for rethinking ordinary people's capacity for basic knowledge of the Bible in the early sixteenth century, the difference between the learned and unlearned remained a fundamental distinction in European culture. In Reformation England, the new Anglican Church attempted to maintain social and religious order after popular risings in the 1530s and 1540s by requiring clergymen to read didactic sermons in the pulpit from *The Books of Homilies*. According to Queen Elizabeth decades later, the "superstitious blindness of the rude and unlearned" justified the abolition of some church ceremonies and the keeping of others.[10]

Pre-Reformation critics of church orthodoxy, most famously in England the Lollards, drew on the early Christian image of the virtuous plowman in calls for the vernacular translation of scriptures and the expansion of literacy.[11]

Though suppressed after the Peasants' Revolt of 1381, Lollardy continued an underground existence up to the Reformation, and Lollard ideas inspired radical Protestant sects into the seventeenth century.[12] Only with the breakdown of state control over the press in the 1640s, however, were claims regarding ordinary people's right to literacy provided to a mass audience in print. Over the course of that decade writers and activists articulated new ideas concerning natural equality, liberty, and common people's ability to participate in the decisions of church and state.[13] Critics of new religious and political doctrines like John Taylor, Thomas Edwards, and Ephraim Pagit—known collectively as heresiographers—attacked promoters of unorthodox religious and political ideas and argued that unlearned preachers seduced common people in order to sow confusion and subvert the authority of the church.[14]

Heresiographers attacked Anabaptists, Brownists, Familists, Seekers, Catholics, and others with extreme vigor in the 1640s. In the mid-1650s critics claimed that Quakers were the direct descendants of Familists (or Family of Love), Seekers, and Ranters.[15] The Familist belief that the Spirit, or Light, of God was in each believer would indeed be a central component of Quaker doctrine.[16] Friends also adopted the Seeker belief in universal salvation and their practice of meeting in silence, speaking only when moved by the Spirit. In his preface to George Fox's *Journal*, William Penn praised Seekers' and Familists' practice of gathering informally in silence, speaking only when inspired by a *"Divine Spring."* However, they failed to retain their original humility and fear of God, evolving instead into antinomian Ranters during the midcentury tumults.[17] Like Familists, Ranters believed God dwelled inside the individual and that Christ's atonement on behalf of humankind was sufficient to place believers in a state of grace on earth.[18] Early Quaker leaders like George Fox and James Nayler proudly proclaimed their "uncivill railing" against "hireling" priests and "conceited hypocrites." Like other critics of university-educated clergy, they were also eager to remind their opponents that Jesus chose "Heardsmen, Fishermen, and Plowmen" over religious authorities of human learning.[19] The famous puritan divine Richard Baxter complained in the mid-1650s that papers sent him by Quakers were filled with "almost nothing but filthy railing words," including "Thou Serpent, thou Liar, thou deceiver, thou childe of the devil, thou cursed hypocrite, thou dumb dogge." The allegations Quakers leveled against Baxter included that he was "called Master," preached from a raised podium and timed sermons with an hourglass, took money for tithes, and was idle because he "did not dig or thresh."[20]

The antiauthoritarian Quaker message of individual conscience found an audience among literate middling traders, artisans, and husbandmen in England, especially in the north. Known for their opposition to tithes in addition to their hostility to the established church and their rejection of predestination, Quakers maintained militant political as well as religious positions throughout the 1650s. As late as 1659 Edward Billing issued manifestos that were as social and political as religious in intent, demanding (in addition to religious freedom) legal equality, an end to capital punishment for theft, prison reforms, the abolition of servile tenures, equal political representation, and other reforms.[21] In the same year Edward Burrough wrote to Parliament requesting the formation of a committee that would include Anabaptists and Quakers for the redress of the many "oppressions and injustices" that remained in civil society despite the great transformations of recent years.[22]

Leading Friends' disavowal of Commonwealth-era calls for social and political reforms were accompanied by an effort to impose doctrinal discipline and church order on members. The theme of order pervaded the writings of Robert Barclay and William Penn in the 1670s. While Quakers continued to refuse to acknowledge man-made social distinctions—most famously in refusing to remove their hats or use formal addresses in the presence of those of higher rank—Barclay and Penn argued for the necessity of submission to authority and conventional norms of social order. Acknowledging the "Malignity of Man's Nature," Barclay castigated the excesses of the civil wars in *The Anarchy of the Ranters,* particularly the "confusion" that resulted from the licentiousness of the 1640s. Recalling organicist metaphors prominent among sixteenth-century Renaissance authors like Thomas Elyot, Barclay argued that all should know "for the good ordering and disposing all Things" their "Place and Station in the Body," since the "uncomely Parts are no less needful than the comely; and the less honourable than the more honourable."[23] Penn similarly instructed Friends that true liberty was a spiritual rather than worldly affair and that in obedience "Everyone in his Order is satisfied."[24]

Friends also adopted a Renaissance and Protestant commitment to "plain speaking" in pamphlets promoting emigration to Pennsylvania, and while recognizing the need for an orderly hierarchy, they also appealed to potential settlers' desire for education. Thomas Budd's *Good Order Established in Pennsilvania & New-Jersey* was delivered in a language "very plain," as it was intended "to be understood by any ordinary Capacity."[25] Gabriel Thomas's appeal to England's poor some years later aimed to ease suspicions among laboring people concerning fraud in the Atlantic passage and exploitation in America. Thomas assured readers that he held no "sinister Design" to impose on "the Ignorant, or Credulous, or to curry Favour with the Rich and Mighty"; his interest was solely in the welfare of England's poor. The poor might also be improved by the existence in Philadelphia of "several Schools of good Learning for Youth, in order to the Attainment of Arts and Sciences, and also Reading, Writing, etc."[26]

While English advocates of overseas plantations had long used printed works to publicize the benefits of colonization, Friends were especially aware of the power of print. For Quakers in the 1650s, freedom of the press was closely related to ideas concerning public education and church disestablishment.[27] After the reintroduction of censorship with the Licensing Act of 1662, Friends developed an elaborate system of clandestine book production and distribution. Quakers were understandably eager to publish without fear of arrest with the founding of Pennsylvania. When William Penn left London for America in 1682, he brought with him a young printer apprentice of Leicestershire named William Bradford. After returning to England to finish his education and marry Elizabeth Sowle, daughter of master printer Andrew Sowle, Bradford set up in Philadelphia in 1685 as the colony's first printer.[28]

Founding Pennsylvania Friends did not support a completely open press, however, and some came to regret the proprietor's choice of Bradford as the colony's printer. George Fox instructed the young man to import and print Quaker books for consumption throughout the North American colonies; he also wanted Philadelphia Friends to closely monitor what Bradford published. The first work printed by Bradford in Philadelphia, Samuel Atkins's 1685 almanac *Kalendarium Pennsilvaniense*, met with disapproval from leading Quakers and was censored. The printer's problems were not limited to establishment Friends; in 1689 Bradford also clashed with the governor, John Blackwell, after publishing the colony's charter and laws. Caught between Philadelphia's ruling factions, Bradford insisted on his right and need to publish as a matter of "my trade and calling."[29]

Print's ability to foment controversy among the general urban population emerged in the 1690s. As noted in chapter 3, antiproprietary critics of taxation published a 1692 petition that appropriated a language of popular sovereignty versus arbitrary bondage and implicitly threatened to remove representatives from office if they approved the bill.[30] Internal doctrinal differences between Friends were brought to the public's attention in a series of publications in the

1690s. After landing in Philadelphia in 1689, George Keith, who had traveled with Fox, Barclay, and Penn on Quaker missions in Europe in the 1670s, criticized local Friends' alleged disavowal of the historical Jesus and their privileging of the Inner Light, or "Christ within." After publishing a series of Keith's tracts in the early 1690s, colonial authorities released Bradford from his contract. Officials accused the printer of libel and, ironically, considering Friends' history of clandestine publishing, of violating England's Licensing Act (which Parliament would allow to lapse in 1695). After the seizure of his papers and printing tools by the colonial government, William Bradford moved to New York City.[31]

The confrontation between Keith and elite Friends Samuel Jennings, John Simcock, Thomas Lloyd, and others demonstrates the potential of the press to contribute to the Quaker schism by placing doctrinal differences before the public.[32] Keith and his supporters presented themselves not only as Friends but as champions of a "court of public opinion," going so far as to place copies of Keith's *An Appeal from the Twenty Eight Judges* on posts in Philadelphia and elsewhere in the colony.[33] The existence of a local printer proved so disruptive that after Bradford's exit, Philadelphia went without one until 1698, when the Dutch lacemaker and printer Reynier Jensen arrived in the town. By this time Keithians had themselves split into factions, and in the late 1690s and early 1700s disaffected Quakers associated with millenarian German Lutherans, Baptists, and Anglicans. Keith returned to publishing religious tracts and polemics in Philadelphia, New York, and Boston in the early 1700s, now as a member of the Church of England.[34]

The primary purveyor of information in early Philadelphia was not the religious polemic, however, but the almanac. The most popular literary genre in England and the colonies, the almanac has been characterized by one historian as "the contemporary equivalent of the tabloid press, both in tone and popularity."[35] In addition to tables and charts describing eclipses, tides, and the position of the sun and moon, almanacs disseminated aphoristic wisdom that both reflected and shaped readers' beliefs and worldviews. The popularity of the form is indicated by the large number of almanac makers throughout the colonies—though producers were concentrated in the highly literate societies of Massachusetts and Pennsylvania. Benjamin Franklin competed with seven other Philadelphia almanacs when he began publishing *Poor Richard's Almanack* in 1732.[36] Competition for readers was reflected in bitter feuds between producers and in their efforts to distinguish their works from those of allegedly inferior quality. Enormously popular in England in the 1640s and

1650s, almanacs remained partisan even after the return of censorship during the Restoration, and this tradition continued in America.[37]

In attempting to reach a broad audience, and, like pamphlets promoting immigration to America, almanacs addressed both lettered and unlettered readers. Samuel Atkins claimed in Philadelphia's first almanac—and the first work published in the town—that in his travels in the Chesapeake and mid-Atlantic he had often heard "the People" complain they had little knowledge of how time passed, while "Ingenious Persons" interested in the mathematical arts desired a printed ephemeris (an astronomical journal) to experiment with. *Kalendarium Pennsilvaniense* was therefore designed to appeal to the plebeian as well as the formally educated, as practical and specialized knowledges found common ground in general education and scientific inquiry. The provincial council's close reading of Atkins's kalendarium, and their subsequent instruction to William Bradford to publish only works approved by the council, testifies to the subversive potential even of everyday almanacs.[38]

The following year the farmer Daniel Leeds published his *American Almanack*, also printed by Bradford. Leeds's self-identification as a "Student in Agriculture"—a common authorial title in almanacs—contrasted with Atkins's more pretentious self-description as a "Student in Mathematics and Astrology," and his single-sheet poster was likely far more affordable than Atkins's forty-page work. While Atkins soon left Philadelphia, Leeds and his son Titan established an American almanac industry, publishing works in Philadelphia, New York, Boston, and Newport well into the eighteenth century.[39] However, like Atkins's *Kalendarium,* Quaker overseers objected to allegedly pagan imagery in Leeds's first almanac, leading him to break with the Society and viciously attack George Fox and other Friends throughout the 1690s and early 1700s.[40]

One of these attacks, *The Great Mistery of Fox-Craft Discovered* (1705), accused Fox and Quakers in America of being hypocrites—no minor insult in early modern culture. With abundant textual support from the New Testament, radical Protestant critiques in the seventeenth century (including those of early Quakers) often portrayed the clergy's pride and vanity as deeply hypocritical.[41] Leeds accused Fox of being an uneducated fraud who deluded his followers through "a Pretence of *Christianity,*" with Friends' doctrine portrayed as a deistical denial of Christ's divinity. Friends' oaths of abjuration constituted further evidence of their duplicity, while Quakers' refusal to provide material support for the War of Spanish Succession revealed a self-interested lack of loyalty.[42] While the prominent Philadelphia Friend Caleb Pusey wrote a number of pamphlets defending Fox and William Penn from Leeds's and John Talbot's assaults, the almanac maker's criticisms, like those of George Keith, gave public expression to anti-Quaker sentiment using a discourse of heresy and hypocrisy.[43]

The disputatious Leeds was also involved in a feud with rival almanac maker Jacob Taylor that lasted through the first decade of the eighteenth century.[44] In addition to lampooning Leeds, Taylor's *Ephemeris Sideralis* (first published in 1699) contained a number of subversive ideas. The 1704 edition claimed religion was the primary cause of the deplorable state of the world, going so far as to assert most Christians differed from Turks and Jews in name only, since contemporary religion was little more than a means to *"Mony and vain glory."* Such an expression of Augustan cynicism in a colonial almanac begs the intriguing question of how widespread such views were in the decades after the Restoration. Taylor's almanac also addressed social and domestic issues, characterizing thieving servants as "Slaves" merely taking revenge on abusive "enslavers" and informing readers that the "inconveniences" of married life were more often a result of men's negligence than of women's faults. Taylor even took aim at "Monster *Custom*," a great tyrant that ruled the mob: "For People love the ways wherein they're bred, / And so, fast hoodwinkd, are by *Levi* led."[45] For the contrarian Taylor, at least, the almanac was a vehicle through which to attack competitors and question received culture through witty aphorism.

The application of Renaissance and Reformation adherence to general comprehensibility through a "Plain and Familiar Form" testifies to the broadening of print's audience in the late seventeenth and early eighteenth centuries. Almanacs' commitment to plain honesty contributed to the conventional image of the virtuous producer and functioned as a form through which to critique luxury. Long before the Father Abraham character in Benjamin Franklin's aphoristic essay "Way to Wealth" criticized colonial luxury, William Birkett appropriated the voice of the "honest country Farmer" to criticize the "superfluous" possessions of the rich and to contrast the "Honour" of lords with the "Honesty" of the poor.[46] Perhaps most indicative of the importance of almanacs to Philadelphia culture is an anonymous, 211-line verse satire attacking them in 1735. City almanac makers Jacob Taylor, Daniel and Titan Leeds, John Jerman, Benjamin Eastbourn, Thomas Godfrey Sr., and John Hughes all came in for ridicule in "The Diarist." Even Franklin, whose Poor Richard would be the most famous plain-spoken almanac producer of all, was characterized as lacking all judgement and good sense, vainly attempting to be "A mungril Son of bald Pernassus."[47]

Making a Popular Political Culture

The author of "The Diarist" argued that printers' and almanac makers' intrusion into the culture of the learned challenged the social order. The political dimensions of disorder were also evident from an early date. In the view of proprietary supporters, the formation of an antiproprietary faction in the 1680s and 1690s, and especially its victory in obtaining the Charter of Privileges in 1701, reinforced the threat of disorderly popular politics. James Logan believed the new charter showed that assemblymen had been seduced by local demagogues and likened the assembly's quest for power to that of the English Parliament in 1641.[48] Since the proper administration of government was exceedingly difficult in such an environment, these Quaker elites saw it as essential that the "best men" be elected to the assembly, as it was they who best understood the true needs of the province. Should the founding establishment lose control of the political order, perhaps Pennsylvania would be better off as a royal colony.[49]

The Keithian schism, almanac feuds, and proprietary and antiproprietary disputes overlapped in the 1690s and early 1700s. It was in the 1720s, however, that a radical-popular political culture cohered and took form in Philadelphia. Not long after the onset of an economic depression early in the decade, the London dissenter Samuel Keimer arrived as the town's second printer, creating an environment in which long-simmering hostilities could be brought before the public. While historians have examined the pamphlet war of the 1720s, it is important to see the polemics of that decade as functioning on multiple levels that used distinctive modes of presentation for different audiences. The first group of pamphlets, though partisan, addressed economic and political problems in a scholarly language of constitutionalism and sovereignty. A second, anonymously authored group of publications deployed dialogues and letters that used allegorical figures and biting satire in an effort to reach a broader audience. While the factional identities surrounding the figures of Governor William Keith and James Logan were important, the popular party's ability to draw on traditional images of producerist virtue in disputes over paper money resonated strongly with local farmers and tradesmen.

Local discussion of the need for a provincial currency in Pennsylvania emerged as early as the 1680s, but the first printed work calling for paper money was Francis Rawle's *Some Remedies Proposed for the Restoring the Sunk Credit of the Province of Pennsylvania,* anonymously published in 1721. Rawle, a Philadelphia merchant and landlord, wrote his pamphlet in a common-wealth language of the public weal that resembled arguments over currency published in London in the 1690s.[50] Though far from inflammatory, Rawle's claim that the colony's credit was in decay led the Pennsylvania government to indict printer Andrew Bradford for libel.[51] When questioned by Governor Keith and the provincial council, Bradford claimed he knew nothing of the printing or publishing of the pamphlet. However implausible Bradford's claim (he was the only printer in town at the time), the absence of publishing information on the tract—a longstanding strategy of clandestine publication among English dissenters—made the printer's involvement in the pamphlet difficult to prove.

Andrew Bradford could not dispute that he was publisher of the *American Weekly Mercury*, whose January 2, 1722, issue was also accused by the council of defaming the colonial government. The offending passage stated: "We have great Expectations from them [assemblymen] at this Juncture, that they will find some effectual Remedy, to revive the dying Credit of this Province, and restore us to our former happy Circumstances." In addition to taking offense at the claim of dying credit, the council was likely also troubled by the coercive implications of the statement. The announcement appropriated the voice of the people and articulated their "expectations" of the government to take action to revive trade. At his appearance before the council, Bradford claimed that the sentence was inserted by a journeyman without the printer's knowledge and successfully obtained a pardon from the governor.[52]

The *Mercury* was not a vehicle for radical political ideas, however. Bradford's paper was created as a business publication for city merchants, with local traders encouraged to inform the printer of current prices and other commercial information.[53] The *Mercury* did regularly reproduce the works of John Trenchard and Thomas Gordon, whose "Independent Whig" and "Cato's Letters" essays were expressed in a patriotic language of rights and liberty that greatly influenced propertied colonists. While colonial essayists consistently deferred to the authority of Trenchard and Gordon, their writings could be interpreted in different ways. Republican tributes to the virtuous plowman who knows good government from bad, and who understands "whether the Fruits of his Labour are his own, and whether he enjoys them in Peace and Security," sounded a distinctly more populist note in a colonial context in which the rural gentry was far less prominent than small freeholders, for example.[54] Comparing Roman imperial governors unfavorably with virtuous plowmen and urban artisans, moreover, had a less metaphorical meaning in a colonial context in which small farmers and mechanics held more social and economic power than did their counterparts in England.[55]

That some in Philadelphia assumed radical Whig essays appearing in the *Mercury* referred to local conditions was made clear in 1722 after an essay translated from Plato by "Americo Britannus" appeared in the paper. The initial essay deplored the hypocrisy of fake "Shews of Wisdom," the success of which depended on the gullibility of "Drones and Coxcombs."[56] Some months later Americo wrote an introduction to another of Cato's letters in the *Mercury* claiming that his earlier essay, "level'd at particular Vice and Humour among the general," was interpreted by some in Philadelphia to be a "Reflection on particular Men in these Parts of the World." The essay, republished from the *London Journal* and repeating a conventional view of human nature, asserted that it was impossible for men to be put under too many restraints because of their inherent lust for wealth and power—a notion repeated some years later in the "Common Sense" essay with which this chapter began.[57] Rather than a statement of general principles, some Philadelphians evidently read the essay as an indictment of the rabble-rousing governor, William Keith, as well as of recent demands for paper money.

If Catonian essays contained both aristocratic and popular republican tendencies, a more unequivocal speech by Governor Keith in 1723 confirmed critics' suspicions of the governor's demagogic (and, as was known in the city, Jacobite) leanings. Keith informed the assembly that the true "Body of any People" was composed of the producing classes, a populist spin on post-Restoration writings on the value of labor and political economy. Keith's reference to the rights and liberties of all regardless of rank, and of the equality of "Fellow Creatures," expounded a radical equalitarianism in a religious idiom.[58] While Philadelphians had complained since the 1680s of the "oppressions" of local creditors and landlords in a language of free subjects' rights and privileges, Keith's call for the political engagement of laboring people in a biblical language of Christian equality—in a speech he knew would be printed for public consumption—was unprecedented.

Keith's oration did not go unanswered. In September James Logan used an address to the Philadelphia grand jury to respond to growing dissention in town. Logan emphasized that only government "delivers us from that Savage and Barbarous State" of lawlessness in which neither possessions, wives, children, nor life (in that order) were secure. Moving from the general to the particular, the address lamented that the Pennsylvania government was not modeled more closely on that of Britain and that as a result of disproportionate popular power in Pennsylvania, grand jurymen were uniquely duty-bound to maintain law and order.[59] Three months later the *Mercury* published a short essay critical of the emergence of factions in the city, suggesting dangerous speeches could "actuate a mighty and many headed Multitude," an allusion to Keith's inflammatory ranting. In a reference to the alcohol-fueled tavern politicking that was becoming prevalent in the town, the writer warned, "A foolish Speech supported with Vehemence and Brandy, will conquer the best Sense, and the best Cause in the World, without Anger or Liquor."[60]

The Philadelphia pamphlet war had its true origins in 1725, however. In contrast to learned and ostensibly "disinterested"—though far from politically neutral—essays and treatises published earlier in the decade, satirical dialogues lambasted opponents while allegorical characters commented on the unique state of affairs in Philadelphia and Pennsylvania. If Keith's critics utilized classical aristocratic republican imagery, radical-popular pamphlets drew on commonwealth social criticisms that contrasted honest commoners with overweening grandees. Importantly, both Andrew Bradford and Samuel Keimer published works for each party, and House Speaker David Lloyd's replacement of Bradford with Keimer as printer to the assembly suggests the extent of publishing competition in the city.[61] More important than personal rivalries was print's placement of "the people" in a position to judge political affairs at the highest levels of provincial government. Though George Keith and his supporters appealed to public opinion in the 1690s, political discussion in the 1720s encompassed a wider segment of the urban and colonial population, and authorities could no longer simply silence critical voices.[62]

Bradford's publication of a speech delivered by Keith to his assembly critics at the beginning of 1725 set the tone in pitting pedantic elites against plain-spoken commoners. While according to the governor the passage of good laws in recent years—especially the two money bills of 1723 and the lowering of the legal interest rate from 8 to 6 percent—had returned the colony to prosperity, some men were still not "contented with sharing the common Benefits of Life freely and equally with their Fellow Creatures." Keith also disparaged men who, under a "conceited Pretence," claimed to subdue ignorance with their own "superiour Knowledge." While the famously well-read Logan may have been the intended target of this barb, the statement also functioned as a criticism of conventional wisdom concerning plebeian ignorance and credulity—a view recently articulated in the *Mercury*. It is also possible Keith was familiar with the true identity of "Americo Britannus," and the governor's comment was a taunt directed at the *Mercury* author specifically. A response to Keith from the House (appended by Bradford to the governor's speech) countered that representatives were aware that "humane Nature" was imperfect and that in most governments there were some who desired unlimited power. The qualification that such appeared not to be the case under the current administration likely fooled no one, especially Keith.[63]

The transferal of hostilities from the halls of the assembly to the public sphere of print advanced further in 1725 with the publication of David Lloyd's *Vindication of the Legislative Power* and James Logan's response, *The Antidote*. Lloyd's *Vindication* championed the assembly's lawmaking supremacy enshrined in the colonial charter, while Logan's *Antidote* argued in favor of proprietary and provincial council authority. Logan's much longer and more elaborate work also expressed a view of history reflective of a deeply conservative social philosophy. According to Logan, current slogans celebrating the supreme judgment of the people were dangerously misplaced. History had shown that parliaments as well as kings could err, as demonstrated by the contemporary agreement among "All men" that the English parliament of the 1640s was characterized by an "excessive Abuse of Power." Logan traced a line from the civil wars in England to the first "fatal Blow" to good order in Pennsylvania, which had arrived in the 1690s in the guise of George Keith, Pennsylvania's "Grand Apollyon." Challenges to proprietary power emanated from those not content to be "grateful and quiet," who were led by the "Sounds" of designing men instead of remaining satisfied with their station. Logan's contempt for recent populist polemics was suggested when he informed the public he would no longer respond to any of those "ingenious Persons" who treated his words with "Scoffs, Invectives, Trifling Cavils, Drollery, Scurrility, &c."[64]

In addition to ridiculing Logan and other grandees, pamphleteers portrayed condescending elitist attitudes intended to provoke ordinary colonists. The author of *The Triumvirate* sought to bring together urban and rural popular interests by having "Negroso Bullico" (probably provincial councilor, assemblyman, merchant, and land bank trustee Richard Hill) refer disdainfully to supporters of paper money as ignorant "Handycraft Tradesmen" and "Country Clowns." The writer claimed the triumvirate were "three notorious Deists, whose Riches have raised their Pride above all Notions of Religion and Humanity," fusing old accusations of anti-Christian Quaker heresy with local class privilege.[65] The theme of irreligion—and, suggestively, hostility to Trenchard and Gordon—resurfaced in 1729, when David Lloyd (by this time out of favor with city radicals) was criticized for promoting deism by permitting Samuel Keimer to print the *Independent Whig* and other "Blasphemies of the Ordinances of Christ" in Philadelphia.[66]

The dialogue, an ancient literary form updated in the sixteenth century by Renaissance authors, was seen by educational authorities as especially suited to the inferior intellectual abilities of common people. One seventeenth-century English author asserted dialogues could be understood even by those of the "weakest capacities," since they presented information to common people in "their own naturall Logick."[67] James Logan's *A Dialogue Shewing what's therein to be found*, though using the popular form, missed the point of anonymous pamphleteers' mocking of such conventions. Instead, his satire was an attack on plebeian politicking and was clearly influenced by Defoe's recently published *Vindication of the Press*, which poked fun at "illiterate Mechanic[s]" who increasingly commented "upon the most material Occurrences, and Judging the Actions of the greatest in *Europe*" in London coffeehouses.[68] In Philadelphia, as in London, public spaces—in this case taverns instead of coffeehouses—had become breeding grounds of popular political discourse. According to *A Dialogue Shewing*, too many in Philadelphia had turned "Politician or Statesmen" and felt emboldened "over a Dram or a Mugg without Doors" to converse on laws, men, and other things of which they "knew little of."[69]

Disorderly politics were directly related to the money issue. If proper government and the public good required social distinctions rooted in nature, the explosion of demands for paper money and antimerchant sentiment signified a dangerous overturning of economic as well as political order. Local talk of "*Medium of Commerce, Ballance of Trade, Publick Good, Funds, Loans, Striking, Sinking*, and such like" were nothing more than a "Parcel of clever Words" to deceive the people. Paper money was "imaginary Stuff" with no intrinsic value; merchants and rich men, who possessed special economic knowledge by virtue of their wealth and profession, were objects of unwarranted hostility in Philadelphia. London newspapers like the *Craftsman* increasingly portrayed historically suspect merchants as the "Heart-Blood of the Body Politic" in the 1720s and 1730s, and *A Dialogue Shewing* similarly argued merchants were the most patriotic and beneficial members of the commonwealth.[70] According to Logan, however, in Philadelphia merchant-creditors were unjustly attacked for charging lawful rates of interest, and "Advertisements" accusing them of usury were published to prevent them from being elected to the assembly. It probably did not help *A Dialogue Shewing*'s popularity to assert that "Everybody that [knew] any Thing of the Matter" knew that good men of good breeding promoted trade and enriched the country in a way common farmers and tradesmen simply could not.[71]

Two responses to *A Dialogue Shewing* were anonymously published in 1726. Francis Rawle's *A Just Rebuke to a Dialogue betwixt Simon and Timothy* primarily addressed the *Dialogue*'s references to Rawle's *Ways and Means,* an economic treatise published the previous year.[72] The other, Keith's satirical dialogue *The Observator's Trip to America,* again utilized the figure of Roger Plowman to attack the aloof and backsliding Logan. The pamphlet contrasted European accounts of unprecedented liberty and prosperity in Pennsylvania with colonial realities, drawing on existing local beliefs in Friends' hypocrisy and worldliness. While acknowledging that he did not experience material deprivation after his arrival in Philadelphia from Gloucester, Plowman informed the Observator that "the Peoples Manners and way of Dealing is quite different from the *Old English* Fashion of plain down-right Honest." Rather than finding a simple and well-meaning people free of pride and luxury in Philadelphia, Plowman found people who "Pamper, Strut, Back-bite and Sharp upon one another, even far beyond the *Londoners* themselves." A "Certain *Quaker*" of Philadelphia with a reputation for being "a mighty Schollard"—Logan—was particularly guilty of such arrogance, refusing to show "the least *Humanity* to those below him." Plowman claimed to have little interest in discourse with the great, preferring to keep company with plain-speaking honest folk. Yet laboring people were as capable of judging their own good as were the learned. After all, Plowman asked, were not all made of the same flesh and bones, sharing in a common desire for happiness, justice, and prosperity?[73]

While the *Observator's Trip* used a populist language evident in other publications, the pamphlet also displayed Keith's traditionalism. In contrast to the plowman character that appeared in other pamphlets, the *Observator*'s Roger Plowman was an exceedingly deferential and even obsequious character, his professed illiteracy reinforcing the superior wisdom of the Observator, a genteel authority figure—like the Scottish baronet Keith, in fact. Social criticism was tempered by a paternalism in which the stability of organic Old English hierarchies was being altered in the exploitative setting of colonial Pennsylvania. The "inhumanity" of Philadelphia grandees disrupted customary reciprocal relations between patricians and plebs, as allegorized by the Observator and Plowman. Keith's sponsorship of two political clubs during his time in power embodied the seemingly given nature of class differences despite the emergence of an organized popular alliance in the city and region. The Gentleman's Club was reserved for the governor's gentry supporters, while the Tiff Club was where the "honest Trades-man" discussed politics "over a Tankard of good Punch."[74] For Keith beliefs in a common humanity and producers' right to comment on politics were perfectly compatible with traditional social distinctions in a deferential culture.

Polemical pamphlets continued to issue from Philadelphia presses over the next two years, and the figures of Keith, Lloyd, Logan, and Isaac Norris continued to loom large in the paper war. Ideological differences were not reducible to personalities, however.[75] In particular, while factional leaders traded insults in the press, the currency issue continued to fuel political animosities. One proprietary partisan alleged in 1727 that unpropertied Philadelphians were illegally voting in the city, while the cry of paper money had become "the grand Machine" of the popular party.[76] A series of tracts published at the end of the decade defended bills of credit, repeated claims of loan office officials hoarding money, and accused Penn's seventeenth-century land agents of corruption. "Philadelphus" (who, as noted in chapter 1, ridiculed accusations of money hoarding) argued that those who peddled such libelous fictions not only had no knowledge of history; they were ignorant of "humane Nature."[77]

While partisan politics rooted in class and culture persisted after Keith's departure, Benjamin Franklin's *A Modest Enquiry into the Nature and Necessity of a Paper-Currency* (1729) characteristically attempted to bridge the gap between learned and popular discourses. *A Modest Enquiry* treated the economic question of paper money in scientifically objective—and therefore politically neutral—terms. Though the pamphlet acknowledged that laboring people were the "chief Strength and Support of a People," perception of the "true Interest" of a country required a specialized knowledge reserved for the few. While it was unsurprising to hear men daily arguing heatedly over some point of politics, it was also the case that neither understood politics any better than they did each other. *A Modest Enquiry* thus expressed a labor theory of value and appealed to the sentiments and needs of working people in calling for paper money, while simultaneously reserving discussion of policy for an enlightened minority.[78]

Prosperity, the People, and Empire

In the early 1730s assemblymen wrote to Lieutenant Governor Patrick Gordon that a feeling of "Unanimity" now existed among "all Sorts of People" in Pennsylvania. This unity led legislators to hope that the "just Sense of the People" had overcome the divisions of the previous decade.[79] Prosperity had returned as trade expanded and local industry revived—thanks, it was generally agreed, to the provincial government's issuance of bills of credit. Franklin's moderation and his desire to establish political consensus in Philadelphia, evident in A Modest Enquiry, fit well with his profit-savvy strategy of an open and nonpartisan press, and by the 1730s a "polite" world of literature and print had come into being in port cities throughout British America.[80] Yet if the Philadelphia press reflected broader trends in Atlantic print culture surrounding the importance of polite discourse and aristocratic republican politics, ideological divisions in the city persisted. While social and political criticism in Philadelphia echoed anxieties over luxury increasingly prominent throughout the British Empire, history and the nature of local rule continued to inform urban political discourse.

A growing number of authors appropriated classical criticisms of luxury and worried over the concomitant decline in imperial power in England and America in the eighteenth century, as an expanding "empire of goods" placed consumption at the center of moral and political discussion.[81] Philadelphia newspapers reprinted English essays hostile to the "Luxuries and expensive Follies" of the better sort, which invariably encouraged similar obsessions among social inferiors who, it was claimed, naturally aped their betters.[82] Justifications of luxurious consumption and inequality were also available, however. Philadelphia merchants read Bernard Mandeville's controversial Fable of the Bees, which argued that hostility to luxury resulted from envy rather than republican virtue and that poverty for the laboring classes was an essential driver of productivity essential to national wealth.[83] Philadelphians could also read defenses of social inequality produced in the mid-Atlantic like Joseph Morgan's The Nature of Riches, published by Franklin in 1732.

Morgan, a Presbyterian minister from New Jersey, had disparate and unorthodox interests. He corresponded with Boston intellectuals and members of the Royal Society, and in 1728 the Synod of Philadelphia received a complaint that Morgan tested judicial astrology before his congregation in Freehold, New Jersey.[84] The Nature of Riches sought to use natural reason as well as the Bible to defend wealth disparities. Morgan began with an assertion prevalent among intellectuals since the early Renaissance: if individuals followed the golden rule and sought the good of others as truly as they sought their own, there would be no reason for economic inequality. However, since it is in people's sinful nature to love themselves above others, it is vain to imagine, let alone attempt to construct, such a society. Necessity therefore dictates that each person be the proper owner of the wealth his or her labor creates, and from this follows the paradox that covetousness is both the support and misery of the world. Morgan argued that individual attempts to make oneself rich actually served the public good through improvements and the expansion of goods. While *Nature of Riches* repeated widely held strictures against usury, theft, and idleness, its claim that human greed is ultimately more beneficial to the public than to rich individuals themselves was a mid-Atlantic manifestation of larger shifts in Anglo-American social, economic, and religious thought.[85]

Morgan's justification of the pursuit of self-interest in the service of the public was accompanied by instructions to the poor concerning their lowly condition. Through "honest Industry" the children of poor families could find happiness in this life and, more importantly, in the next. In fact, the poor were paradoxically freer than the rich, since although the wealthy believed others were their slaves, in reality it was they who were slaves to the public. The lives of the rich were "miserable" because wealth brought an excess of "Fear and Care"; those prosperous enough to avoid labor with their hands worked even more arduously with their minds and therefore received less rest than the toilers. The poor, who obtained only food and clothing from their honest labor, were free from such weighty responsibilities. Similar to Mandeville's opposition to charity schools, Morgan justified not educating the working classes, claiming that the ignorant laborer "who has no Expectation of rising higher" eats and drinks with comfort and sleeps with a cheerful mind.[86]

After listening to the "famous philosopher" Morgan discourse on a variety of subjects at a New Jersey inn on his way to New York in 1744, the Maryland doctor Alexander Hamilton noted that on his way out, "the old don" seemed "well satisfied with his own learning and knowledge."[87] In Philadelphia Constant Truman articulated an association between wealth and formal learning when he distinguished between the gentleman and the farmers and mechanics who supplied the former with "all his fine Cloaths, his gay Houses and Furniture, and his Train of Servants and Attendants." Truman wanted "nothing to do with your Cricks and Scholars and Book Learned Men," who were too proud to receive instructions from a commoner like Truman in any case. He was "a plain Man" who wrote for "plain People, and desire to be understood." While Truman's friends and neighbors may not have as much wit as those more learned, "yet they may have as much Honesty as others."[88]

Truman's pamphlet celebrated William Penn and Pennsylvania's Charter of Privileges in a plain-spoken populist discourse critical of a small group's monopolization of power in the colony. In 1736 the editor and lawyer John Webbe took a more radical position by taking explicit aim at the structure of Pennsylvania government in a series of letters published in the *Gazette* appearing under the pseudonym "Z." Webbe criticized the allegedly oligarchic concentration of power in the colonial legislature using an architectural metaphor: "If the Superstructure is too heavy for the Foundation, the Building totters, though assisted by the outward Props of Art." Though the metaphor was not uncommon in early modern political theory, Webbe's was a novel criticism of Pennsylvania considering that criticisms from proprietary supporters typically lamented the colony's excessively "popular" government. Calling for a wider foundation that implied a broader franchise and more representative assembly, Webbe claimed political liberty was the "Birth-right" of every man and the extent of freedom in society was proportionate to the level of popular political participation. Echoes of civil war–era ideas from radical groups like the Levellers concerning natural equality were prominent: "Nature has made no Distinction; from the same Clod of Dirt she forms a Monarch and a Cobbler." Indeed, in contrast to the populist agitators of the 1720s, Webbe openly sided with seventeenth-century revolutionaries. Stuart tyranny rather than a power-hungry Parliament was responsible for the English civil wars, and the story of history in general was one of a perpetual struggle between rulers and ruled.[89]

In an autobiographical account in the last Z letter, Webbe framed his egalitarian politics as a product of his upbringing and education. During the Restoration, Webbe's father's political sentiments were "wholly founded on Revolution Principles," though his mother was more status-conscious and thought it a great misfortune to be the daughter of a lowly tradesman. This produced in her son a belief in the necessity of placing all "Mankind on a Level, by proving we are all naturally equal." While studying at Cambridge, Webbe regularly sent his mother satirical accounts of the "Fopperies of the young Nobility" in an attempt to dissuade her from her "Foible" of aristocratic envy. Webbe's time at university was itself largely an effort to appease his mother, as was, apparently, his entrance into legal training at Temple Inn after Cambridge, for after her death he immediately volunteered to serve in the War of Spanish Succession. In this period the doctrines of hereditary right and passive resistance resurfaced in England, according to Webbe. English priests "bellowed out Damnation" against any who challenged the divine right of kings, while to say the aggressions of Charles I caused the civil wars became a "horrid Blasphemy." After the 1713 Treaty of Utrecht formally ended the war, Webbe toured continental Europe and found little but tyranny, oppression, and slavery under the dominion of Rome. Shortly after the South Sea Bubble burst in 1720, Webbe immigrated to the colonies, where he hoped to live in "uninterrupted Tranquility."[90]

The relevance of all this for contemporary Pennsylvanians was that recent proceedings in the provincial assembly had allegedly "struck at the Roots of *Liberty*"; Webbe therefore felt compelled to relay his personal experience of arbitrary power to colonists. The impetus for the Z letters seems to have been related to the creation of a chancery (or equity) court in Philadelphia, made lawful under the governorship of William Keith in 1720 but not established until the mid-1730s. If Webbe was indeed referencing the chancery in the *Gazette*, he gave public expression to a number of assembly petitioners' belief that the court signified the emergence of arbitrary power in Pennsylvania.[91] Webbe accused the "inconsiderable Scribe" who devised the plan of attempting to introduce "popish Politicks" to the colony, suggesting the court was a siren of arbitrary rule.[92] If assembly elections were largely uncontested in the 1730s, specific policies continued to be sources of debate and controversy in Philadelphia. Equally important, Webbe's historical-political analysis went further than the populist pamphlets of the previous decade in proclaiming natural equality and popular sovereignty to be universal principles unalterable by man.

Letters printed in the *Mercury* quickly responded to Webbe's radical arguments. According to "Anti-Z," Webbe's political theory was dangerously republican and promoted a "licentious *ungovernable Freedom*" in defiance of all knowledge of human nature. Furthermore, neither Penn nor his proprietary successors had ever attempted to violate the English constitution, as Webbe suggested, and the balanced British constitutional monarchy was far superior to the dissolute Roman republic evidently favored by Z. As scandalous as the treatment of Penn and his descendants was Webbe's slander against the Stuarts, a family from whom "we derive our *Royal Charter*, which like the *Magna Charta*, is the firm Basis of all our Privileges."[93]

Webbe chose not to respond to his *Mercury* critic (or critics) with specifics, instead referring to them as "grave solemn Coxcombs," whose "*little smattering in learning*" had distorted their natural sense. Despite their education they failed to understand Z's arguments, which according to Webbe followed logically from self-evident principles.[94] The fundamental ideological difference between Webbe and his *Mercury* critics reflected competing views of human nature. Webbe's egalitarianism was rooted in a belief in natural equality and right; therefore for him, "*Vox Dei est Populi Vox*" (The voice of the people is the voice of God).[95] Anti-Z adhered to a more pessimistic view of human capacities, which corresponded to a rejection of Z's natural right argument in favor of precedent and tradition as embodied in law and lineage.

Fears of challenges to Pennsylvania governance persisted after the Z/Anti-Z exchange of 1736. According to one Philadelphia critic of the British constitution, a number of inhabitants frequently took the opportunity to call for introducing a different form of government closer to that of the metropole. In a place like Pennsylvania, ruled by principles of reason and equity and "suited to the sober dispositions and independent circumstances of the first adventurers," proposals to alter the form of rule were "almost as wicked, as was the attempt to change the *English Constitution* into a *Democracy*."[96] Speculative scholars like Webbe, who argued for popular sovereignty and universal natural rights, denied particular people's experience as well as human nature in general. In Pennsylvania the character of the people necessitated rule by those of "sober dispositions"—Quaker men of wealth and property who could trace their ancestry to the colony's founders. And once again, the frame of reference for critics of popular politics in Pennsylvania was the "democratic" turmoil of seventeenth-century England.

If political debate in the middle decades of the eighteenth century never reached the intensity of that of the 1720s, the availability and diversity of ideas expanded considerably. Between 1746 and 1767 at least a dozen new printers established themselves in Philadelphia and its hinterland, while in the same period the importation of books from England increased dramatically. From Philadelphia, the rising center of American intellectual life, Benjamin Franklin established a network with fellow printers in New York, New Haven, Annapolis, Lancaster, and Antigua. By 1760 nine printers resided in Philadelphia, and the Delaware River port rivaled Boston (with fourteen printers) for publishing supremacy in the Americas.[97] While the development of reading publics was essential to the expansion of cosmopolitan urban cultures in Philadelphia,

Boston, and New York, print also helped spread new evangelical ideas that questioned religious orthodoxies and learned religious authorities.[98]

The expanding world of print impacted all of Philadelphia society, albeit in different ways. In 1742 a third city newspaper, William Bradford III's *Pennsylvania Journal*, began publication (the *Mercury* would cease in 1746), and Bradford's London Coffee House at the southwest corner of Front and Market Streets became the center of Philadelphia's polite literary culture.[99] Yet gentility was only one aspect of colonial print culture; the diffusion of printed works enabled those further down the social ladder to consume books, pamphlets, chapbooks, and broadsides in homes and taverns. In Philadelphia local almanacs remained popular, though imported devotional books were the most important support of city booksellers. Educational works, pamphlets, and compendiums were purchased by farmers and artisans; works of fiction—the poetry of Shakespeare, Milton, and Pope as well as the prose of Bunyan and Defoe—were regularly sold in Philadelphia bookstores. If in times of political conflict ordinary Philadelphians displayed a traditional suspicion of university learning, Reverend Jacob Duché observed of Philadelphians in 1772 that "such is the prevailing taste for books of every kind, that almost every man is a reader."[100]

Print served a variety of functions in Philadelphia, including that of cheap entertainment, but serious literary works sold in the city focused on history and politics. History and biography formed the largest subject category in the city's subscription libraries, with Bishop Gilbert Burnet's history of the English Reformation and his Whiggish *History of His Own Time* especially popular. These interests dovetailed with the influence in the city of political writers including Sidney, Harrington, Locke, Trenchard, Gordon, and radical republicans like Milton. Those of more conservative political orientations like James Logan, Isaac Norris, Jonathan Dickinson, and William Allen read Edward Hyde's multivolume *History of the Rebellion and Civil Wars in England*.[101] First published in 1702, it is very likely that the Earl of Clarendon's history was the main source for Philadelphians' frequent references to the alleged democratic excesses of the 1640s.

While some colonists continued to believe in the need to keep ordinary people in ignorance, print culture's deference to public judgment fostered a belief among most Philadelphians that they had a right to speak on political matters. During his visit to the city, Alexander Hamilton claimed that among townspeople of the "better sort," men of "good learning" and "polite conversation" were abundant. ("Ladies," however, were rarely seen in public.) At a plebeian tavern Hamilton also "observed severall comicall, grotesque phizzes" who "afforded [a] variety of hints for a painter of Hogarth's turn." However comical they may have appeared to the Maryland physician, tavern-goers discoursed on a variety of subjects, including politics, religion, and the economy. Hamilton even admitted some of them spoke "tollerably well" on issues he believed to typically be beyond the generality's understanding.[102] Some years later Reverend Duché wrote that the "poorest labourer" in Philadelphia thought himself "entitled to deliver his sentiments in matters of religion or politics with as much freedom as the Gentleman or scholar." Inhabitants' forwardness in offering criticisms of printed works puts all "upon a level, in point of knowledge, with their several authors."[103]

Anxieties surrounding the threat of invasion during the 1740s strengthened the belief that ordinary, or at least middling, colonists were equipped to comment on government policy. Franklin's *Plain Truth* (1747) expressed most clearly how many Philadelphians' identity as Britons intersected with class, gender, and racial dynamics during King George's War. Signed by a "Tradesman of Philadelphia," Franklin emphasized that since the rich had the means to flee the city should an invasion occur, it was the "middling People"—the artisans, shopkeepers, and farmers who lived by their "Labour and Industry"— who would bear the brunt of the enemy's extortions (which, Franklin noted sardonically, was not all that different from the colony's system of taxation). To avoid alienating middling Quakers, Franklin claimed it was not Friends but rich men in general who failed to protect the colony. As things stood it was likely Philadelphia would soon fall to "licentious" privateers; the town's women would be subject to "the wanton and unbridled Rage, Rapine and Lust, of *Negroes, Molattoes*, and others, the vilest and most abandoned of Mankind." Most colonists, by contrast, were of the "British Race," and, like the inhabitants besieged by James II in the Northern Ireland town of Londonderry in 1689, Philadelphians would succeed in resisting the Catholic invaders.[104]

Despite the intensity of urban fears of invasion and the bitter hostility to the assembly's inaction as outlined in *Plain Truth*, Franklin and other Philadelphia printers remained committed to publishing disparate views. In the same year he published *Plain Truth*, Franklin also published James Burgh's *Britain's Remembrancer*, a critique of luxury very different from that of almanac makers like Franklin. First published in the aftermath of the Jacobite rising of 1745, *Britain's Remembrancer* claimed that all great states had degenerated because of the "inseparable Companies" of irreligion and luxury. What distinguished contemporary Britain was that whereas historically it was only "the Rich and Great" who had the ability to consume their lives in pleasure and disregard religion, "with us no Rank or Station is too low for either of these polite Vices." And according to Burgh it was British print culture—specifically newspapers—that were the primary sowers of irreligion.[105] Franklin and his partner David Hall, as well as their competitor William Bradford, also published works that attacked as well as defended the Quaker position on war. If dense biblical exegetics defending Quaker beliefs were no match for the polemical force of pro-defense pamphlets in shaping popular opinion, no one could argue that pacifist Friends were denied a public platform.[106]

The creation of the Association in 1748, as had been called for in a print campaign by Franklin, signaled the triumph of a popular vision of local self-defense. The voluntary organization confirmed the view that honest and virtuous freemen would have to overcome disloyal politicians to save the city and commonwealth. While Friends objected to the organization on religious grounds, Thomas Penn expressed a conventional political theory in thinking that the Association took power from the king and gave it to the people. Penn (who had been burned in effigy on leaving Philadelphia in 1741) referred to Franklin as dangerous and "a sort of Tribune of the People" and believed that considering the "Licenciousness" of the people of the colony, the Association could only end in "Anarchy and Confusion."[107]

Though the Association would be short-lived (it dissolved with the ending of the war in the fall of 1748), political arguments involving defense and popular participation were revived after war broke out again in 1754. If in the 1740s Thomas Penn thought Franklin was a dangerous populist, it was the Reverend William Smith who most forcefully attacked Franklin and what he believed to be republicanism in Pennsylvania in the context of the Seven Years' War. As in the previous decade, in the second half of the 1750s Philadelphians petitioned the provincial government requesting defensive measures; governors James Hamilton and Robert Morris complained about representatives' refusal to raise money and Philadelphia merchants' trading with the enemy.[108] Franklin attempted to appease pacifist Friends as well as supporters of defense with a bill for the creation of a voluntary militia in the city. He tried to win public support for the bill in the *Gazette* with a plain-spoken dialogue between three virtuous men; it defended the exemption of Friends from service as consonant with "the Liberty and Genius of our Constitution." The dialogue also addressed criticisms concerning the act's provision for the election of officers—a radical democratic proposal—by arguing that the Crown had invested settlers with additional liberties not in force in England. The act was therefore agreeable to both England's and Pennsylvania's constitutions.[109]

Franklin's attempt to create a citywide patriotic consensus "as Englishmen and Pennsylvanians" was ultimately unsuccessful. Leaders of the proprietary faction condemned the act in the assembly, and Smith attacked Pennsylvania's government in the London and Philadelphia press. Smith's *A Brief State of the Province of Pennsylvania*, published in 1755, acknowledged that most Quakers "without Doors" did indeed oppose war as a matter of conscience; powerful Friends within, however, resisted out of self-interest. Smith also claimed that German immigrants were a menacing fifth column and criticized the colony's "popular" form of government. While his call for the introduction of English methods of rule in Pennsylvania was not new, Smith's belief in the colony's republican excesses had more in common with James Logan and Isaac Norris than populist Keithian pamphleteers or the democratic doctrines of John Webbe.[110]

Satirical pamphlets and letters to local newspapers lambasted Smith and proprietary elites, with both sides deploying vituperative rhetoric that again recalled the 1640s. *Tit for Tat, Or the Score Wip'd off,* penned by "Humphrey Scourge," satirized "sycophantic Courtiers"—meaning Smith.[111] Letters to the *Journal* similarly implored "a Certain Parson" (also Smith) not to offend God and the parson's own conscience for the sake of pleasing "a few *small Grandees*" in what was an effort to be made the "BISHOP of *America.*"[112] For his part, Smith recalled the "Days of *Cromwell*" when referring to a local regiment that had recently appeared at an organizational meeting for the Philadelphia militia, implicitly comparing the regiment to Parliament's New Model Army, led by Oliver Cromwell. Smith portrayed Franklin as a democrat who aimed to "level all *Distinctions*" in the colony by sowing social discord and enflaming party heats.[113] Smith's opponents channeled seventeenth-century Independents' scathing criticisms of state-funded clergy, calling Smith an "infamous Hireling" whose "Vomitings" against Franklin were not becoming of a follower of Jesus but were rather demonstrative of a "Frantick Incendiary."[114]

A response to Smith's pamphlet published in 1759 suggests the limits of popular radicalism in Philadelphia before the revolutionary conflicts of the 1760s and 1770s, however. Published anonymously, *A True and Impartial State of the Province of Pennsylvania* represented the colonial legislature as heroically resisting the tyranny of the proprietary faction, an "*exorbitant Power*" desirous of "*unlimited Authority.*" It argued that proprietaries had repeatedly endeavored to establish a system of despotism in Pennsylvania at the expense of the people's rights and liberties and in violation of the Frame of Government, which stood as a testament to British liberty and constitutionalism. Yet, in keeping with a Franklinian discourse of moderation, *A True and Impartial State* disavowed any affinity for popular government. The colony's system of government, like that in Britain, was a mixed one that did not incline more to the republican than to the monarchical form. It was, in fact, founded on the same principles of liberty and industry as those of the parent constitution. Suggestively, *A True and Impartial State* accused Smith of a form of demagoguery not dissimilar to the accusations leveled by Isaac Norris and James Logan against opponents of the proprietary party decades earlier. Assembly critics like Smith had attempted to raise a "popular Clamour" against the legislature with his spurious claims. *A True and Impartial State* also forcefully rejected any notion of popular sovereignty, ridiculing as absurd the idea that "a *fickle,* and *confused Multitude*" should direct the assembly in any way.[115]

Conclusion

The fundamental premises of *A True and Impartial State of the Province of Pennsylvania* were widely shared by British Americans in the mid-eighteenth century. Indicative of a post-1688 consensus among the political classes regarding the virtues of a mixed government in which powerful assemblies stood for the rights and liberties of propertied freemen, the defense of "the people" was balanced by fears of the disorderly multitude out of doors. A similar view was expressed in 1764 when colonists under Franklin's leadership unsuccessfully attempted to make Pennsylvania a royal government. A published petition to King George emphasized proprietors throughout the colonies had consistently abused their power and placed their private interests above those of the public—this was why most proprietary governments no longer existed. Disputes, often involving property and "mutual Opinions of Injustice," were in the very nature of proprietary governments, creating in proprietors a "Dislike of the People" and among the populace a "Want of Respect" for government. Were the privileges, happiness, and security enjoyed by other colonies under royal control granted to inhabitants of Pennsylvania, both proprietors' abuses and the people's hostility would be eliminated.[116]

Yet how to establish the proper balance of power between rulers and ruled was always a difficult question, and the perennial early modern problem of order was manifested in unique ways in early Philadelphia. The founding of Pennsylvania by Quakers raised novel questions of social order, despite Restoration-era leaders' disavowal of the group's antiauthoritarianism during the Commonwealth period. The Keithian schism and the formation of proprietary and antiproprietary factions in the 1690s and early 1700s were expressions of theological and political issues unresolved by the 1688 settlement. When, in the early eighteenth century, urban grandees like James Logan and Isaac Norris voiced classical elite fears of disorderly multitudes, they opened the door to populist criticisms of excessively learned men lacking in religion and humanity who were disconnected from the populace. Proprietary leaders repeatedly cited the chaos and confusion of the civil wars when referring to popular politics in Philadelphia, while their opponents deployed satirical and polemical pamphlets to attack the abuses of local elites. In some ways the seventeenth century never went away in the most modern of eighteenth-century cities.

At the same time, few cities could match the volume and diversity of ideas that circulated in and through eighteenth-century Philadelphia. Franklin's and other printers' commitment to a free press, together with inhabitants' diverse religious and cultural interests, produced a thriving print culture in which the judgment of the public was, at least rhetorically, supreme. Like the difficult question of social order, however, what exactly constituted the public and its interest, and who was entitled to speak in its name, was never completely clear. Learned theoretical tracts and Catonian arguments addressed a different audience than did plain-spoken almanacs and allegories. Benjamin Franklin tried to bridge a conventional lettered/unlettered cultural divide; his successes as well as his failures suggest the complex nature of ideological contestation in early Philadelphia.

6

POLITE SPACES AND NURSERIES OF VICE

Place, Disorder, and Cultural Practice

The importance of the concept of order in early Philadelphia was not limited to the city's print culture. Authorities' fears of disorder were also social, rooted in the physical spaces of the city and with certain peoples and places especially prone to turbulence. While in many ways the early modern obsession with order echoed ideas originating in antiquity, in the late seventeenth and early eighteenth centuries new ideas about urban refinement and the "reformation of manners" influenced city planners and campaigners in Europe and the Americas.[1] European metropolises like Amsterdam, Paris, and London built public walks and pleasure gardens and lit public streets, while coffeehouses and genteel taverns provided new spaces for public displays of refinement. Such places were also highly exclusionary, of course; "politeness," as expressed in urban spaces as well as in individual manners, only made sense in relation to its contrary, the "vulgar."

William Penn and surveyor Thomas Holme's plan for Philadelphia was a notable manifestation of the urban transformation in Restoration America, as Penn's orderly New World utopia was to be embodied in the structure and spaces of the city. Planners throughout Europe endeavored to open up overcrowded, "organic" medieval cities by creating broad streets and open spaces in the sixteenth and seventeenth centuries. Unlike Boston and New York, with their crooked and narrow streets, Philadelphia was modeled on new urban principles. In addition to its rectangular pattern and wide streets, a ten-acre square anchored the center of the grid at the intersection of High (Market) and Broad Streets. Four additional squares were intended "for the like Uses, as the Moore-fields in London," evidence for the influence on Philadelphia's planners of Richard Newcourt's plan for London after the Great Fire of 1666.[2]

Early visitors to Philadelphia frequently commented on the town's broad, straight streets and on new buildings constructed after the "English fashion."[3] By the 1730s the city exemplified the British phenomenon of civic associations and clubs with the Junto (the Leather-Apron Club), the Carpenters' Company, the Library Club, the Ancient Society of Britons, and the Schuylkill Fishing Company, to name a few.[4] Townspeople consumed news and conversed and debated in the city's numerous taverns and coffeehouses. By the 1750s a visitor sailing up the Delaware River to the city would have seen to their left, on the river's west bank, a skyline dotted with the spires of several new churches, most prominently the 196-foot steeple of the Anglican Christ Church, then the tallest building in North America.[5] By this time newspapers advertised the sale of maps and prospects of the city, perhaps most notably George Heap's *East Prospect of the City of Philadelphia*, a view of the city from the New Jersey shore measuring more than seven feet wide and two feet tall. The prospect was engraved by "one of the best Artists in London" and functioned as a testament to a sense of civic pride among Philadelphians as well as to the preeminence of British crafts in the colonies.[6] After midcentury, inhabitants could stroll down the city's broad avenues comfortably after dark, as the city joined large European metropolises in lighting its streets with whale-oil lamps.[7]

Philadelphia was also a place in which refined colonists rubbed elbows with a rowdy and multiethnic seafaring population and where a surfeit of peoples, sights, and sounds contrasted with the more homogenous rhythms of rural life.

FIGURE 3. Prospect of Philadelphia from the Jersey shore, 1754. City prospects were increasingly popular in the eighteenth century. Measuring more than seven feet wide and two feet tall, this image was a visual testament to Philadelphians' growing sense of civic pride. (*An east prospect of the city of Philadelphia; taken by George Heap from the Jersey shore, under the direction of Nicholas Scull surveyor general of the Province of Pennsylvania;* courtesy of the Library Company of Philadelphia)

Throughout the colonial period residents clustered in the city's commercial district along the Delaware River, frustrating Penn's plans for an even, spacious distribution of the population between the Delaware and Schuylkill Rivers. The formation of a popular political tavern culture—as well as the frequency with which many publicans violated the law by serving unfree workers—regularly frustrated provincial elites and urban authorities. As polite English norms became embedded in a number of urban spaces, a creole culture characterized by noisy festivity occupied other parts of the city. If the lighting of Philadelphia's streets at midcentury gave visual expression to the city's status as a refined center of Atlantic commerce and culture, it is telling that the legislative justification for illumination lay in "the preservation of the persons and properties of the inhabitants and [was] very necessary to prevent fires, murders, burglaries, robberies and other outrages and disorders."[8] Early Philadelphia was a place with an increasingly rich and refined associational and civic life; it was also one of the most disorderly cities in the British Atlantic world.[9]

The Early City: Ideal and Reality

At Philadelphia's founding William Penn offered prime urban building lots to First Purchasers—those who bought five-thousand-acre tracts in the new colony—and other wealthy settlers. The proprietor also reserved the largest properties lining the town's central square for the colony's substantial landowners; smaller lots extending from the Delaware and Schuylkill to the square were available for more modest purchasers. Penn also set aside eight thousand acres as "liberty lands" outside the town limits, where First Purchasers were awarded an additional eighty acres. A number of scholars have recognized the relationship between the orderly plan for the city and Penn's moral vision of discipline and individual reformation.[10] Similarly, the reservation of differentiated lots according to wealth and status signified the proprietor's traditional corporatist belief in the necessity of an orderly hierarchy.

Penn's holy experiment was also indicative of evolving seventeenth-century conceptions of "improvement": the belief that the rational application of technology and labor could enhance human happiness. Though most often associated by historians with the process of enclosure, consolidation, and the intensification of agricultural production, the concept of improvement also applied to cities.[11] Similar to agricultural improvement, urban improvement involved altering the landscape through technology to increase property's monetary value.[12] According to Penn, in less than three years after the founding the values of the worst lots Philadelphia had increased by a factor of four; the best had risen by a factor of forty. The monetary success of property holders was matched by urban aesthetic and civilizational advances, including the creation of tree-lined streets and multistoried brick houses and civic structures. Grumbling over who profited from improvements in the town seems to have surfaced rather quickly, however, for Penn noted that while it "seems unequal" that absentee property holders should benefit from the improvements made by those present, all in fact profited from the development of town and colony.[13]

Around the time he was developing plans for Philadelphia, Penn published *A Brief Examination and State of Liberty Spiritual*, a religious work addressing the perennially fine line between liberty and licentiousness. The distinction between natural and civil liberty was an old one, and Penn sided with those who argued that freedom did not mean a right to dissent from instituted authority.[14] According to Penn, freedom of conscience in religious matters was very different from social permissiveness or political liberty. It is perhaps not coincidental that after the Laws Agreed Upon in England mandated religious liberty and the keeping of the Sabbath (articles 35 and 36), article 37 attempted to restrain "wildness and looseness" among the people. In addition to making a number of verbal and sexual acts criminal offenses, the law also banned plays, gambling, Mayday games, and other customary revelries. For Penn, as for most learned Europeans, the tolerance of minor infractions against the moral order portended societal decay. Just as the corrupt administration of justice brought the wrath of God to magistrates, "looseness" among the multitude provoked God's wrath against the people.[15]

Carefully planned and laid out streets, squares, and neighborhoods were therefore accompanied by the creation of a well-regulated urban environment in which clearly delineated city spaces were mirrored by an economic and social order in which place was acknowledged and respected. Such austere conditions were in part demonstrative of Friends' emphasis on plain living and, in the case of the ban on bear-baiting and cockfights, their opposition to inflicting unnecessary pain on living creatures.[16] It is also probable that Penn's concern with order, discipline, and unity was intended to mitigate any potential antagonisms arising from religious or national differences. The proprietor emphasized in 1685 that all inhabitants of the new colony "are of one kind, and in one Place and under One Allegiance, so they live like People of one Country," to counter conventional beliefs in the impossibility of diverse peoples peacefully coexisting.[17] In Philadelphia municipal order would guarantee religious liberty, and ethnonational heterogeneity would not devolve into unruly licentiousness. English ways would be perfected, not abandoned.

Penn's professions of harmony notwithstanding, it was clear early on that unlicensed taverns and the immoral activities these spaces supposedly engendered would pose challenges to the proprietor's orderly ideal. Particularly problematic in the early 1680s were the makeshift dwellings dug into the banks of the Delaware River that also served as riverside taverns. The caves were formed by digging approximately three feet into the ground near the verge of the riverfront; half of the establishment was thus underground, with an aboveground chamber formed of earth and brush.[18] In 1685 the Philadelphia grand jury indicted the proprietors of a number of cave taverns, characterizing the places as sites of drunkenness and debauchery. After receiving complaints from magistrates later that year, families inhabiting the caves were summoned to appear before the provincial council. None of those summoned to appear before the council did so, however, and the following year Penn ordered the dwellings destroyed.[19]

Penn claimed that the taverns encouraged the spread of "clandestine looseness" in the town and complained about authorities' inability (or disinclination) to repress such moral laxity. Should provincial councilmen have the caves demolished and encourage magistrates to maintain sobriety, those of "inferior stations" would surely follow the example of their social betters. Discipline and order were especially necessary in the "wilderness of America," which Penn contrasted with more settled parts of the world.[20] Penn's objections were financial as well as moral. The caves' removal would allow the development of wharves on Front Street, enhancing the value of the property and facilitating trade. The year after his letter to the council, the proprietor allowed for an exception to the wholesale destruction of the taverns. Cave publicans able to pay a hundred-pound security and a yearly rent of fifty pounds to the proprietor would be allowed to remain; establishments worth less than thirty pounds—by definition "not of Sober Conversation"—were to be destroyed.[21]

While cave taverns were an improvised response to local conditions, officials were also scandalized by townspeople's importation of traditional festive practices. In late December 1701 music and laughter emanated from John Simes's tavern in Strawberry Alley, between Second and Third streets. At Simes's establishment John Smith, Edward James, Dorothy Cantorill, and Sarah Stivee held a party in which celebrants danced, sang, wore masks, and cross-dressed. Late in the evening Smith and Stivee strolled down Chestnut Street, knocking on inhabitants' doors and bringing their revels to other residents' dwellings. The Philadelphia grand jury indicted the celebrants as well as Simes for keeping a disorderly house. The presentment claimed the revel brought "Greef and Disturbance" to the neighborhood and propagated the "Throne of wickedness" among the urban population.[22]

Though since the nineteenth century scholars have puzzled over precisely what was going on in Strawberry Alley and along Chestnut Street, the event was in fact an example of "mumming," or "mummering."[23] Mumming was a Twelve Days celebration in which men and women cross-dressed and traveled house to house giving masked musical performances to neighbors in exchange for gifts. The practice had long been discouraged by urban authorities in England. In the fifteenth and sixteenth centuries, for example, the corporations of London, Bristol, and Chester banned walking openly masked during the Christmas season.[24] In 1725 the Newcastle curate Henry Bourne wrote in his ethnography of plebeian customs, Antiquitates Vulgares, that, as a remnant of the pagan Roman festive of Saturnalia, mumming received a "deserved blow" from the church in the Middle Ages. Unfortunately, however, the holiday was still practiced, remaining an "Occasion of much Uncleanness and Debauchery."[25]

Philadelphia authorities' hostility to mumming recalled a Lancashire dispute between puritans and their Anglican neighbors in the early seventeenth century that resulted in King James's Book of Sports (1618), which declared a number of sports and traditional festivities permissible. Though opposition from the godly in Parliament forced the king to withdraw the command, in 1633 Charles I reissued his father's declaration and confirmed the legality of church ales and subjects' right to sports on Sundays.[26] Seven decades later Queen Anne disallowed a number of Pennsylvania laws, including a 1705 act against riotous sports, plays, and games, with the justification that the act "restrains her Matys Subjects from Innocent Sports and Diversions." After the law's repeal assemblymen passed a revised bill banning sports and gaming and, once again, the act was disallowed by the Crown.[27]

An important component of early modern popular culture signaling order or its contrary was that of sound. The ringing of bells signaled work, curfew, and church times as well as special events; deferential speech also reinforced social order in European and American towns.[28] Disorderly sounds, or "noise," disturbed an ideal of public peace—especially in the decades after the Revolution of 1688, when the gentry and middling sorts adopted new standards of politeness and civility. In the 1680s Pennsylvania and New York made swearing and cursing a crime; shortly after the founding of the Society for the Reformation of Manners in London in 1691, King William issued a proclamation against swearing, cursing, drunkenness, and a number of other moral offenses.[29] The significance of "noise" to disorder in Philadelphia is indicated by grand jury complaints over the "tumultuous" gatherings of enslaved people on First Days (Quakers' term for Sundays) and the sounds from taverns that disturbed the peace after curfew. The music resulting from the mumming celebration at Simes's tavern brought "Greef and Disturbance" to the neighborhood in addition to promoting vice in the city.[30]

Like King William, colonial legislators associated subversive speech and other vulgar sounds with alcohol consumption. A 1683 Pennsylvania law linked excessive drinking with cursing, swearing, and obscene speech. Officials, who theoretically set behavioral examples for common people, were to be punished double for convictions of drunkenness and swearing. In 1693, 1700, and 1705 assemblymen passed laws against publicans allowing drunkenness (described as permitting "self-abuse") and against the drinking of healths, since the latter ritual encouraged people's "disordering" themselves. Profane language and cursing were punished by the same five-shilling fine or five days' imprisonment and hard labor; blasphemers were to pay ten pounds.[31] City authorities fined particularly troublesome inhabitants like William Orion for drunkenly "fighting, quarreling and challenging his neighbours & for molesting them in the night."[32] Weekly markets also provided spaces in which unruly townspeople mixed alcohol consumption and subversive speech, most often the swearing of oaths.[33] And it was likely in the market or at a tavern that the merchant William Wright publicly—and probably drunkenly—blasphemously declared in 1718 that Jesus Christ was a bastard.[34]

Disorderly sounds, like other moral offenses, were also highly gendered. Women like the cave publican Hannah Gooding often ran plebeian taverns, and women were accused in disproportionate numbers of keeping bawdy houses throughout the colonial era.[35] Though Friends held relatively progressive beliefs regarding women's participation in meetings, civil authorities prioritized regulating women's speech. Philadelphia grand juries petitioned provincial lawmakers for a ducking stool and cage for drunkards on a number of occasions, and magistrates continued to punish "scolding Drunken Women" like Mary Hutchins and other "profligate" urban elements into the 1720s.[36] While grand jury requests for the construction of stocks and a whipping post bore fruit, as indicated by the weekly public punishments at the entrance to the market by the 1720s, it appears no ducking stool was built.[37] Yet norms of womanly silence remained in force in Philadelphia until the mid-eighteenth century, at least. According to Alexander Hamilton, respectable women in Philadelphia were confined to the home to a much greater extent than in New York, appearing publicly only in church or at Quaker meetings.[38]

In face-to-face communities in which the individual's reputation for honest dealing was crucial to economic survival, slander was a serious offense. John Smolenski has noted that, while hearings for speech offenses constituted nearly half of Pennsylvania's early legislative output, compared to other colonies Pennsylvanians were not particularly inclined to bring accusations of slander before legal authorities.[39] That may be because of the severity of the offense. In 1709 Elizabeth Hardin publicly called blacksmith Anthony Moore a thief to his face and informed listeners she could prove the charge. Moore then sued Hardin for slander. Not only was Moore's "Good Name & fame" tarnished by the accusation, his business suffered as well. It is possible that Hardin accused the blacksmith of stealing silver from a customer (perhaps Hardin herself), leading potential customers to avoid the tradesman. Moore therefore demanded the significant sum of one hundred pounds as recompense. Unable to pay, Hardin requested permission to leave the city after throwing herself on the mercy of the court.[40] Whether Hardin's status as a woman factored into the court ruling cannot be known, though her alleged accusation fit with an image of women as naturally prone to "scolding."

Gendered violations of moral order were not only public offenses. A private offense that Philadelphia officials continued to punish into the revolutionary era was fornication, an activity loaded with standards of female virtue.[41] Defined simply as sexual intercourse between an unmarried man and woman, fornication in Pennsylvania was a criminal offense—in contrast to England, where it was a matter for church courts.[42] Rape was also a criminal offense, though not a capital crime until 1718, though as elsewhere the crime was rarely prosecuted in Philadelphia.[43] In 1685 John Rambo was charged with fornication and "craftily designing the good Name, State, Credit & reputation of the said Peter Cooke and Bridgett his daughter," though whether Bridgett was forced by Rambo or consented to sex was disputed. The court therefore ordered Rambo to marry Bridgett according to the law; if she refused, Rambo was to pay a ten-pound fine. Whether outraged over the court's failure to charge Rambo with rape or dissatisfied with the amount of the fine (or both), as patriarch Peter defended his and his family's honor, he swore "in the open fase of the Court" and received his own five-shilling fine.[44]

Masters and mistresses considered economic concerns regarding fornication as important as moral ones. In 1685 town justices found out about the pregnancy of servant Martha Wilbins, and under a grand jury examination Wilbins confessed that John Moon, her master, was the father. Following Moon's indictment, the court ordered the pair to be married. It was Wilbins, however, who received a fine of ten pounds and was chastised by the court for dishonoring God—likely because, as she admitted, Moon did not promise marriage before intercourse.[45] Within a decade of Pennsylvania's founding, women were regularly prosecuted for fornication in Philadelphia. In one 1695 quarter session alone Gertea Bore, Mary Hopkins, Mary Lugger, and Mary Duke were all indicted for the offense. Mary Rowland, forced to appear in court in 1695 for her "Loose and Idle Life," expressed her desire to move to Maryland or enter into service in Philadelphia to avoid the lash.[46]

The frequency of fornication offenses led the legislature to modify the law in 1700, expressly for the "preservation of the virtue, chastity and purity" of the colony's inhabitants—namely women. Thereafter whipping, property forfeiture, and hard labor could be visited on fornicators; female servants who bore children were to serve an extra year to compensate masters and mistresses for their losses.[47] In the 1710s unwed mothers were whipped alongside runaway laborers at the entrance to the biweekly market, though as the century progressed (and similar to those convicted of passing counterfeited currency) people in the city jail unable to pay fines for fornication petitioned the common council for the remission of fines.[48] As early as 1706 John Dodd petitioned the common council on behalf of Thomas Raymond for the remission of all or part of a nine-pound fine Raymond received for fornication with Eliza Owen, probably a servant like Raymond.[49] Though by the late 1750s and early 1760s theft was overwhelmingly the most frequently prosecuted offense in Philadelphia, fornication remained, along with theft and assault, among the most prominent crimes in Philadelphia mayor's court dockets and courts of quarter sessions.[50]

Visitors to early Philadelphia rarely commented on the illicit intimate practices of the town's servant and lower-sort populations. Of more interest were the city's architecture, food, and natural environment. When he visited Philadelphia after a stay in New York in the summer of 1697, the Boston physician Benjamin Bullivant noted that after just fifteen years the town was "a very magnificent City." Bullivant admired the design and layout of the riverine port, was impressed with the "large and stately dwellings of some eminent Merchants," and noted the town's streets and shops appeared "after the English mode." According to Bullivant, Philadelphia also had the "purest bread and strongest beere in America." This was no trivial observation—food and drink were crucial markers of health and status in the early modern world. The white "manchet" consumed by the nobility and gentry in England was a notable contrast from the darker, inferior grains eaten by the laboring classes. Similarly, while most commoners drank ale made from malted barley, "small beer" (beer with a low alcohol content), and even water, the middling and better sorts brewed hopped beer and distilled aqua vita. The wealthiest increasingly imbibed wines and spirits imported from abroad.[51]

Access to pure wheat bread and good strong beer across a relatively wide spectrum of the Philadelphia population testified to the area's natural abundance and the industry of local farmers, bakers, and brewers. And at a time when fruit—historically gathered as a dietary supplement by the "poorer sort"—was becoming fashionable to cultivate among England's upper ranks, the abundance of apples, pears, peaches, apricots, mulberries, and cherries in Philadelphia further demonstrated the healthful and diverse diet available to colonial inhabitants.[52] For servants like William Moraley, the general availability of the fruits of nature contrasted with the comparatively enclosed physical environment of early eighteenth-century England.[53]

While elite Friends retained a concern with moral propriety, their adoption of English ideals of gentility was increasingly evident in urban architecture and social practices. In the years around the turn of the eighteenth century, wealthy colonists began to construct two- and three-story brick Georgian houses with balconies and front porches. According to Bullivant, urban gentlewomen were particularly proud of their refinement; "having a large retinue of servants" to perform domestic labor, some women devoted themselves to painting and needlework. Such freedom from labor in the home increasingly signified respectable status in the eighteenth century and contributed to a gendered ideology of separate spheres. Bullivant claimed that Philadelphia Quakers were generous in their entertainments, though male Friends generally refused to give their "very pretty" daughters to "men of the world."[54] For leading Quakers, religious affiliation and endogamy in marriage were not incompatible with the adoption of English models of gentility in architecture, consumption, and leisure.

The formation of refined people and places was also not inimical to a level of social and cultural diversity exceeding that of provincial English towns. By 1700 the construction of Philadelphia's Lutheran Gloria Dei Church was completed, Anglican Christ Church was opened in 1702, and the creation of Presbyterian and Baptist churches soon followed.[55] Departures from metropolitan norms were evident in other ways. Even admirers like Bullivant commented on Philadelphia's unpaved and therefore dirty and muddy streets. While well-to-do merchants' houses were large and stately, homes in general "exceed not our second rate buildings in London, and many lower." More primitive still were the city's "natural" inhabitants: Indians and enslaved Africans. Though he did not comment on the institution of slavery in the mid-Atlantic, Bullivant did observe that in Philadelphia summers non-Europeans went "quite naked except what covered the Secrets of nature."[56] If European civilization, expressed in the physical development of the town and its inhabitants' gentility, had arrived in colonial Philadelphia by the early 1700s, evidence of American distinctiveness remained unavoidable.

Power, Commerce, and Mixed Multitudes

A new courthouse at Second and Market Streets across from the Quaker Meeting House in the center of Philadelphia was completed in 1710. The structure stood on arched brick pillars, the ground floor was open for the erection of market stalls, and provincial governors gave speeches and read proclamations from the balcony. Though some complained that the new building's placement marred the beauty of the city, the Old Courthouse functioned as the seat of government power in Philadelphia until the construction of the neoclassical State House in the 1730s.[57] The city also undertook projects like mending and repairing streets, wharfs, and bridges in the 1710s and 1720s, changes made possible by incorporation in 1701.[58]

Architecture served practical functions while also symbolizing institutional power. Some projects responded to the needs of a growing urban population; an expanding non-English population led longtime residents like James Logan to worry in 1713 that "Great numbers of People are Crowded in upon us," and in the same year the grand jury urged the common council to build a new prison.[59] The construction of instruments of public punishment also followed increased immigration from Ireland and Germany in the 1720s and 1730s.

Placing the stocks and pillory next to the courthouse and market created a spatial connection in the city between law, commerce, and government—related manifestations of order, wealth, and power. The link between economic and social development is demonstrated by the completion of Stone Prison in April 1723. The completion of the new jail prompted the city government to auction the Old Prison; money from the sale was to be used to repair the Arch Street wharf.[60]

While an expanding empire of trade meant imported commodities were increasingly sold in local shops, weekly markets remained important for the distribution of regionally produced provisions and goods. The central market was also a site of festive culture and revelry, as well as a place of disputation. Market rents were essential sources of municipal revenue, and in the summer of 1707 the common council appointed William Carter and Robert Yeldhall to collect fees for the use of market stalls. Some tradesmen neglected to pay, however, and the difficulty of collecting rents was a frequent source of official frustration. In 1710 the common council threatened Philadelphia butchers with removal if they continued to resist paying rents, though more than a decade later the council was still complaining of the tradesmen's recalcitrance.[61] In 1718 the municipality discovered that some renters sublet their stalls at five times the price they paid the city.[62] Customary norms regarding market regulations persisted, as when the council recommended ringing a bell to signify market times to prevent hucksters from engrossing provisions. Complaints against the "Irregular Methods" of selling goods at vendues rather than the market similarly testify to some townspeople's suspicions regarding excessive profit-seeking in the city.[63]

Market days, like the Sabbath and seasonal holidays and fairs, were times of liberty that if not regulated held the potential for licentiousness. Moral reformers objected to the debaucheries of holidays and fairs in Europe beginning in the late seventeenth century, but in the Americas the presence of large numbers of enslaved people posed novel challenges to critics of traditional festive culture.[64] English visitors to the West Indies like Richard Ligon commented on African cultural practices in Barbados in the late 1640s, often with an emphasis on music and others sounds. Ligon, an exiled royalist who fled to Barbados during the civil wars, noted that on days of "Liberty" the enslaved made music with kettle drums, fifes, and singing. Ligon found the music melodically simplistic but complexly timed. It was, in his characteristically ambivalent manner, both "a pleasure to the most curious eares" and "one of the strangest noyses that ever

I heard."[65] The Anglican missionary Morgan Godwyn claimed in the 1680s that the *"Idolatrous Dances* and Revels" practiced by enslaved people in Barbados were no longer found in Virginia.[66] Hans Sloane wrote around the same time of how enslaved people in Jamaica, "although hard wrought," gathered in the evening or on feast days to "Dance and Sing" to songs which were "all bawdy, and leading that way." Sloane also described the stringed musical instruments made from hollowed out gourds used by island musicians and published the first known transcription of Afro-Caribbean music.[67]

Gatherings of enslaved people functioned rather differently in the middle colonies, in large part because of the concentration of enslaved people in the urban environments of New York and Philadelphia. In 1682 the New York City court of assizes condemned the gatherings of "Negroes and Indian Slaves" on Sundays and other "Unseasonable" times. Slaves' "Rude and Unlawfull Sports and Pastetimes" not only disturbed the peace and quiet of Christian subjects; many were "Drawed asside and mislead to be Spectators of Such their Evill Practices and thereby Diverted From the more suitable And Pious Duty and Service of the Day."[68] Though Philadelphia's enslaved population in the late seventeenth century (less than 10 percent of the whole) was smaller than New York's (approximately 20 percent), official concerns were similar. In the 1690s and early 1700s Philadelphia magistrates and grand juries complained of "Negroes & loose people" gathering in large numbers on First Days. As early as 1693 city magistrates complained enslaved people were often found roaming the town without passes, and public celebrations included the tumultuous mixing of the enslaved with "Divers Infants" and "bond Servants."[69]

According to Benjamin Franklin, Philadelphia's biannual fair was where lower-sort debauchery was most pronounced and damaging to the social order. In late 1731 Franklin presented a petition to the Pennsylvania assembly that claimed the fairs were of little economic benefit for sellers or buyers, since all the goods on offer could be purchased at any time in a variety of places in the city. The twenty-five-year-old printer also claimed that fairs corrupted youth, who were "induc'd" to gaming and drinking "in mix'd Companies of vicious Servants and Negroes." In addition to debauching the town's and region's young people, fairs threatened property. For it was at these large gatherings that bound laborers joined together to flee servitude; the environment also provided opportunities for thieves who could blend into the crowd and disappear with their plunder. Equally troubling for Franklin was that unfree laborers claimed fair revels as a customary right. They had "by Custom" established a

"Right to Liberty" at such times, and the hangovers resulting from this customary right led to the loss of many days of labor afterward.[70]

For magistrates and grand jurymen, fair day tumults were simply accentuated reflections of daily insubordinations evident in city taverns, streets, and
squares. Though grand juries complained of slave and servant gatherings and
alcohol consumption as early as the 1690s, worries over interracial socializa-
tion and lower-sort disorder intensified in the 1730s and early 1740s, decades
when the unfree population peaked as a percentage of the population. In
April 1732 the common council took note of the gambling, cursing, swearing,
and other disorders that terrorized law-abiding townspeople on the Sabbath.
Youth and "White Servants" also met in great numbers on the Sabbath "to
play Games & make disturbances & noise in this City."[71] The grand jury delivered reports to urban officials regarding Sunday gatherings of servants and
slaves who could be seen during church services "at almost every Corner of
the Streets of this City" or in tippling houses whose doors were open to all.
The jury claimed toleration of this "growing Evil" would inevitably lead to the
overturning of all human and divine laws.[72]

Violations of dominant norms of propriety often occurred under cover of
darkness. Early modern authors often associated disorder with the chaos of
night's darkness in rural areas where authority was minimal or absent. The
lighting of streets and the creation of new forms of policing in eighteenth-
century European cities were responses to urban growth and accompanying
social problems. Despite reforms aimed to curb nighttime activities, darkness
retained its traditional associations with danger and misrule. The existence of
urban spaces hidden from the view of authorities obtained a new importance
in expanding cities like Philadelphia. Franklin wrote that "the Riot and Confusion of the Rabble after Night" at fair times not only offended "sober People";
such disorders were bound to increase in the growing city if left unreformed.[73]
At midcentury dangerous activities and ideas were exchanged in the habitations of newly arrived Black strangers, "especially in the Night time."[74] If conventional associations between the darkness of night and witchcraft and other
demonic practices were waning by the late seventeenth century, nighttime disorders presaged crime and secular disorders in the eighteenth-century city.

The persistence of noisy disorders in the 1730s and 1740s contrasted with
emerging norms of politeness. The first half of the eighteenth century witnessed
a reversal in thinking about gender as men, rather than women, came to be
seen as the naturally lustful sex. Accompanying this intellectual shift was the

notion that quietness connoted restraint and self-discipline; literature on man-ners therefore urged controlled, soft speech—especially for women.[75] Colonists eagerly consumed the prescriptive cultural writings of Joseph Addison and Richard Steele in the *Spectator,* and at midcentury readers of the *Gazette* learned that women's unique natural capacities included, in addition to the politeness necessary for a "civil Life," a "Voice and Way of speaking more musical and entertaining" than men's. While according to the "Female Advocate" history had shown that women could excel in politics and science, men were indebted to them above all because of women's distinguishing politeness, neatness, and engaging behavior—those things that constitute "the Pleasures of a civil Life."[76]

If many colonists associated politeness with English gentility, politeness's con-trary, vulgarity, acquired ethnic and racial as well as class and gender connota-tions. Newspaper advertisements informed colonists that the runaway "Dutch" (meaning German) servant Elizabeth Cowren was noticeable by her "loud and course" way of talking (though she spoke "good English"), the antithesis of proper feminine speech.[77] In addition to pretending to be a Quaker and spending time among local Native Americans, the fugitive servant John Reddy masked his Irish accent with "a smooth Tongue without much of the Brogue."[78] According to the grand jury, the tolerance of unlicensed tippling houses—"Nurseries of Vice and Debauchery"—led inexorably to the "profane Language, horrid Oaths, and Imprecations, grown of late so common in our Streets."[79] Some elite Philadel-phians did not see vulgar speech as being as menacing to the moral order as did grand juries, however. In 1744 the grand jury indicted the magistrate, alderman, and former mayor Samuel Hassell for refusing to pursue a complaint against an inhabitant accused of swearing; moreover, he had himself set an "Evil example" by cursing on a previous occasion.[80]

The language of enslaved people became a source of ridicule and racial-ization in the mid-Atlantic press beginning in the 1730s. Franklin's *Gazette* reported on the trial of an enslaved man known as Sampson, accused of burn-ing James Logan's country house in 1737. The reporter, most likely Franklin, characterized Sampson's self-defense as "long, artful and pathetick" and as wanting "nothing to make it effective but good English and Truth."[81] Around the same time the *Gazette* covered Sampson's trial, some Philadelphians read a satirical account of a "mixed" holiday in the *New-York Weekly Journal.* The narrator, ostensibly an English gentleman who called himself "The Spy" (in imitation of Ned Ward's popular turn-of-the-century periodical the *London Spy*) mimicked the speech of an enslaved man and characterized the festival as a cacophonous assortment of music and vulgar cursing and shouting.[82] In the spring and summer of 1741, the *Mercury* and *Gazette* reported an alleged slave conspiracy in New York, which recounted countless "frolics" involving music (especially fiddling), dance, and revolutionary talk in taverns and homes throughout the city.[83] Additional representations of enslaved people's alleged incomprehensibility and propensity to dissimulate were available a few years later, when New York City Recorder Daniel Horsmanden published a book-length report of the conspiracy and slave trials.[84]

In the view of middling and better-sort Philadelphians, vulgar noises and nefarious activities seeped from taverns into city streets and public spaces. This was made possible by the alleged permissiveness of city authorities, who failed in their duty to maintain order. A complaint delivered to the common council in August 1741—as townspeople consumed weekly reports of the trials of slave rebels in New York—claimed "great numbers of Negroes and others" met every evening in the vicinity of the courthouse on Market Street. Laboring-class Philadelphians turned milk pails into drums after the day's work, and festive disorders continued out of doors late into the night. Aural, temporal, and spatial boundaries of order were crossed as revelries lasted late into the night in the very center of town.[85] When, three years later, the grand jury claimed an investigation of disorderly houses revealed a neighborhood so "vitiated" that it obtained among the "common People the shocking name of *Hell-Town*," its criticism was directed toward magistrates who, jurymen believed, too freely awarded liquor licenses.[86]

Urban Space, Property, and the Public

The decades between the 1730s and 1760s witnessed the "adorning and beautifying" of English provincial cities, including in the colonies.[87] In 1729 Pennsylvania lawmakers approved plans for the construction of the new State House in Philadelphia, as the center of state power on Market Street shifted further inland from the Delaware to Chestnut between Fifth and Sixth Streets. Costing an estimated £5,600 and demonstrating the "liberality and public spirit of the times," the State House was completed five years later, in 1734. Master craftsmen like the architect and carpenter Edmund Woolley and bricklayers Thomas Boude, John Palmer, and Thomas Redman earned between four and eleven shillings per day working on the structure. Piece rates were paid to diggers and carters for hauling soil, bricks, lime, boards, and shingles to the site;

wages for other manual laborers were set at two shillings and sixpence per day.[88] Construction of the new Anglican Christ Church was begun around the same time, and during the 1750s Philadelphians built a new Presbyterian Church, the Pennsylvania Hospital, the College of Philadelphia, and the London Coffeehouse. While different in function, new midcentury structures testified to the increasing importance of civic identity to Philadelphia and Anglo-American culture as well as to a growing population.

Evolving social identities and patterns of consumption in the British Atlantic world that were reflected in urban spaces and architecture were accompanied by demonstrations of discontent and protest. Some scholars have seen the emergence of customary forms of rough justice in British America in the 1730s as evidence of strains between cosmopolitan elites and common people defending traditional communal norms.[89] Two controversies in Philadelphia in the late 1730s and early 1740s testify to the existence of new social tensions centered around an important spatial dynamic while also complicating a binary distinction between traditionalist commoners and genteel elites. The disputes involved competing perspectives on acceptable practices and reforms in the city, and all participants cited traditional commonwealth norms to justify their positions. At the same time, in both cases the Philadelphia press brought contests over city space to the attention of the urban public to gain popular support and in the process demonstrating the growing significance of print to urban life.

The first case involved the craft of tanning leather.[90] In sixteenth-century Italy Tommaso Garzoni called leatherworkers "vile" and "dirty," though he noted "they make good money." In 1651 the Flemish lawyer Theodor Ameyden referred to the "smelly art of leather-tanning" when noting the artisan origins of a number of elite Roman families.[91] In Thomas Middleton's play *The Mayor of Queenborough* (1619), a journeyman tanner symbolized for civic aristocrats the dangers of a growing group of politically assertive burgesses in England.[92] Tanners, as much as any other craftsmen, exemplified early modern elite fears of a prosperous, growing, and politically confident artisanal middling sort. Like shopkeepers, masons, and blacksmiths, tanners were often wealthy freemen of the city. However, like butchers, tanners' craft was a dirty and malodorous one. While privileged in terms of skill and wealth, tanners were also stigmatized as a result of the smells and materials (alum, lime, oil, lard, blood, and urine) associated with their trade.

The craft of tanning and competing ideas concerning the urban communitas came together in Philadelphia in the summer and fall of 1739. As noted in chapter 1, by the early eighteenth century a powerful group of Quaker artisans had established tanneries around Dock Creek, or the Dock, as it was commonly known in the city. (Tanneries required large amounts of water.) By the late 1730s, in addition to William Hudson and his son William Jr., Samuel Morris, John Snowden, John Howell, and John Ogden operated tanneries along the Dock.[93] The noxious smells and effluvia that resulted from the curing, soaking, cleaning, de-hairing, tanning, washing, drying, and softening of leather produced a "witches' brew" of industrial byproducts in European and American towns and cities.[94] In the spring of 1739 a petition to the provincial assembly called for the removal of tanyards and slaughterhouses from the neighborhood around the Dock, citing the "great Annoyance" arising from slaughterhouses, tanyards, and lime pits. According to petitioners, the convenience, reputation, and health of the city required the removal of the annoyances in a "reasonable" period of time. The petition deployed customary commonwealth keywords—convenience, reasonableness, reputation, the public good—as well as a discourse of improvement, since tanners' removal would increase the value of lots in the neighborhood.[95]

The desire to remove tanyards from American towns was not unique to Philadelphia. As early as 1676 the municipality of New York banished the city's tanners to the Fresh Water Pond north of the city.[96] The powerful tanners of Philadelphia would not go quietly, however. The artisans responded to the petition calling for their removal by sending a counterpetition to the assembly, and they proceeded to publish an account of their hearing before legislators in the *American Weekly Mercury*. (The tradesmen likely chose the *Mercury* because Benjamin Franklin, proprietor of the *Gazette*, was active in the effort to remove them.) The tanners' newspaper narrative portrayed the artisans as an oppressed group of mechanics whose political sagacity saved them from banishment. Tanners refuted the petitioners' claims before the assembly point by point and placed blame for the "disorderly" state of the public Dock on the municipality. Tanners offered their own ideas concerning the regulation of the Dock, to which they claimed "the House readily agreed." The artisans obtained the approval of representatives and rallied the support of many urban citizens who signed a protanner counterpetition. "Upon the whole, the Petition was Rejected, the Tanners right to follow their Trades within the City, according to their own Proposals asserted, and the Corporation to see that they comply'd with such a Regulation."[97]

Tanners' populist rhetoric in the *Mercury* was ironic considering other local leatherworkers and local consumers had often complained of tanners'

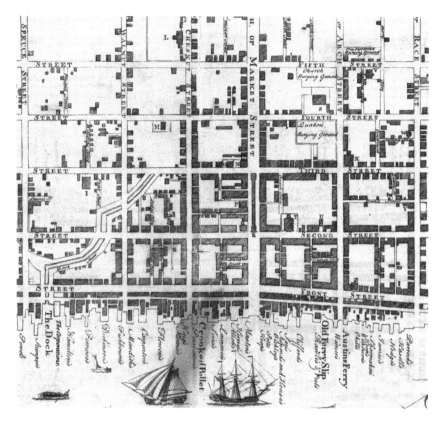

FIGURE 4. Map detail of downtown Philadelphia between Spruce and Race Streets, circa 1762. Dock Street is visible on the lower left, and Robert Bolton's dancing school was located on Second Street, near Chestnut Street and just below the Dock. (*To the mayor, recorder, aldermen, common council, and freemen of Philadelphia this plan of the improved part of the city surveyed and laid down by the late Nicholas Scull;* Library of Congress, Geography and Map Division)

violations of customary practices in the past.[98] Yet rather than recalling tanners' previous disputes, a response in the *Gazette* emphasized tanners' disingenuous portrayal of the assembly hearing; their version of the event failed to uphold the public's right to an accurate representation. The *Gazette* account clarified the original petition's request and emphasized the unwholesome smells from the yards and the refuse in the creek—whose water, if unclogged, could be used to fight fires. If the artisans were removed, the properties near the Dock would increase in value. The author inserted the tanners' proposal and included the names of the signatories (William Hudson Jr., Samuel Morris,

John Ogden, John Howell, William Smith, and John Ogden), an unusual practice in early modern print culture.[99] Also included was an extract of the assembly's decision, which served as evidence for the *Mercury* writer's dishonesty, since it was clear that the House acknowledged the legitimacy of the petitioners' grievance. To answer the claim that the petition was an attack on the liberties of local tradesmen, the *Gazette* mocked the tanners' account in declaring it was but a modest attempt to "deliver a *great Number* of Tradesmen from being poisoned by *a few,* and restore to them the *Liberty* of Breathing freely in their own Houses." Tanners were a group of "Hot-Heads" attempting to "stir up Faction, Heats and Animosities" among urban citizens. Whereas tanners claimed to act in the interests of the town's workmen, the *Gazette* attempted to isolate those around the Dock as a small group of troublemakers who would rightly be shunned by other city mechanics—even their own "Brethren."[100]

With the publication of the *Gazette* letter, the "Affair of the Tanners" became a source of discussion in town, and the artisans' *Mercury* representative account felt obliged to respond. The third front-page letter in the controversy appeared on September 13. The tanner vigorously defended the initial protanner account of the dispute while further attacking the motives of the "Gentlemen who principally had the Management of the Affair" in front of assemblymen. The *Gazette's* pitting of the interests of a few tanners against a great many others was untrue, since those who would benefit from tanners' removal were in fact a cabal of two or three men set on "improving" the Dock neighborhood for their own gain. The author again represented prosperous tanners as ordinary laboring folk who, had petitioners succeeded, would be denied the liberty of following their trades in the city and banished from "the greatest Pleasure that the World affords, the Society of their Relations and Friends, to sit down where-ever their little means can cheapest furnish them with Ground and Conveniences." Further factual details of the hearing followed, with emphasis again placed on the acumen of tanners in counterpetitioning and convincing "almost all" of the original petitioners to withdraw their names from the call for removal.[101]

Samuel Morris was likely the author of the *Mercury* accounts, for the final *Gazette* letter in the tanners' affair targeted Morris specifically, and tanners generally, as a group of undeferential clowns utterly unfit for colonial politics. The longest work in the affair at two pages and four full columns, a short preface claimed the letter had been written after the *Mercury's* September 13 defense of the tanners. But because "we (in this Town) abound with Learning and Politicks," the author ("E.F.") delayed its publication until after the assembly election in early October, since some "mighty Genius" would probably have used the letter for electoral purposes. It was then asserted that the anonymous *Mercury* writers, though they attempted to hide their identities, were surely the same men who had "for Years past polluted and fill'd our Publick Papers with the most false and infamous insinuations." In the view of the *Gazette* the urban press had allowed designing men to repeatedly make seditious and libelous claims, and the *Mercury*'s representation of the tanners' affair was yet another attempt to sever the "Bands of Society."[102]

After a lengthy indictment of the *Mercury*'s alleged lack of regard for truth, justice, and modesty, the *Gazette* writer returned to the assembly hearing. "Young M——s" (Samuel Morris), "who appeared as the Chief of the Tanners," erroneously claimed tanyards were allowed in London's Southwark. As "all Men knew," however, Southwark was on the south side of the Thames River, outside the city limits. Tanners' were also too young to remember the sickness of 1699 (a yellow fever epidemic), which killed many Philadelphians, including one of two tanners in the city and many others who resided near the Dock.[103] Current tanners' knowledge of the distemper came from "an antient Brother, or rather Father of the Pit"—the elderly William Hudson—whose memory could no longer be trusted. The youth of the tanners, especially Morris, was referenced to make the artisans' appearance in the House appear outlandish and disrespectful. In addition to claiming their foul-smelling trade was in fact "sweet," the behavior and mannerisms of the "Youth" that spoke for tanners was "extraordinary and amazing," as he gesticulated before spectators with his handkerchief and looked to his shocked opponents with "an Air of Grandeur, Self-sufficiency, and Contempt." By contrast, the gentlemen on the other side said little, preferring to patiently defer to the reasoned judgment of their superiors.[104] In thus contrasting the behavior of juvenile and politically inexperienced tradesmen with the sober and respectful manner of gentlemen petitioners, the *Gazette* author sought to reinforce a deferential social order without explicitly saying so.

One final point needed to be made, which related to the *Mercury* writers' appeal to Philadelphia tradesmen. For such a scheme to successfully divide the urban community, writers like those in the *Mercury* would have to persuade city artisans that their crafts were as "offensive, infectious and injurious" to their neighbors as were the tanners'. Until this "mean Artifice" was completed, tanners and their advocates had no right to make such an inference, since no "modest Man" would rank clean and healthy trades with tanners' employment, which was justly prohibited in most well-regulated towns and cities. This closing by the *Gazette* left open the possibility that the machinations of plotters like those in the *Mercury* could ultimately seduce other city tradesmen, however, a peril to be borne in mind by readers. Yet the *Gazette* ended by professing faith in the wisdom of Philadelphia's "modest Men," who would ultimately see through the nefarious plans of those who sought to subvert the public peace.[105]

The passage of the tanyard controversy from the neighborhood around the Dock to the State House, and eventually to the city's public sphere, indicates how disputes over urban space and property could become politicized through the press. Drawing on traditional languages of the common good using competing newspapers, both sides deferred to the public as the ultimate arbiters of truth and justice. The primary difference lay in emphasis: tanners' *Mercury* supporters articulated a populist, class-based language of oppression and resistance, while the *Gazette* expressed a vision of order and improvement in the interests of the corporate community. Whichever account was more truthful, tanners continued to practice their craft around the Dock, and the tradesmen and their trade continued to be a source of urban discord through the 1770s.[106]

Just a few months later similar themes involving urban space, social rank, and the public-as-arbiter emerged in what was, on the surface, a very different kind of urban dispute. In 1738 dance teacher Robert Bolton opened a dancing school in Philadelphia on Second Street between Walnut and Chestnut Streets—just around the corner from Dock Street, in fact. Annual membership dues cost £3 15s, and members included proprietor Thomas Penn, Governor George Thomas, provincial politicians, and leading city merchants. The hall's dances and concerts were particularly extravagant at assembly meeting time in autumn and spring, as rural representatives and elite townspeople congregated after political business for genteel entertainment. Like the Schuylkill Fishing Company, the dancing assembly illustrates the formation of a self-conscious urban gentry in Philadelphia.[107]

The famed evangelical preacher George Whitefield arrived in America in the same year the dancing assembly opened. Philadelphians could already purchase a collection of Whitefield's sermons from Andrew Bradford's shop on Front Street.[108] Whitefield preached in Christ Church on Second Street and to larger outdoor audiences near the Court House in 1739; in April 1740 the press estimated more than fifteen thousand people gathered in town to hear one of his charismatic sermons.[109] One of Whitefield's listeners was evidently Robert Bolton, for he converted to the evangelical cause shortly after the 1740 visit.

Inspired by the New Light message of universal salvation and social reform, Bolton decided to close the dancing assembly and turn the space into a school for Philadelphia's Black population.[110]

When, on an April evening, dancing assembly members gathered at Bolton's as was their custom, they found the doors locked. Enraged, they broke down the door and forcibly entered the premises. At the beginning of May Franklin inserted a short notice in the *Gazette* from Reverend Whitefield's assistant, William Seward, describing the "great Stir" of a few weeks earlier. The passage stated that since Whitefield's preaching in the city, the dancing school assembly and concert room had been deemed inconsistent with the Gospel and was subsequently closed. (It was, in fact, a "devilish diversion," and no mention of Bolton was made.) Though "the gentlemen concern'd caus'd the Door to be broke open again, we are inform'd that no Company came to the last assembly Night."[111]

Dancing school members were deeply offended by the announcement, and the following week the *Gazette* published a letter from an anonymous member of the club.[112] Members were affronted not because they were accused of breaking into the school and violating Bolton's property but because their inability to meet on assembly night implied that they had been converted to New Light doctrines. The *real* reason school members did not meet on assembly night was because they thought Bolton's shuttering of the dancehall to be "a romantick Piece of Conduct" beneath the dignity of gentlemen to notice. Far from being converted by Whitefield, as Seward allegedly implied, members regularly met—though where was unstated—the following two weeks, as usual. The author accused Seward of imposing a great "Iniquity" on the public in his dishonest attempt to spread Whitefield's fame before he left for England by suggesting that the city's "better Sort of People" were converted by the itinerant preacher. In fact, members held both Whitefield "and his mischievous Tenets in the utmost Contempt."[113]

If members were scandalized by Seward's statement implying that the dancing school's supporters had decided not to meet, the *Gazette* writer's reference to the city's "better sort" raised Franklin's hackles.[114] Franklin quickly published a response to the offended school member under the suggestive pseudonym "Obadiah Plainman." The alleged offense was, according to Plainman, wholly imaginary, since there was nothing in the *Gazette* report to justify the claim that Seward insinuated dancing school members had converted. Of seemingly more import, however, was the writer's appropriation of the term "better sort." Assuming a dichotomous social structure (the better sort and the mob), Plainman wondered why the dancing school author submitted his defense to an ignorant public—or, using a suggestive urban metaphor, placed his complaint "in the publick street." Why appeal to "the *Mob* as *Judges* of this IMPORTANT Controversy?" Franklin gestured toward a contradiction that had confounded aristocratic republicans since the seventeenth-century emergence of serial publication in England: how to maintain traditional norms of hierarchy and deference in a medium whose nature was to appeal to as large an audience as possible? Plainman embraced historically derogatory terms for the people, informing the gentleman that "We" are not displeased with the monikers "meaner sort," "mob," or "rabble" when used or bestowed by "Us" or our friends, since the Demosthenes, Ciceros, Sidneys, and Trenchards of the world always approached "Us" with reverence. In contemporary Philadelphia, however, "Scriblers expect our Applause for reviling us to our Faces."[115] Franklin's populist equation of the public with the "meaner sort," in stark contrast to previous letter's linkage of the public with the "better sort," suggests the ambiguous and contested meaning of the concept of the public by midcentury.

Despite his embrace of the label "meaner sort," Franklin's reference to republican philosophers assumed a certain amount of cultural capital among readers, and dance assembly members quickly pointed to Plainman's contradictions in both Philadelphia papers. In the *Gazette,* "Cadiz" hinted at Franklin's identity when he accused the writer of not truly understanding Whitefield's evangelical message, since Plainman was "only a temporizing Convert, drawn in with Regard to your Worldly Gain"—a reference to Franklin's profiting from the sale of Whitefield's works. More pointedly, Plainman had misrepresented Cadiz's earlier use of the category "better sort" in insinuating that all to whom the label was not applied were "Mob and Rabble." If a visitor to Philadelphia who heard there was a Library Company in town (another clue as to Franklin's identity) inquired as to what kind of people composed the society, since men of "various Persuasions and Employments" were members, an answer of the "*better Sort* of People" would be reasonable. Would it follow that all those not belonging to the Company were mob and rabble? By "better sort," Cadiz claimed to have meant simply some respectable inhabitants from the city, thereby refuting Plainman's populist binary while more subtly challenging Franklin's everyman persona.[116]

A *Mercury* letter published on the same day by "Tom Trueman" similarly attacked Franklin's divisiveness. Claiming to be a simple country-born member of the dancing school (and thereby adding an urban-rural dimension to the conflict), Trueman, like Cadiz, used examples of other groups—young men playing ball, Quakers, judges—to problematize Plainman's social dichotomy.[117] Plainman's use of "the mob" was also problematic, since, according to Trueman, this term customarily referred only to the "low, idle, dissolute and abandon'd Part of the People without Property." Trueman never knew "the honest Housekeeper, the industrious Tradesman, or laborious Ploughman" to be classed as part of the mob, since it was well known that the strength and wealth of Great Britain lay in its honest and useful inhabitants. In addition to accusing Franklin of demagoguery, Trueman evoked a traditional political paternalism as an antidote to Plainman's leveling republicanism. Admirable honesty and industry among ordinary housekeepers, artisans, and farmers did not translate into political rights or equality. The lives and liberties of such "useful" folk were protected by English law, and virtuous commoners were "justly us'd with Kindness and Humanity by the best in the Kingdom, if the Word BEST don't offend you."[118]

The controversy then descended into trivial name-calling before its exit from public attention in early June. Yet, like the tanners' affair, the dancing school controversy illustrates how everyday power struggles over urban space took on wider significance with the help of the press. The representations of disputes involving artisans, evangelicals, the gentry, and city printers in town newspapers also worked to blur a traditional distinction between a learned public and an unlearned people, as readers were encouraged to identify with competing interests while being elevated to judges of truth and the public good. By the 1730s the notion that the "public" was the preserve of a minority possessing cultural and literary capital denied to the unlettered majority was no longer hegemonic in Philadelphia. The belief that the people were also the public was at least in part facilitated by disputes over urban space and property.[119]

While acrimonious, the controversies surrounding the Dock and the dancing assembly did not descend into physical violence (though assembly members used force in entering Bolton's property). The popular demonstrations over the devaluation of the copper halfpence discussed in chapter 1 involved property damage, but there is no evidence anyone was injured. The most violent conflict in early Philadelphia occurred in 1742 and involved political tensions that were literally, not metaphorically, manifested on the public street. In the weeks before the assembly elections of that year, rumors circulated that Quaker assemblymen would allow unnaturalized Germans to vote, as legislators opposed to Governor Thomas attempted to form an alliance with recent immigrants. Conversely, antiproprietary leaders spread rumors that the city recorder and partisan of the proprietary party, William Allen, had enlisted hundreds of sailors to attack the election site in the center of town. As political factions argued over who should serve as election inspectors in front of the Philadelphia courthouse on election day, between fifty and eighty sailors approached from Market Street and attacked magistrates, constables, and aldermen after being instructed to disperse. Many fled from the courthouse into Second Street and the market house for safety; when sailors returned a short time later, however, the "crowd turned against them" and fought back. More than fifty people were apprehended in the melee, after which the election was conducted without further incident.[120]

It is not surprising that the involvement of noncitizens in a local election provoked charges of interference with the sacred British privilege of choosing representatives. Yet the vehemence with which some present at the riot referred to sailors as "strangers" and victims as "freemen" or "citizens" is noteworthy. According to the *Gazette*, sailors were strangers with "no kind of Right to intermeddle with the Election."[121] Similar characterizations of rioters as "Strangers lately arrived at the Port of Philadelphia" or "Strangers, and not Inhabitants" featured prominently in accounts of the riot.[122] This hostility to alien interference made the accusations against Mayor Clement Plumsted, Recorder Allen, and aldermen Joseph Turner, Abraham Taylor, and Septimus Robinson for refusing to suppress the attack especially reprehensible. Plumsted acknowledged the damage incurred to his reputation in the community in a remonstrance against his accusers. There was, according to the mayor, nothing more sacred than good character among neighbors, and one's credit in a community, once injured, was difficult to repair.[123]

Though townspeople's depositions emphasized how proprietary supporters solicited the help of outside forces to interfere with the privileges of residents, evidence also testifies to hostile views of elite Friends within the city. Peter Thompson has detailed how the young Quaker patrician Israel Pemberton Jr. harried sailors from city streets to Masters' Wharf and then to the Indian King Tavern. If they were strangers to the city, seamen apparently knew who the young Quaker was, declaring at one point "by God we will kill Pemberton." The owner of the Indian King Tavern, Peter Robinson, defied Pemberton and continued to serve sailors and their leader, a Captain Mitchell. Robinson went so far as to offer the captain a glass of rum in front of the prominent young Friend. Alderman Joseph Turner later testified that it was Pemberton's haughty treatment of mariners that caused the riot.[124] Sailors shouted "broad brims," "men with no pockets," "damned Quakers," and "Enemies to King George" as they approached the election site, which suggests a view of Philadelphia Friends as unpatriotic men whose dress and mannerisms separated them from the national-imperial community.[125] The proprietary party would suffer an election defeat as a result of the tumult, and the anti-Quaker epithets and assaults stirred a few inhabitants to action. Laboring Philadelphians like the sailor Abraham Cribb and the apprentice Michael Lester joined mariners in their attack against Quakers and immigrants.[126]

If local hostility to Quakers—particularly in the context of war with Spain in the early 1740s—was still evident in the mid-eighteenth century, the formation of genteel places and practices among respectable Philadelphians helped bridge denominational divides. William Bradford's London Coffeehouse, opened in 1754 at the southwest corner of Front and Market Streets, became the city's center of polite culture. The opening of the New Theatre on Water Street in the same year signaled the defeat of a historic Quaker hostility to "wicked" entertainments like the theater.[127] Philadelphians' desire to emulate English architecture was demonstrated by the construction of new Georgian mansions by wealthy merchants like Charles Norris, Edward Shippen, and Charles Willing.[128] Merchants attempted to emulate metropolitan commercial culture by building an exchange in the city, "for the like uses with that of the Royal Exchange in London."[129] The physical transformation of the city was an outward expression of individuals' attempt to fashion polite identities through clothing, manners, plays, and concerts. The obverse of the coarse and vulgar sounds heard on city streets and in taverns was the conscious adoption of genteel English speech and manners by respectable inhabitants. Lord Adam Gordon (a Scotsman) was pleasantly surprised in the 1760s by Philadelphians' "propriety of Language," for example; proper English was spoken "in a degree of purity and perfection, surpassing any, but the polite part of London."[130]

New sites of leisure and display constituted crucial sources of civic, as well as British, identity. Also important to the physical transformation of the city and the making of local civic identities were efforts to address social problems. Between the 1690s and 1720s more than a hundred workhouses were built in England; a 1725 account declared the movement a remarkable success.[131] Like Boston, New York, and Newport, Philadelphia built workhouses that isolated the poor from other townspeople in the early eighteenth century. Modeled on the English workhouse movement, American workhouses separated the "deserving" poor from the "idle" (the term now connoting laziness rather than simple unemployment, as was the case in the sixteenth century), while forced labor was designed to inculcate habits of industry and make paupers useful to society. The majority of those forced into the Philadelphia almshouse (built in 1732) were impoverished women, and women's prominence in needing relief grew dramatically in the 1760s and 1770s as urban poverty reached new heights.[132]

The most illustrative demonstration of the relationship between social reform and civic identity was perhaps the establishment of the Pennsylvania Hospital in 1751. Cofounded by Benjamin Franklin and Dr. Thomas Bond, the petition (written by Franklin) requesting the hospital began by emphasizing the recent growth in "Lunaticks" in the colony. The "distemper'd Poor" regularly made their way to Philadelphia, where they were a "Terror to their Neighbours" and were taken advantage of by "ill disposed Persons." Franklin acknowledged that few would voluntarily submit to confinement, but if put in proper care such people could again be made "useful Members of the Community, able to provide for themselves and Families." The hospital would also reduce public expenditures and rid the city's public spaces of the mentally ill (who wandered about the city "disorder'd in their Senses") by confining them in a centralized location. Like workhouses, the hospital would help those who could not help themselves—and like workhouses, would do so at a reduced cost and therefore for the benefit of the public. Few efforts were of so "useful, pious and charitable a Design."[133]

In cities like Philadelphia the emergence of workhouses and hospitals, the lighting of city streets, and the creation of more punitive laws were responses to social processes occurring throughout the Atlantic world. For the objects of such reforms the most important identity to be fashioned was not genteel status but more simply status as a free person. Fugitive bound laborers regularly "pretended" to be free (most often sailors), and, as noted in chapter 2, servants and slaves in the Americas created elaborate networks of shelter.[134] It is perhaps appropriately ironic that not long before the opening of Bradford's London Coffeehouse, in front of which captives of African descent were regularly purchased, an ad appeared in the *Gazette* from William Fitzhugh of Westmoreland County, Virginia, for the apprehension of the transported felon Thomas Winey and "a Molattoe slave, nam'd James." On interrogation, "confederates" of the men informed Fitzhugh that Thomas and James were traveling to New England by way of Pennsylvania. If possible, they would try to find passage to England at some Atlantic port, since James had an uncle who had opened a coffeehouse in London after similarly fleeing bondage in the Chesapeake.[135]

Like the city itself, the bodies of unfree Philadelphians became contested spaces in the mid-eighteenth century. Beginning in the 1730s Pennsylvania masters and mistresses began to brand runaway servants after capture, using gunpowder to mark their initials, usually on the left hand near the thumb.[136] The West African origin of young women like Rose, a "Whedaw Negroe" from the Gold Coast, was, according to Philadelphia slaveholder John Richardson, evident by the three rows of beadlike tattoos across her neck. Rose's previous efforts to free herself were indicated by a branding near her tattoo.[137] For Rose, bodily reminders of her preenslavement self were contrasted by New World markers of possession and subordination. The potter Samuel Hale informed newspaper readers in Philadelphia and New York that the runaway laborer Edward Pain had a "lively look"—suggestive of a bearing different than servants' deferential "down look." Though skilled in pottery, Pain also claimed to have labored as a sailor. However, Pain's status as a servant and runaway were indicated by the branding of his initials between the thumb and forefinger. Another identifier was the blue tattoo of Jesus Christ on the cross on the inside of his arm, an image likely indicating Pain's time as a mariner in addition to his religion.[138] Tattoos and other bodily signs of personal and work history performed essential, if multivalent, functions in the eighteenth-century city.

People forced into workhouses in the early modern Atlantic world often did not see the benefits of their confinement. The "poor Folks" of Rumford, England, viewed workhouse detention as a "State of Slavery"; according to managers the fear of such slavery was workhouses' primary virtue.[139] As urban poverty worsened dramatically in Philadelphia in the early 1760s, reformers promoted a new subscription-funded linen manufactory; while it employed several hundred individuals for brief periods, it failed within two years.[140] Soon a new almshouse and workhouse called the "Bettering House" was constructed on Spruce Street beyond the limits of residential development. The notion that workhouses operated primarily as a deterrent, drawn from the English case, influenced managers of the house, and as in England and other colonies, the poor in Philadelphia resisted confinement. A visitor who received a tour of the house soon after its opening reported a number of inmates "begged me to try to get them out," and in the late 1760s overseers of the poor informed Quaker merchant-managers that many in their wards declared they would "rather perish through want" than enter the institution.[141] That city overseers also resisted imposing separation and confinement on the city's poor testifies once again to how consensus over legitimate practices were elusive in early Philadelphia.

Conclusion

William Penn adapted Renaissance principles of urban symmetry and order to his intended New World metropolis. The proprietor attempted to embed social order in the structure of the city, as urban streets, squares, and areas of commerce were spatial expressions of the proprietor's lofty aspirations. For Penn and many other seventeenth-century reformers, moral order was indistinguishable from social order, and the elimination, or at least the minimization, of customary cultural practices was essential to the betterment of the commonwealth. That the proprietor's vision of a virtuous, green country town was illusory quickly became apparent. The emergence of vice in Philadelphia was facilitated by the formation of disorderly taverns; and blasphemous talk on streets and in markets, vocal and unruly women, and raucous gatherings of enslaved people on the Sabbath indicated that the orderly ideal was unattainable. But if the utopian dream of Penn's green country town was unrealistic, for many colonists the town as a site of economic improvement, cultural sophistication, and civic virtue was triumphantly realized.

The changing urban landscape between the 1710s and 1760s demonstrates how evolving standards of cultural propriety accompanied economic transformation. For the middling sort and elites, architectural change and the establishment of refined public places provided physical manifestations of English civilization. Many townspeople believed Philadelphia embodied the best qualities of British society and government. Religious toleration (demonstrated in the churches of various denominations throughout the city), commerce (shown in bustling wharves, docks, and shops), and political rights (indicated by regular elections and a free press) were examples of the fulfillment of British liberties in America. Urban reforms, inspired by developments in England but uniquely embraced in Philadelphia, demonstrated local civic-mindedness as well as an aversion to traditional popular culture evident on both sides of the Atlantic. Yet Anglicization is at best a partial explanation for urban cultural change in early modern Philadelphia. For the contrary of politeness, vulgarity, was in American cities like Philadelphia often associated by the genteel with lower-sort strangers and the enslaved. By midcentury "mixed multitudes" and disorderly sounds on streets, squares, and in taverns testified to the persistence of a decidedly nongenteel urban Atlantic culture. This urban history is a story of creole cultural formation in which spaces were appropriated through practice and custom as well as commerce.

The urban press played an important role in reproducing English standards of politeness and in celebrating local manifestations of gentility. Yet print also provided a forum in which minor conflicts over property and the use of urban space could take on broader social and political meanings. Tanners and their opponents deployed competing languages of local rights and the common good to plead their respective cases before a hegemonic, though ill-defined, urban "public." The dancing school controversy evolved from differences over evangelicalism into a battle between a republican "mob" and the self-described "better sort." Representations that revealed the fiction of an early modern ideal of corporate harmony were products of competing visions of the urban public interest and competition between rival printers.

But if the press made possible the expression of competing conceptualizations of people and public, in the last instance printers acted as guarantors of order. No mention was made in the *Mercury* of the riotous destruction of the town's pillory, stocks, and butcher stalls after the assembly election in 1726, for example. Local papers were also silent about the attacks and intimidation directed against legislators and constables in 1729 and 1738, respectively. In the early 1740s the *Gazette* reprinted the acrimonious assembly exchanges between Governor Thomas and representatives over servant enlistment, yet the public demonstrations over the devaluation of the British copper halfpence around the same time were absent from both city papers. Proprietor Thomas Penn's grand exit from Philadelphia in August 1741 was described by the *Gazette;* the burning of his image in effigy earlier in the year was not.[142] Since printers were quite willing to publish stories of riot and rebellion in other places, the decision not to report on local disturbances hinged on whether such reports might provoke strife in Philadelphia.

Historians have emphasized how the booming midcentury city became more segregated and exclusive beginning in the 1760s, as laboring people were driven outward while the homes and leisure places of the wealthy moved to the center of the city.[143] In the decades between the 1680s and 1760s, a less segregated and more compact city produced a situation in which proprietary and reformist norms of order clashed with an evolving festive culture. If new ideas around improvement, health, and beautification emerged in the early eighteenth century, traditional beliefs in reasonableness, convenience, and corporate rights and privileges continued to shape Philadelphians' experience of urban life. Bells informed townspeople when to work and when to go home; officials prosecuted disturbers of the peace and fornicators; and conventional notions of industry and idleness shaped responses to immigration and poverty. It was in the lived spaces of the city, in which traditional understandings were adapted to new circumstances, that individual and collective identities were made.

CONCLUSION

At the turn of 1764 people walking the streets of Philadelphia could purchase "The New-Year Verses of the Printers' Lads," a humorous broadside summarizing the preceding year's events hawked by *Pennsylvania Gazette* newspaper boys since the 1740s. That year's edition celebrated peace in Europe and Britain—though it warned against antagonizing Highland Scots, those "Warriors without Breeches." The verses also poked fun at the British MP John Wilkes, whose arrest after criticizing King George's speech at the end of the Seven Years' War became a cause célèbre in England and America.[1] The broadside also addressed issues closer to home. It ridiculed colonists who coddled local Native Americans, a reference to growing hostility toward provincial authorities in the Pennsylvania metropolis who allegedly favored local Indians over vulnerable backcountry settlers. The lads apologized for their "Sauciness and Noise" in criticizing government policy and acknowledged that few cities could compare to the blessings then enjoyed in Philadelphia. Townspeople had a "close and dear Alliance" with "every gentle Art and Science," while "of good Living there's such Plenty." As the severe cold of January approached, the *Gazette* encouraged townspeople to gather close together and pass the night with a drink in mirth and fellowship.[2]

There was, of course, much more reading material that could be purchased as winter set in. In his printing shop on Market Street, David Hall offered hundreds of works of literature newly imported from Europe. From Homer and Ovid to Bunyan, Locke, and Defoe, as well as bound collections of numerous English periodicals, Philadelphians could immerse themselves in an expanding British Atlantic culture of print.[3] A surplus of locally produced newspapers, almanacs, captivity narratives, and other ephemera also testified to Philadelphia's and Pennsylvania's lively local print culture and to the region's importance as a center of culture in the Americas. Consumption of English goods was not confined to print: per capita consumption of imports in the northern colonies increased significantly in the 1740s and peaked in the early 1760s.[4] The claim that Pennsylvania had "made great Advances towards Commerce and Opulence, notwithstanding the short Era of her Settlement" was axiomatic in midcentury Philadelphia.[5]

Yet celebratory accounts of the local and imperial past and a prosperous and (for the moment) peaceful present masked an urban history of contested development that testified to the scale and complexity of transformation in the early modern Atlantic world. Around the time that colonists celebrated the British victory in the Seven Years' War, the octogenarian John Smith expressed how the Society of Friends had changed over the preceding decades in the Philadelphia Yearly Meeting. At the turn of the eighteenth century, when Smith joined the Quakers, Friends "were a plain, lowly-minded people" and there was much "tenderness and contrition" in their meetings. By the 1720s, however, many members became wealthy and had conformed to the "fashions of the world." The virtue of humility was now less apparent at meetings, which were no longer lively or edifying. By the fourth decade after Smith's joining the Society, some Friends had grown "very rich." Wealthy Quakers began to wear fine clothes and jewelry, and elite families made a "spacious appearance in the world, which marks of outward wealth and greatness appeared on many in our meetings of ministers and elders." In proportion to outward displays of worldliness becoming more prevalent, "so the powerful overshadowings of the Holy Ghost were less manifest" among Friends, leading to the current spiritual "barrenness" evident among local Quakers.[6] Smith contrasted the crass materialism of the present with an idealized earlier era of simplicity and plainness that had fostered a sense of community, humility, and sympathy among mid-Atlantic Friends.

Other local social critics—people like John of Blockley but also well-known Quakers like John Woolman—similarly lamented the lust for wealth and power that had allegedly overtaken the region and the British Atlantic world.[7] These criticisms would have resonated with those who complained of a lack of circulating money and the loss of property and freedom that followed an inability to repay debts. Yet while debtors and their sympathizers held that avarice and a corresponding lack of commitment to the common good were similarly responsible for the concentration of power among a small group of men, their solution lay not in a voluntarist return to founding-era morality. Rather than spiritual backsliding, official policies that favored certain men over others were responsible for the hardship that plagued debtors. And, as in earlier years, only an active government could relieve local people from the oppressions of those who wielded economic power. The history of Philadelphia was, from this perspective, less a story of spiritual declension than one of a perennial contest between rulers and the people for a just social order.

Those lacking social and political power—the enslaved, servants, women, and laboring-class immigrants—would undoubtedly have characterized the city's past and present differently. Servants who wrote of their experiences, such as William Moraley and Peter Williamson, left favorable impressions of early Philadelphia. Both pointed out, however, that masters frequently abused their authority over servants and that success in the early modern mid-Atlantic was highly contingent on the whims of fortune. Moraley's quest for success in America failed, while Williamson emphasized that his achievements were dependent on his finding a "good master," an unusually "humane" and honest fellow Scotsman who, like Williamson, had been kidnapped and forced into service in America.[8] Servants like Moraley passed along a popular narrative of colonial prosperity, emphasizing that the origins of American wealth lay in the exploitation of unpaid labor. Richard Allen, founder of the African Methodist Episcopal Church and born into slavery in Philadelphia in 1760, noted that the man who had owned him, the Quaker lawyer Benjamin Chew, was "what the world called a good master," a "tender, humane man." Yet despite many years of loyal service from Richard's parents, when Chew ran into financial trouble he readily sold Allen's mother and three siblings.[9] Many enslaved Philadelphians would have recalled, in addition to humane or inhumane masters and mistresses, the First Day frolics, fair revelries, and tavern gatherings that characterized nonworking life in the city. For them, meaning and identity lay in the unofficial power of custom and community.

Philadelphia's passage from seventeenth-century colonial outpost to eighteenth-century imperial metropolis was a contradictory one. The different memories of the local past in and around Philadelphia testify to the diversity of interests and values in the city, and to the variety of experiences and struggles that resulted from the profound urban changes that took place between the 1680s and 1760s. Newcomers to the city brought with them worldviews and belief systems from throughout the Atlantic world and adapted them to the mid-Atlantic urban context, and these were reflected in competing and evolving economic, legal, and popular cultures. As was (and is) common, nostalgic recollections of an earlier period of harmony and justice provided key reference points for urban controversies and disagreements. In the early nineteenth century the antiquarian John Fanning Watson wistfully recalled a deferential pre-revolutionary Philadelphia—recollections that, in their idealization of reciprocal relations between urban free people and their subordinates, were not substantially different from languages of social order developed between the sixteenth and eighteenth centuries.[10] Radical-popular critics of new state and national governments in Philadelphia and Pennsylvania in the late eighteenth century recalled an earlier period of fair dealing and justice in their calls for debt relief and paper money.[11]

Claims to legitimacy originating in past practices shaped contemporary struggles in early modern Philadelphia. Rooted in the material world, contests involving power and authority were articulated in competing conceptions of justice and right, and they pervaded all levels of society. They encompassed differences over provincial laws and economic policies as well as disputes concerning who had a right to which urban spaces and everyday leisure practices. Similar differences could be found in England and in all of Britain's colonies, though in each locale their manifestations were necessarily determined by local conditions. By the 1760s most people in Philadelphia were very much aware that the City of Brotherly Love was a part of a larger world that spanned the Atlantic and that their city was a distinctive example of an imperial British society. That they disagreed profoundly over the virtues and vices of such a world speaks to the contested nature of the making of early modern Philadelphia.

NOTES

ABBREVIATIONS

Ancient Records	Ancient Records of Philadelphia
Annals	*Annals of Philadelphia and Pennsylvania* (John F. Watson)
Archives	*Pennsylvania Archives*
Assembly	*Votes and Proceedings of the House of Representatives of the Province of Pennsylvania*
Common Council	*Minutes of the Common Council of the City of Philadelphia*
Franklin Papers	*The Papers of Benjamin Franklin*
Gazette	*Pennsylvania Gazette*
HSP	Historical Society of Pennsylvania
Journal	*Pennsylvania Journal*
Mercury	*American Weekly Mercury*
Narratives	*Narratives of Early Pennsylvania, West New Jersey and Delaware* (Albert Cook Myers)
NYWPB	*New-York Weekly Post Boy*
PCA	Philadelphia City Archives
Provincial Council	*Minutes of the Provincial Council of Pennsylvania*
Statutes	*Statutes at Large of Pennsylvania from 1682 to 1801*

INTRODUCTION

1. Prophecy and Dream, 1757–68, HSPp. Spelling and punctuation in John's idiosyncratic journal have been modernized.
2. *Gazette*, September 8, 1763.
3. *Petition of divers of the Inhabitants of the County of Chester.*
4. *Whereas the Number of Poor in and around this City.*
5. *Prophecy, Lately Discovered.* For Quakers and dreams, see Gerona, *Night Journeys.*

6. Gordon, "Journal of an Officer's Travels," 410–11; Kalm, *Travels in North America*, 1:33; Burnaby, *Travels through the Middle Settlements*, 99.

7. *New-Year Verses of the Printers Lads, who Carry the* Pennsylvania Gazette *to the Customers,* January 1, 1764. Benjamin Rush quoted in Foner, *Tom Paine and Revolutionary America*, 19.

8. *Independent Reflector,* November 30, 1752.

9. Le Goff, "Learned and Popular Dimensions of Journeys in the Otherworld." The importance of the prophetic dream vision in late medieval England was evident in the popularity of Julian of Norwich and in its use as a literary device in the epic poetry of Geoffrey Chaucer and John Langland. The latter's allegorical *Piers Plowman* would provide a model of the honest, simple producer that would resonate through the centuries, including in colonial cities like Philadelphia. See chap. 5.

10. The classic statement is E. P. Thompson, "Moral Economy of the English Crowd." For the development of liberal economic thought, see Appleby, *Economic Thought and Ideology;* MacPherson, *Political Theory of Possessive Individualism.*

11. For debates over usury in sixteenth-century England, see Tawney and Power, *Tudor Economic Documents,* 2:154–64.

12. Levy, *Quakers and the American Family,* 6–9; Marietta and Rowe, *Troubled Experiment,* 17–18.

13. Milroy, "For the like Uses, as the Moore-fields"; Fries, *Urban Idea in Colonial America.*

14. Dunn and Dunn, "The Founding, 1681–1701," 2.

15. Schwartz, *"Mixed Multitude";* Lemon, *Best Poor Man's Country;* Wokeck, *Trade in Strangers,* 58–60.

16. Green, "English Books and Printing in the Age of Franklin," 248–97.

17. Nash, "Poverty and Poor Relief"; B. Smith, *"Lower Sort";* Salinger, *"To Serve Well and Faithfully."* These scholars have also argued that it was during the 1760s that waged labor became increasingly dominant in the city, though Christopher Tomlins has recently argued for an earlier transition to free labor: see *Freedom Bound.*

18. P. Thompson, *Rum Punch and Revolution;* Smolenski, *Friends and Strangers;* Finger, *Contagious City;* Roney, *Governed by a Spirit of Opposition.*

19. For a recent work on Boston that challenges common periodization and nation-centrism, see Peterson, *City-State of Boston.*

20. In contrast to the rest of Europe, where urban growth was concentrated in large cities, in England the number of small towns doubled between 1600 and 1750. Daunton, *Progress and Poverty,* 136. See also Wrigley, "Urban Growth and Agricultural Change."

21. Stein, Boele, and Blockmans, "Whose Community?," 169.
22. Isenmann, "Notion of the Common Good," 110. For the concept in England, see Withington, *Politics of Commonwealth*.
23. Prevenier, "Utilitas Communis in the Low Countries," 205.
24. "The Statute of Artificers, 1563," in Archer and Price, *English Historical Documents*, 5(A):68–75; Withington, *Politics of Commonwealth*, 29–30.
25. Hindle, *State and Social Change*, 28, 226; Wrightson, "Two Concepts of Order."
26. T. Smith, *De Republica Anglorum*, 41–45.
27. T. Smith, *Discourse of the Common*, esp. 54–55, 121–24; Slack, *Invention of Improvement*.
28. Canny, *Elizabethan Conquest of Ireland*, 85–88; Mancall, *Envisioning America*; Appelbaum and Sweet, *Envisioning an English Empire*.
29. Reay, *Quakers and the English Revolution*, 38, 57, 104–6; Davies, *Quakers in English Society*, 23, 67; Hill, *World Turned Upside Down*.
30. Penn, *A Further Account of the Province of Pennsylvania*, reprinted in Myers, *Narratives*, 261.
31. Ibid.
32. Nash, "Early Merchants of Philadelphia."
33. It is difficult to imagine the genteel Penn or Barclay characterizing their critics as liars, reprobates, dragons, Jesuits, or "dead beasts," as did Burrough in *Answers to Severall Queries*. For early Quaker incivility see also Naylor, *Vindication of Truth*; Baxter, *Quakers Catechism*. For conservative humanism, see Elyot, *Boke Named the Governour*.
34. Davies, *Quakers in English Society*, 129–31; Spufford, *World of Rural Dissenters*.
35. For the literature of rural complaint, see McRae, *God Speed the Plough*.
36. For the emergence in the 1730s of customary forms of protest in the colonies, see Pencak, Dennis, and Newman, *Riot and Revelry in Early America*.
37. For the concept of appropriation, see Chartier, "Culture as Appropriation." Useful for understanding the relationship between society and culture is Chartier, *Cultural History*; Sewell, "Concept(s) of Culture."
38. Withington, *Society in Early Modern England*, parts 1 and 2; Wrightson, *Social History of England*, 1–16.
39. Wrightson, *Social History of England*, 3–5.
40. J. Thompson, "Late Early Modern"; Starn, "Early Modern Muddle."
41. Subrahmanyam, *Empires between Islam and Christianity*; S. White, *Climate of Rebellion*. The launching of the *Journal of Early Modern History* by the University of Minnesota's Center for Early Modern History in 1997 is another indication of the growing prominence of comparative and global approaches to early modernity.

42. Greene and Pole, *Colonial British America*; Greene, *Pursuits of Happiness*; Guasco, *Slaves and Englishmen*.
43. For the overlap between "early modern" and "early American" and other forms of historical categorization, see St. George, *Possible Pasts*, 1–32.
44. See the preface to Bradburn and Coombs, *Early Modern Virginia*, viii.
45. Ibid.
46. Ryerson, *Revolution Is Now Begun*; Meranze, *Laboratories of Virtue*; Pencak, *Pennsylvania's Revolution*; Pearl, *Conceived in Crisis*.
47. This is not to say, however, that older sources of social conflict—currency, law, sources of cultural legitimacy—were eradicated after the revolution.
48. Wrightson, *Social History of England*, 3.
49. For the notion of human rights, see Hunt, *Inventing Human Rights*; Blackburn, *American Crucible*.
50. See Suny, "Back and Beyond": 1485–86. Key works for the "cultural turn" discussed by Suny include Hunt, *New Cultural History*; and Bonnell, *Beyond the Cultural Turn*.
51. Chartier, *Cultural History*, 4–5; E. P. Thompson, *Making of the English Working Class*, 9–16.
52. The concepts of "way of life" and "structure of feeling" as developed by Raymond Williams have been useful in developing this approach. Williams, *Long Revolution*, esp. 39, 46, 48.
53. While slavery and indentured servitude in colonial Philadelphia and Pennsylvania have received significant attention, they have most often been analyzed separately. See Nash, *Forging Freedom*; Nash and Soderlund, *Freedom by Degrees*; Salinger, "To Serve Well and Faithfully."

1. "NOTHING WILL SATISFY YOU BUT MONEY"

1. Philadelphia Exports for the Year 1752, Miscellaneous Collection, 1676–1937, box 7b, folder 7, HSP; "Notes and Queries, Exports: 1759–1763," 508–16; McCusker and Menard, *Economy of British America*, 205.
2. Shepard, *Accounting for Oneself*, 118–19.
3. *Petition of divers of the Inhabitants of the County of Chester.*
4. B. Smith, "*Lower Sort*"; Salinger, "Artisans, Journeymen."
5. Vickers, "Competency and Competition," esp. 20–21. See also Johnson, "Nothing Will Satisfy You."
6. A strong (or "hard") money is one of high value relative to competing currencies. Strong currencies can have high value and lead to low or stable prices but can restrain growth; a weak or soft currency can lead to growth but runs

the risk of inflation. In medieval and early modern Europe, people of wealth tended to favor a strong currency, while commoners typically favored a more abundant currency and therefore a "soft" money policy. Desan, *Making Money*, 153–60; Mayhew, "Wages and Currency."

7. *Petition of divers Inhabitants of the County of Chester.* For money-saving as an antisocial practice in England, see Muldrew, "Hard Food for Midas," 98; Valenze, *Social Life of Money*, 155.

8. Ray, *Compleat Collection of English Proverbs*, 18.

9. Bacon repeated the proverb "Money is like muck, not good unless it be spread," after a 1607 Midlands rising. Bacon, "Of Seditions and Troubles," in *Major Works*, 369.

10. Johnson, "Nothing Will Satisfy You."

11. Woodfine, "Debtors, Prisons, and Petitions." For revolutionary-era petitions, see *Humble Remonstrance and Complaint of many Thousands of Poore Distressed Prisoners.*

12. Hakluyt, *Discourse of Western Planting*, 54.

13. McCormick, *William Petty*, 157, 191; Armitage, *Ideological Origins of the British Empire*, 147, 151–53.

14. Slack, *Invention of Improvement*, 53, 62, 80–81; chap. 5.

15. Penn, *Some Account of the Province of Pennsylvania*, reprinted in Myers, *Narratives*, 202–7, 209–10. For a representative view to which Penn was responding, see Coke, *Discourse of Trade in Two Parts.*

16. Penn, *Some Account of the Province of Pennsylvania*, reprinted in Myers, *Narratives*, 203–4. Penn's contemporary, the English merchant Josiah Child, claimed one English colonist with ten slaves in Barbados created work for four men in England, while ten colonists in New England would not employ one man in England. Mulcahy, *Hubs of Empire*, 182.

17. Quoted in Nash, *Quakers and Politics*, 10. See also Penn's detailed instructions to his commissioners concerning property and the search for natural resources (especially mines) in 1686 and 1687 in Philadelphia County Records, 1671–1855, Collection 1014, box 1, folder 1, HSP.

18. Budd, *Good Order Established*, 2.

19. Penn, *Some Account of the Province of Pennsylvania*, reprinted in Myers, *Narratives*, 260; Nash, *Quakers and Politics*, 50.

20. "Letter from William Penn to the Committee of the Free Society of Traders, 1683," in Myers, *Narratives*, 139–40; Penn, *Further Account of the Province of Pennsylvania*, reprinted in ibid., 260–62, 269–72.

21. Tim Stretton, "People and the Law," in Wrightson, *Social History of England*, 199–202; Cohen, "History of Imprisonment for Debt."

22. W. Bullock, *Virginia Impartially examined*, 13–14; K. Morgan, *Slavery and Servitude in North America*, 21; Beckles, *White Servitude and Black Slavery*, 91; Revel, "Poor Unhappy Transported Felon," 192.

23. Caesar, *A General Discovrse Against the damnable sect of Vsurers*, 6, 7, 13–14, 15 (quote), 18. For debtor rebellions in ancient Rome, see Brunt, *Social Conflicts in the Roman Republic*, 56–58. At the turn of the eighteenth century, the English agricultural writer Timothy Nourse argued that the customary seven-year system of apprenticeship was a legacy of the ancient Hebrew jubilee, when after seven years of service poor debtors were to be freed and treated as "hired Servants or Sojourners." Nourse, *Campania Fœlix*, 185.

24. Morris, *Government and Labor*, 355–56.

25. Exquemelin, *Bucaniers of America*, 38, 43–44.

26. For the politics of the Pennsylvania charter, see Nash, *Quakers and Politics*.

27. *Statutes*, 1:49, 60, 65; Priest, "Creating an American Property Law," 408–16; *Colonial Laws of New York*, 1:14.

28. Staughton, *Charter to William Penn*, 151–52. This situation was in contrast to the Chesapeake colonies, which allowed the seizure of slaves but not land for debt.

29. Hanna, *Pirate Nests*, 97, 170–71, 349.

30. Blackwell, *Model for Erecting a Bank of Credit*. Blackwell also contributed to monetary debates in London during England's recoinage controversy of the 1690s and was certainly familiar with arguments from the 1640s for a land bank on the Dutch model. Blackwell, *Essay Towards Carrying on the Present War with France*. For paper money in New England, see Priest, "Currency Policies"; Peterson, *City-State of Boston*, 43–54, chap. 2.

31. Nash, *Quakers and Politics*, 117–26; Dunn and Dunn, "The Founding," 22.

32. "Original Letters and Documents," 363–64; Dorfman, "Captain John Blackwell," 233–37. The itinerant Labadist Jasper Dankaerts wrote of similarly exploitative merchant practices in New York. Danckaerts, *Journal*, 245–46.

33. *An Historical and Geographical Account of Pensilvania and of West New-Jersey*, reprinted in Myers, *Narratives*, 317, 326–29, 332–33.

34. Pennsylvania assemblymen had in fact broached the subject of placing a ceiling on workers' pay as early as 1683, though they ultimately decided "every Man" could "agree with his Artificer to his best Advantage." *Assembly*, 1:9–10.

35. Shepard, *Accounting for Oneself*, table 2.8 (74). In Worcestershire in 1663, sawyers earned 2s 4d per hundred, meaning—if Blackwell's wage claims are correct—that Boston sawyers earned wages roughly equivalent to their English counterparts. "Wage Assessments," in Archer and Price, *English Historical Documents*, 6:469.

36. Dorfman, "Captain John Blackwell," 237; Johnson, "Nothing Will Satisfy You," 111–12.
37. Dunn and Dunn, "The Founding," 20, 25–27.
38. See, for example, Child, *New Discourse of Trade*, preface, 46–47, 122–23.
39. Miller, "Crown and Borough Charters"; Brooks, "Apprenticeship, Social Mobility," 65, 72; Musselwhite, *Urban Dreams, Rural Commonwealths*, chap. 5.
40. "Remonstrance from the Inhabitants of Philadelphia," in M. M. Dunn, *Papers of William Penn*, 2:570–73. Penn's charter granted the proprietors the right to incorporate towns and boroughs. *Provincial Council*, 1:21–22.
41. In a 1683 petition for the reconfirmation of the New York charter (first issued by Governor Richard Nicolls in 1665), New Yorkers claimed that without the grain export monopoly the city would be "ruined." *Minutes of the Common Council of the City of New York*, 1:104.
42. "First Charter of the City of Philadelphia, 1691."
43. *Assembly*, 393–401; Nash, *Quakers and Politics*, 232–33; Diamondstone, "Philadelphia's Municipal Corporation."
44. *Common Council*, 9, 11, 22, 23, 57, 84, 86, 136.
45. Wood, wine, sugar, rum, molasses, and salt were the main commodities carters moved around the city. Ibid., 6–7, 20, 147, 163, 164.
46. Ibid., 17.
47. Ibid., 25.
48. Ibid., 16, 20, 34.
49. Ibid., 25.
50. Glenn, "William Hudson"; Johnson, "Hot-Heads, Gentlemen," 354.
51. Peter Thompson makes a similar case for publicans in *Rum Punch and Revolution*, 24. For a controversy involving city tanners, see chap. 6 of this work.
52. Thomas, *Historical and Geographical Account of Pensilvania*; Pastorius, *Circumstantial Geographical Description of Pennsylvania*, both reprinted in Myers, *Narratives*, 327, 409; Welsh, *Tanning in the United States to 1850*, 4–7.
53. *Assembly*, 1:411–12.
54. Ibid., 2:1294, 1301, 1375–76. The assembly finally responded with an act regulating the price of leather, banning its export, and prohibiting all leatherworkers from practicing others' trades. *Statutes*, 3:258–60.
55. Salinger, *"To Serve Well and Faithfully,"* 54–56; Wokeck, *Trade in Strangers*.
56. *Common Council*, 115.
57. While female shopkeepers whose husbands were away at sea were accorded the status of *feme sole* around this time, urban citizenship became overwhelmingly male, while unmarried women increasingly resorted to poor relief or ran lower-sort taverns. *Statutes*, 3:157–59; Overseers of the poor, 1709–10, II: Joseph B. Francus Collection, Miscellaneous Documents, HSP.

58. Three carters paid the high cost of £2 for membership, likely in exchange for long-term or lifetime licenses to cart in the city. *Common Council,* 118–35.
59. Ibid., 146–47.
60. Morris, *Government and Labor,* 141–42.
61. *Common Council,* 145–47.
62. Teaford, *Municipal Revolution,* 47.
63. Watson, *Annals,* 1:98; *Assembly,* 2:1477, 1485.
64. *Common Council,* 16, 19.
65. "The Humble Petition of Diverse poor Inhabitants of the City and County of Philadelphia," Philadelphia County Records, 1671–1855, Collection 1014, box 1, folder 6, HSP. Though the petition is undated, it is addressed to Evans. For the second, similar (though differently worded) petition, see Watson, *Annals,* 1:358.
66. Stretton, "People and the Law," in Wrightson, *Social History of England,* 200–203, 205; Woodfine, "Debtors, Prisons, and Petitions," 1–31.
67. "Humble Petition of Diverse poor Inhabitants."
68. Philadelphia County Records, 1671–1855, Collection 1014, box 1, folder 7 (Davis), folder 8 (Roe, Shelley, Callowhill and Pinnoll), HSP.
69. For the lending practices of Sisom and others, see ibid., folders 6–10, HSP. See also Gillingham, "Cesar Ghiselin, Philadelphia's First Gold and Silversmith"; Account Book of Joseph Richardson, 1733–39, Joseph Richardson Papers, HSP.
70. Philadelphia Court of Common Pleas (1697–1732), 1712, 1714, James T. Mitchell Collection, box 19, HSP. Credit arrangements could themselves be highly exploitative. In 1723 George Ward, a bricklayer, promised to repay David Evans the £3 5s 4d he owed by the following November; the "Penal Sum" if Ward was unable to clear the debt was doubled to £6 10s 8d. Philadelphia County Records, 1671–1855, box 1, folder 11, HSP.
71. McCusker, *Money and Exchange,* 126; Hanna, *Pirate Nests,* 97.
72. *Assembly,* 1:461.
73. *Statutes,* 2:277–78; *Assembly,* 1:481, 533, 534, 541.
74. *Colonial Laws of New York,* 1:666–68, 695–700, 737–40, 819–26, 847–48, 853–57, 938–46.
75. *Assembly,* 2:840.
76. Debtors would also be permitted to repay loans in old currency rates. *Statutes,* 2:294–99.
77. *Assembly,* 2:889, 921–22, 955, 1124, 1237, 1262, 1263, 1266, 1269, 1394–95; Johnson, "What Must Poor People Do?," 121–22; Johnson, "Nothing Will Satisfy You," 120–22.
78. Schweitzer, *Custom and Contract,* 115–19; Nash, *Urban Crucible,* 149–53; Wendel, "Keith-Lloyd Alliance."

79. This is a suggestive statement considering Rawle was one of the landlords who allegedly charged Philadelphia tenants rents in proclamation money. See note 77 above.
80. Rawle, *Some Remedies Proposed; Provincial Council*, 3:143, 145.
81. Logan, *Charge Delivered from the Bench;* Lloyd, *Vindication of the Legislative Power;* Logan, "The Antidote."
82. McRae, *God Speed the Plough.*
83. *Dialogue between Mr. Robert Rich and Roger Plowman.*
84. Ibid.; Johnson, "Nothing Will Satisfy You," 123–24.
85. *Triumvirate of Pennsylvania.* Type and font indicate this pamphlet was also printed by Keimer. More commentary on money in the populist vein can be found in William Keith's *Observator's Trip to America,* 10, 25, 34–37. See also Johnson, "Nothing Will Satisfy You," 124–25.
86. Logan, *Dialogue Shewing what's therein to be found,* 12–13, 15, 19–20, 22–23.
87. Wendel, "Keith-Lloyd Alliance," 302.
88. *Statutes,* 3:326.
89. *Assembly,* 2:1739.
90. *Provincial Council,* 3:260–61; *Archives,* 2nd Ser., 7:94–97; Wendel, "Keith-Lloyd Alliance," 301–2.
91. *Revisal of the Intreagues of the Triumvirate.*
92. *View of the Calumnies Lately Spread.*
93. Overseers of the poor claimed at this time that they were unable to provide for the "great Number" of insolvent debtors and immigrants from Europe and neighboring colonies. *Archives,* 1st Ser., 1:186–87.
94. *Provincial Council,* 3:293–94, 351–52; Watson, *Annals,* 1:79. While approximately eight hundred German immigrants arrived in Pennsylvania between 1683 and 1726, many thousands arrived in the 1730s alone. After 1726, moreover, German immigrants were increasingly similar to their Irish counterparts in being young, male, and poor. *Provincial Council,* 3:282–83; McCoy, "Absconding Servants, Anxious Germans, ," 432–33, 438.
95. "Strangers" were blamed for the Knowles Riot in Boston in 1747 and for a coin devaluation riot in New York in 1754, for example. Pencak and Lax, "The Knowles Riot," 29; Johnson, "Nothing Will Satisfy You," 132–35.
96. Gordon and the assembly eventually agreed to emit £30,000 in bills of credit. *Statutes,* 4:98–116.
97. McCusker and Menard, *Economy of British America,* 194–95, 205; B. Smith, "*Lower Sort,*" 84, 88–89.
98. While the population of Pennsylvania increased 160 percent between 1740 and 1770, English imports increased more than a thousand percent. Price,

"Economic Function and Growth," 154. For Pennsylvania's trade imbalance, see Jensen, *Maritime Commerce of Colonial Philadelphia*, 89.

99. B. Smith, *"Lower Sort,"* 104; Roney, *Governed by a Spirit of Opposition*, 113.

100. Jessica Choppin Roney has counted sixty formal associations in Philadelphia before the revolution. Roney, *Governed by a Spirit of Opposition*, 5. See also chap. 6 in this work.

101. P. Thompson, *Rum Punch and Revolution*, 127.

102. *Act to Incorporate the Carpenters' Company of Philadelphia*, vi.

103. *Franklin Papers*, 1:255; S. Newman, "Benjamin Franklin and the Leather-Apron Men."

104. Morris, *Government and Labor*, 142; Nash, "Artisans and Politics," 80.

105. *Assembly*, 3:2246, 2249–50, 2264–65; Watson, *Annals*, 1:381–82, 396, 398; Morrison, *Early American Architecture*, 532, 537.

106. *Gazette*, October 2, 1729, and March 19, 1741.

107. Ibid., April 21, 1737.

108. Account Book of Joseph Richardson, 1733–39, Joseph Richardson Papers, HSP.

109. *Archives*, 1st Ser., 1:186–87.

110. Ibid., 325–26.

111. Ibid., 4th Ser., 1:669, 676–81, 682–83.

112. Ibid., 1st Ser., 1:306.

113. *Report from the Committee Appointed to Enquire into the State of the Gaols of this Kingdom.* The committee's "fearless and shocking revelations quickly won it lasting celebrity." White, "Pain and Degradation," 77.

114. *Provincial Council*, 3:376–77.

115. Ibid., 376.

116. Debts made before the law would no longer apply, and unmarried people under forty would also be exempt from the law. *Statutes*, 4:211–15. Residents unsurprisingly followed debt law closely, as is suggested by the petition of Joseph Sturgis, who cited revised debt law requesting release from debtors' prison in 1737. Petition of Joseph Sturgis, June 15, 1737, Philadelphia Court of Common Pleas, 1732–44, James T. Mitchell Collection, box 19, HSP.

117. For this reason Truman proposed banning loan office trustees from sitting in the assembly. *Advice to the Free-holders and Electors of Pennsylvania*, 4.

118. Muldrew, "Hard Cash for Midas," 98.

119. *Advice to the Free-Holders and Electors of Pennsylvania*, 2.

120. The copper halfpence was first minted in 1672 as a token currency to help relieve England's coin shortage. As part of major economic reforms and at a time of war with France, in the 1690s Parliament banned the exportation of silver abroad, a development that encouraged colonies to manufacture coins

and use English copper coins. C. Smith and Mossman, "Eighteenth-Century Counterfeit."

121. An emergency charity collection organized by the municipality produced more than two hundred pounds in aid. *Common Council*, 396–99.

122. *Gazette*, January 8, 1741; *New-York Weekly Journal*, January 26, 1741.

123. *Whereas Great Quantities of English Copper.*

124. *Common Council*, 402.

125. *Mercury*, July 2, 1741.

126. *Common Council*, 405.

127. B. Smith, *"Lower Sort,"* 71, 78, 82, 89; Theodore Thayer, "Town into City, 1746–1765," in Weigley, *Philadelphia*, 74–75.

128. *New-York Gazette, or Weekly Post-Boy*, January 3, 1757; *New-York Mercury*, March 18, 1765; *New-York Journal or General Advertiser*, August 17, 1769; *New-York Gazette and Weekly Mercury*, March 15, 1773.

129. Franklin, *Autobiography*, 182.

130. *Franklin Papers*, 1:143–46.

131. E. Newman, "Franklin Making Money More Plentiful," 341.

132. The title of Franklin's essay was taken from Robert Crowley's *Waie to Wealth* (1550), an anti-enclosure tract with a very different moral message than that of Franklin.

133. Franklin, "Way to Wealth," 812–13; Johnson, "Nothing Will Satisfy You," 135–36.

134. For more on Webbe's "Z" writings in the 1730s, see chap. 5 in this work.

135. Webbe, *Discourse Concerning Paper Money*, esp. A2, 4, 5, 7.

136. Society Miscellaneous Collection, 1676–1937, Miscellaneous Collection 425, box 7b, folder 6, HSP.

137. Mittelberger, *Journey to Pennsylvania*, 28, 36–37, 49–51, 68–69, 76, 89.

138. *Assembly*, 4:3483, 3515, 3518, 3520.

139. *Statutes*, 5:189.

140. Ibid., 5:243–62, 303–8, 337–52, 379–96, 6:344–67.

141. Organization began with the association of master cordwainers, carpenters, and tailors in the 1760s and 1770s, while by the 1780s and 1790s journeymen formed labor unions and engaged in the city's first strikes. Morris, *Government and Labor*, 199, 201; Salinger, "Artisans, Journeymen," 77–79.

142. Woolman, *Considerations on Pure Wisdom*, 3, 11, 14, 21, 23–24.

2. "A GREAT NUMBER OF HANDS"

1. In 1740 servants constituted 7.2 percent of the urban population (575), the enslaved 15.1 percent (1,209); together bound workers were 22.3 percent

of the urban population (1,784) and 34.3 percent of the labor force (1,457). Tomlins, *Freedom Bound*, tables 1.9–1.12 (46–50); Salinger, "To Serve Well and Faithfully," appendix A, table 3 (178–80). Nash, "Slaves and Slaveowners."

2. Moraley was one of tens of thousands of indentured servants to arrive at the port of Philadelphia in the 1720s and 1730s. In *The Infortunate* he chronicled in colorful prose his experiences as an indentured servant between 1729 and 1734, beginning with his downward social slide as a watchmaker in London to his roguish representation of tramping on the social and spatial fringes of Philadelphia. For details of Moraley's life, see Klepp and Smith's introduction to the *Infortunate*, 1–36.

3. Ibid., 66, 88–89. In fact, real wages in England had begun a steady climb after the Restoration that would continue until the middle of the eighteenth century. Wrightson, *Earthly Necessities*, 230–31.

4. Moraley, *Infortunate*, 93.

5. Ibid., 50; Shepard, *Accounting for Oneself*, 203.

6. Advertisements with rewards ranging from thirty shillings to five pounds for the return of fugitives were posted on trees, in public places, and in newspapers throughout the colonies. Moraley, *Infortunate*, 96.

7. Ibid., 94–95. This popular understanding was corroborated some years later, when Gottlieb Mittelberger noted slaves were commonly "given in marriage by their masters, so that they may raise young blackamoors who are sold in their turn." Mittelberger, *Journey to Pennsylvania*, 81.

8. Dyer, *Making a Living*; Steinfeld, *Invention of Free Labor.*

9. S. Newman, *New World of Labor*; Blackburn, *Making of New World Slavery*; Pettigrew, *Freedom's Debt.*

10. Armitage, *Ideological Origins of the British Empire*; Pettigrew, *Freedom's Debt.*

11. Tomlins, *Freedom Bound*, 288–89. In practice, as will be seen below, laws were frequently ignored by townspeople and officials, leaving public oversight uneven, at best. The literature on Quaker antislavery is large, but see Nash and Soderlund, *Freedom by Degrees*; Soderlund, *Quakers and Slavery*; Carey, *From Peace to Freedom.*

12. Tomlins, *Freedom Bound*, 287. See also Canny, *Elizabethan Conquest of Ireland.*

13. More and Claypoole, "Articles, Settlement, and Offices," 43, 45; Salinger, "To Serve Well and Faithfully," 19–20; Nash, "Free Society of Traders."

14. Racialist laws were passed in Barbados and Virginia in the 1660s, and in 1661 a Council of Foreign Plantations Committee noted that American "servants are either Blacks or Whites" and that blacks (typically costing twenty pounds) were "perpetual servants," whereas whites (transported for six pounds) labored four or five years in servitude. Wareing, *Indentured Migration*, 41.

15. Wright, *Negro in Pennsylvania*, 7.

16. Watson, *Annals*, 2:262.

17. Salinger, *"To Serve Well and Faithfully,"* 34; Herrick, *White Servitude in Pennsylvania*, 35.

18. Beckles, *White Servitude and Black Slavery*, 71; Horn, *Adapting to a New World*, 66; Morris, *Government and Labor*, 396–97.

19. Horne, *Brief Description of the Province of Carolina*, 71. The Duke's Laws of 1665 in New York stated only that on the expiration of terms of service, servants "shall not be Sent empty away," a vagueness copied from Massachusetts. *Colonial Laws of New York*, 1:48.

20. *Provincial Council*, 1:37; Tomlins, *Freedom Bound*, 287.

21. P. Wood, *Black Majority*, 41; K. Morgan, *Slavery and Servitude*, chap. 1.

22. *Statutes*, 1:100–101. Ten years later Pennsylvania's custom of the country was slightly revised again, with ages reduced to sixteen and twenty-one. *Statutes*, 1:210.

23. Register of Arrivals, 1682–86, Am. 213, HSP.

24. Salinger, *"To Serve Well and Faithfully,"* table 2.1 (33–34).

25. Thomas, *Historical and Geographical Account of Pensilvania*, reprinted in Myers, *Narratives*, 328.

26. Steinfeld, *Invention of Free Labor*, 19–21; Kussmaul, *Servants in Husbandry*, 5–7.

27. For by-employments in England, see Kussmaul, *Servants in Husbandry*, 23–24.

28. *Minutes of the Council and General Court of Colonial Virginia*, 467; O'Callaghan, *Laws and Ordinances of New Netherland*, 32, 35.

29. The third law concerning servitude made it illegal to harbor and trade with servants. *Statutes*, 1: 99–100.

30. *Statutes*, 1:99–101, 110. Maryland passed the most draconian punishments for runaways in colonial North America: a 1641 law mandating the death penalty was dropped in 1649, when two days' service for every day missed was substituted. In 1661 this penalty was raised to ten days for every day of absence. Morris, *Government and Labor*, 450, 456.

31. Moraley, *Infortunate*, 97.

32. *Documents Relative to the Colonial History of the State of New York*, 4:160.

33. *Statutes*, 2:398–99. See also *Provincial Council*, 2:113.

34. Nash, "Slaves and Slaveowners," 225. Nicholas More informed William Penn that the purchase of slaves drained the colony of already scarce specie. M. M. Dunn, *Papers of William Penn*, 2:608.

35. Nash and Soderlund, *Freedom by Degrees*, 15–16; Soderlund, *Quakers and Slavery*, 64. If Philadelphia's population in 1710 was between 2,400 and 2,600, as Susan Klepp has estimated, then there were approximately 250 enslaved people in the town, if Nash and Soderlund's estimates are accurate. Klepp, "Demography in Early Philadelphia," tables 1 and 2.

36. Nash and Soderlund, *Freedom by Degrees,* 19–20.

37. For a discussion of Black culture in the city, see chap. 6 in this work.

38. Keith, *An Exhortation & Caution to Friends Concerning buying or keeping of Negroes, Archives,* 8th Ser., 3:1012; Soderlund, *Quakers and Slavery,* 19, 22; Gerbner, "Antislavery in Print."

39. *Provincial Council,* 2:112.

40. *New York State Library Calendar of Council Minutes,* 61.

41. *Statutes,* 2:236–37.

42. Ibid., 280–91, 382–83.

43. *Assembly,* 2:1387.

44. Foote, "Some Hard Usage."

45. *Statutes,* 2:433–36.

46. *Provincial Council,* 1:380. For idle servants gadding in England, see Gouge, *Of Domesticall Duties,* 617.

47. Bronner, "Philadelphia County Court of Quarter Sessions," 92; Grand Jury Petition to the Mayor and Commonalty, 1702, Ancient Records, HSP.

48. *Provincial Council,* 1:380; *Statutes,* 4:59–64.

49. For population in the early eighteenth century, see Klepp, "Demography in Philadelphia," 103–4.

50. Salinger, *"To Serve Well and Faithfully,"* 52–54; Dickson, *Ulster Emigration to Colonial America,* 6, 30, 33; Wokeck, *Trade in Strangers,* 169.

51. Salinger, *"To Serve Well and Faithfully,"* 55–56; Wokeck, *Trade in Strangers,* 41–42.

52. Herrick, *White Servitude,* 4; Grubb, "Auction of Redemptioner Servants, Philadelphia."

53. *Archives,* 2nd Ser., 7:39.

54. Nash, *Quakers and Politics,* 322; *Provincial Council,* 3:29.

55. *Archives,* 2nd Ser., 7:103–4, 114.

56. *Statutes,* 3:167, 4:135–40; Archer and Price, *English Historical Documents, 1558–1603,* 5(A):663–82.

57. Petition of William Spencer to the Mayor, Recorder, and Aldermen of Philadelphia, 1713, James T. Mitchell Collection, box 16, HSP. For extensions of service, see also Moraley, *Infortunate,* 96; Mittelberger, *Journey to Pennsylvania,* 19.

58. Grand Inquest presentation of Francis Philipps, 1715, Ancient Records, HSP.

59. Watson, *Annals,* 1:308–9; *Statutes,* 3:167–68.

60. For a detailed discussion of grand juries, see chap. 3 in this work.

61. *Assembly,* 2:1464.

62. Petition of Hannah Cherry, 1722, Ancient Records, HSP.

63. *Statutes,* 4:59–60.

64. Ibid.; Tomlins, *Freedom Bound,* 497.

65. *Common Council*, 314–15 (1732), 326 (1733), 342 (1735), 376–77 (1738); Grand Inquest Remonstrance, "To the worshipful the Mayor Recorder & Aldermen of the City of Philadelphia," 1736, Philadelphia County Records, 1671–1855, Collection 1014, box 1, folder 14, HSP.

66. See the introduction to Ehmer and Lis, *Idea of Work in Europe*, 18; Dyer, *Making a Living*, 281–82.

67. Slack, *English Poor Law*, 14–15.

68. Bullock, *Virginia Impartially Examined*, 13–14.

69. Harris, *Revolution*, 143. The pamphleteers claimed that the natural abundance in which the Irish lived, which promoted sloth, also led to comparisons with similarly lazy Native Americans. McCormick, *William Petty*, 191.

70. P. Wood, *Black Majority*, 46. For the discursive shift to alleged African idleness in the eighteenth century, see J. Morgan, *Laboring Women*, 42, 45.

71. New York and New Jersey used the phrase in laws to regulate Black populations in 1712 and 1714, respectively. Tomlins, *Freedom Bound*, 497n.297.

72. Wrightson, *Earthly Necessities*, 320–21; Jordan, *Anxieties of Idleness*, 44–45, 135–36.

73. P. Morgan, *Slave Counterpoint*, 153–55, 202. For differing English valuations of leisure and labor, see Wrightson, *Earthly Necessities*, 321.

74. *Statutes*, 4:63–64. The practice of "self-hiring" was well established by this time in the southern colonies.

75. Defoe, *Great Law of Insubordination Consider'd*.

76. Nash and Soderlund, *Freedom by Degrees*, 19; Salinger, "To Serve Well and Faithfully," 15.

77. Amussen, *Caribbean Exchanges*, 221–22.

78. *Mercury*, December 29, 1719, and March 8, 17, 1720. For Franklin's *Gazette* and slavery, see Waldstreicher, *Runaway America*.

79. *Mercury*, March 8, 1720; *Gazette*, December 28, 1732.

80. *Gazette*, October 11, 1733.

81. Ibid., February 7, 1740, and June 18, 1730.

82. Ibid., October 9, November 20, 1729; Salinger, "To Serve Well and Faithfully," 54; Dickson, *Ulster Emigration*, 43.

83. *Statutes*, 3:264–68, 4:135–40.

84. Unsurprisingly, the Pennsylvania statute was repealed by the Crown.

85. Sandiford, *Mystery of Iniquity*; Lay, *All Slave-Keepers*.

86. *Mercury*, November 7, 1728, November 7, 1734, January 16, May 10, and June 14, 1739; *Gazette*, November 29, 1728, and December 28, 1731.

87. *Gazette*, October 23, 1729.

88. *Mercury*, October 9, 1729, and April–August 1741; *Gazette*, May 2, 1734, and March 17, 24, 1737; Brown, *Tacky's Revolt*, 228–29.

89. Herrick, *White Servitude*, 23; *Gazette*, April 27, 1738; *Mercury*, May 10, 1739.
90. *Provincial Council*, 4:318–20, 323–28. Thomas and the Penns eventually agreed to the emission in exchange for £1,200 in Pennsylvania bills and an annual £130 when bills of credit were re-emitted. *Statutes*, 4:322–26, 344–59.
91. *Provincial Council*, 4:351; *Assembly*, 4:165–67; *Mercury*, September 28, 1738; Wilson, *Sense of the People*, 140–42.
92. "Notes and Queries: Two Letters of Governor Thomas," 98.
93. *Provincial Council*, 4:354.
94. Ibid., 350–51, 354, 355–56; *Assembly*, 3:2527–28, 2529–31, 2532; Chew, *Speech of Samuel Chew.*
95. *Archives*, 1st Ser., 1:616–19. For hostility to impressment in the seventeenth and eighteenth centuries, see Donoghue, *Fire Under the Ashes;* Brunsman, *Evil Necessity.*
96. *Provincial Council*, 4:395–97, esp. 396.
97. Ibid., 397–98.
98. As of June 1741 fifty-eight servants had fled neighboring Chester County, and nineteen left Bucks County. *Assembly*, 3:2656, 2677. Sharon Salinger has claimed close to half of the servant population fled during the war, a probable overestimate. *"To Serve Well and Faithfully,"* 59. Taking the total servant population in 1740 to be 575, the 188 claimed by representatives to have enlisted is 32.7 percent—still a significant proportion of the urban servant population. For population figures, see Tomlins, *Freedom Bound*, tables 1.9, 1.11 (46, 49).
99. Rediker, *Fearless Benjamin Lay*, 68–69, 93–94, 131–32.
100. *Assembly*, 3:2564.
101. Ibid., 2570, 2600, 2628.
102. *Provincial Council*, 4:437.
103. *Assembly*, 3:2614–15.
104. *Provincial Council*, 4:437; *Assembly*, 3:2603.
105. Mather, *Brief Discourse on the Necessary Properties & Practices*, 38.
106. For this ideology in the South, see P. Morgan, *Slave Counterpoint*, 259.
107. *Assembly*, 3:2619–20.
108. Ibid., 2535–38, 2652–53. For crime and punishment in Philadelphia, see chap. 4 in this work.
109. Ibid., 2542.
110. Ibid., 4:439–40, 449.
111. Ibid., 455–56.
112. Ibid., 4:440, 3:2607–8.
113. *Provincial Council*, 4:467.
114. A. E. Smith, *Colonists in Bondage*, 118–19; Galenson, *White Servitude in Colonial America*, 8, 101; Revel, "Poor Unhappy Transported Felon," 190, 192.

115. Chaplin, "Slavery and the Principle of Humanity."
116. *Provincial Council*, 4:468–69.
117. Servants continued to volunteer for service well into 1742, and masters' applications for compensation continued to arrive at the Philadelphia State House. *Assembly*, 3:2671–75, 2677, 2679–80, 4:2709, 2722, 2787, 2786–803, 2815, 2823.
118. Ibid., 5:4186; Nash, "Slaves and Slaveowners," 229.
119. *Assembly*, 5:4196; Nash, "Slaves and Slaveowners," 229.
120. *Provincial Council*, 6:45.
121. Quoted in Nash, "Slaves and Slaveowners," 230.
122. Ibid., 229–30.
123. Salinger, *"To Serve Well and Faithfully,"* appendix A, table A.3 (179).
124. See Waldstreicher, "Reading the Runaways," table 1 (250).
125. *Gazette*, October 31, 1745.
126. Conversely, a number of "Spanish Negroes" seized by Philadelphia privateers demanded their freedom. *Provincial Council*, 71, 79, 92–93, 200, 201, 227, 262.
127. *Gazette*, September 10, 1761.
128. Ibid., December 3, 1747.
129. Ibid., May 23, 1751.
130. Ibid., June 8, 1749. For fines for harboring slaves, see *Statutes*, 4:62. For free Black people in New York and East Jersey, see Hodges, *Root and Branch*; and for South Carolina, see J. Morgan, *Laboring Women*, 159; P. Wood, *Black Majority*, 271; P. Morgan, *Slave Counterpoint*, 552.
131. For the growth of luxury and idleness among those dependent on slave labor in Barbados and Virginia in the years of Philadelphia's founding, see Godwyn, *Negro's and Indians Advocate*, 81, 110.
132. Woolman, *Journal and Major Essays*, 51–93, 198–239. Recent studies of Woolman include Slaughter, *Beautiful Soul*; and Plank, *John Woolman's Path*.
133. Hornick, "Anthony Benezet and the Africans' School," 400.
134. Benezet, *Short Account of that Part of Africa*; Benezet, *Caution and a Warning to Great Britain*, 3. See also Jackson, *Let This Voice Be Heard*.
135. According to Christopher Tomlins, in 1740 slaves and servants were 15.1 and 7.2 percent of the Philadelphia population, respectively. By 1775 these percentages had fallen to 7.5 and 2.4. Tomlins, *Freedom Bound*, tables 1.10, 1.11 (48–49). See also Salinger, *"To Serve Well and Faithfully,"* appendix A, table A.3 (178–79).
136. For the text of the act, see *Statutes*, 10:67–73.
137. Tomlins, *Freedom Bound*, table 1.9 (46); Salinger, *"To Serve Well and Faithfully,"* 128–33, 148–49. Traditional forms of service in husbandry remained important, however. In 1775 an agricultural writer noted that in Pennsylvania, while

some planters used "negroe slaves" in cultivation, there were far more white servants. And throughout North America white servants were distinguished by those hired by the year (both men and women) who earned wages as in England, and new arrivals who were poor and sold into servitude. *American Husbandry*, 169–70.

138. They also point out that no Philadelphia Quakers are known to have manumitted slaves before 1720. Nash and Soderlund, *Freedom by Degrees*, 57, 61.

139. Watson, *Annals*, 1:261, 265.

140. *Journal*, July 23, 1752; *Gazette*, March 17, 1763.

141. During the war male servants accused of theft were simply banished if they were willing to board privateers. *Common Council*, 587, 594, 595, 596, 603.

142. *True and Impartial State of the Province of Pennsylvania*, 42.

143. Mackraby, "Philadelphia Society before the Revolution," 492.

144. Moraley, *Infortunate*, 109–10.

145. Most of those enslaved (to use Williamson's terminology) were by contrast driven through the country "like cattle to a Smithfield market and exposed to sale in public fairs as so many brute beasts." Williamson, *Life and Curious Adventures*, 11, 13; Shannon, "King of the Indians." For youth "spirited" from Ireland to Philadelphia in the eighteenth century, see the petition of Dennis Galhor, October 1732, Court of Common Pleas, Philadelphia Court Records, 1676–1825, AM3039, HSP; and the petition of Ann Dempsey, December 1753, Quarter Sessions Court Docket, 1753–60, PCA.

3. "UNINTELLIGIBLE STUFF CALLED LAW"

1. Moraley, *Infortunate*, 94–96.

2. A. Wood, *Riot, Rebellion, and Popular Politics*. For colonists' growing identification with Britain, see McConville, *The King's Three Faces*. For the key role of law in early Virginia, see Billings and Tarter, "Esteemed Bookes of Lawe."

3. Davies, *Quakers in English Society*, 67; Hill, *World Turned Upside Down*, 297–304. For Commonwealth influences on the founding Frame of Government, see Ryerson, "William Penn's Gentry Commonwealth."

4. *Provincial Council*, 1:29–30.

5. Smolenski, *Friends and Strangers*, 3–4, 9–10.

6. One scholar has argued that law was the main device through which Quakers maintained economic and political dominance in early Pennsylvania. Nelson, "Government by Judiciary."

7. As early as the 1680s members of the Board of Trade envisioned getting rid of the proprietary system in favor of a centralized royal system of governance. Tomlins, *Freedom Bound*, 183.

8. Wrightson, "Two Concepts of Order"; Barbara Smith, *Freedoms We Lost*.

9. Court days were important cultural gatherings throughout the colonies. For their importance in Virginia, see Isaac, *Transformation of Virginia*, 92; and in the colonies generally, see Barbara Smith, *Freedoms We Lost*, chap. 1.

10. John of Salisbury, *Policraticus*, 25, 28. See also Rollison, *Commonwealth of the People*, 47–60; Duby, *Three Orders*, 264.

11. Dyer, *Making a Living*, 137–43, 178–83; Guasco, *Slaves and Englishmen*, 25–26.

12. Fortescue, *On the Laws and Governance of England*, 17, 20–21, 26.

13. "Sir Thomas Smith on penal sanctions," in Archer and Price, *English Historical Documents*, 5(A):698.

14. Collinson, *Elizabethan Essays*.

15. Sidney, a friend of William Penn, told friends that Penn's conservative early draft of the Pennsylvania constitution contained "the basest laws in the world, not to be endured or lived under, and the Turk was not more absolute" than Penn. Quoted in Ryerson, "William Penn's Gentry Commonwealth," 401. For examples of Commonwealth thought, see Harrington, *Commonwealth of Oceana*; Sidney, *Discourses Concerning Government*; Locke, *Two Treatises of Government*.

16. Hilton, *Bond Men Made Free*, 139, 151–52, 156; Dyer, *Making a Living*, 284–89.

17. More, *Utopia*, 529–35, 554–55, 572–73.

18. Brinklow, *Complaynt of Roderyck Mors*, chaps. 7–10.

19. Como, *Blown by the Spirit*.

20. Baxter, *Quakers Catechism*; Hill, *World Turned Upside Down*, chap. 10; Davies, *Quakers in English Society*, chap. 13. Some colonists believed Catholics disguised themselves as Quakers to foment religious controversy as late as the 1760s. "Remonstrance and petition of the South Carolina back country (7 November 1767)," in Archer and Price, *English Historical Documents*, 9:596.

21. The Clarendon Code was a series of acts establishing the supremacy of the Church of England and included the Corporation Act (1661), the Act of Uniformity (1662), the Conventicle Act (1664), and the Five-Mile Act (1665).

22. Gerona, *Night Journeys*; D. Hitchcock, "He is a Vagabond."

23. Barclay, *Anarchy of the Ranters*, iii, v, vi, 9, 11–12, 40. See also his *Catechism and Confession of Faith* (1673) and *Apology* (1678), discussed by Reay in *Quakers and the English Revolution*, 111–12.

24. Barclay, *Anarchy of the Ranters*, 40.

25. Hall, *Worlds of Wonder*, 186; Norris, *Early Friends (Or Quakers)*, 9; *Statutes at Large of Virginia*, 532–33.

26. O'Callaghan, *Laws and Ordinances of New Netherland*, 439–40; *Ecclesiastical Records of New York*, 1:399–400, 413, 415, 432–33.

27. Quoted in Hill, *Liberty Against the Law*, 300.

28. Quoted in Ryerson, "William Penn's Gentry Commonwealth," 401.
29. *Provincial Council*, 1:38.
30. Ibid., 29–30. See also Offutt, *Of "Good Men,"* 2–3.
31. Though Quakers were vocal in demands for radical legal reforms in the 1650s, their views grew more ambivalent in England in subsequent decades. Davies, *Quakers in English Society*, 173–75.
32. "Remonstrance from the Inhabitants of Philadelphia, 1684," in Souderland, *William Penn and the Founding*, 377–81; Nash, *Quakers and Politics*, 77–79; Dunn and Dunn, "The Founding," in Weigley, *Philadelphia*, 16–17.
33. *Provincial Council*, 1:48–55; Nash, *Quakers and Politics*, 202–3.
34. "Remonstrance of divers of the peaceable and well affected inhabitants of the county of Philadelphia, March 12, 1696–7," in Hazard, *Register of Pennsylvania*, 6:258–59.
35. William Penn to Thomas Lloyd, June 15, 1685, *Papers of William Penn*, 3:50. See also Ryerson, "William Penn's Gentry Commonwealth."
36. *Archives*, 7:15–20.
37. I. Norris, *Friendly Advice*.
38. Wrightson, "Two Concepts of Order," 25.
39. *Provincial Council*, 1:41; *Colonial Laws of Massachusetts*, 87; *Colonial Laws of New York*, 1:26.
40. Smolenski, *Friends and Strangers*, 73–74.
41. Indictment of Peter Cook, Court of Quarter Sessions, 1685, Philadelphia Court Records, 1685–86, HSP; Indictments of George Robinson and George Thompson, in Bronner, "Philadelphia County Court of Quarter Sessions," 88; Indictment of George Robinson, 1702, Ancient Records, HSP.
42. For refusal to pay market stall rents, see *Common Council*, 48, 51, 210, 221–22. For new settlers' refusal to pay quitrents in the new Northern Liberties, see the 1694 complaint in Philadelphia County Records, 1671–1855, box 1, folder 3, HSP.
43. Ekirch, *At Day's Close*, 80–82, 250; Koslofsky, *Evening's Empire*, 169, 171, 172; Wrightson, "Two Concepts of Order," 26–27, 31.
44. Presentment of Samuel Holt, March 5, 1695, Bronner, "Philadelphia Court of Quarter Sessions," 90; Presentments of Francis Jones, Samuel Perry, Samuel Stacy, James Metcalf, and Thomas Merriot, August 6, 1695, ibid., 236–37. For a strikingly similar event in Lancashire in 1652, see Wrightson, "Two Concepts of Order," 21.
45. *Provincial Council*, 2:210.
46. Roney, *Governed by a Spirit of Opposition*, 50–51; P. Thompson, *Rum Punch and Revolution*, 102–3.
47. *Provincial Council*, 2:161–62; *Common Council*, 35.

48. Liddy and Haemers, "Popular Politics"; Almbjär, "Problem with Early-Modern Petitions."

49. "Act against tumultuous petitioning, 1661," in Archer and Price, *English Historical Documents*, 6:66.

50. *To the Representatives of the Free-Men of this Province of Pennsilvania.*

51. *Assembly*, 1:292, 298, 319, 411–12, 445, 531, 2:889.

52. Mittelberger, *Journey to Pennsylvania*, 38–39.

53. *Provincial Council*, 3:33–37.

54. *Nature and Importance of Oaths and Juries*; Barbara Smith, *Freedoms We Lost*, 33–34.

55. The taking of oaths or affirmations was, however, a source of conflict between Governor Evans and local Quakers in the early eighteenth century. See "The Humble Address of the Mayor and Commonalty of the City of Philadelphia," December 11, 1704, James Logan Papers, Coll. 379, Vol. 3, f101, HSP.

56. *Provincial Council*, 3:40–41.

57. Ibid., 41–42.

58. T. Smith, *De Republica Anglorum*, 46.

59. Hindle, *State and Social Change*, 28; Braddick, *State Formation*, 162–63.

60. In 1700 the assembly attempted to limit grand jury presentments in the House by disallowing those that could be determined by local JPs. *Statutes*, 2:24, 188–89.

61. *Provincial Council*, 1:380; Offutt, *Of "Good Men,"* 54–60. For juries in New York, see Geobel and Naughton, *Law Enforcement in Colonial New York*, 466–67. For the activist grand jury in post-1720 Richmond, Virginia, see G. Morgan, "Law and Social Change." For grand juries in the colonies generally, see Barbara Smith, *Freedoms We Lost*, 21–26.

62. Logan, *Charge Delivered from the Bench to the Grand-Jury*, 6 (quote).

63. Keith, *Observator's Trip to America*, 28–29.

64. I. Norris, *Speech Delivered from the Bench in the Court of Common Pleas.*

65. *To My Respected Friend I.N.*, 2–3.

66. *Advice to the Freeholders and Electors of Pennsylvania*, 2.

67. Ibid., 4–5.

68. *The Tripple-Plea.*

69. Sandiford, *Mystery of Iniquity*, [12].

70. For the growth of professional education in medicine and law in England, see Jewell, *Education in Early Modern England*, 60–79. For the European context of popular suspicion of clergy, doctors, and lawyers, see Burke, *Social History of Knowledge*, 21, 26.

71. "The Benefit of Going to LAW," *Poor Richard's Almanack*. A few years earlier, as noted in chap. 1, Franklin argued in *A Modest Enquiry* that it was mainly

lawyers who benefitted from monetary scarcity, since it was they who profited from creditors bringing debtors to court.

72. Birkett, *Almanack for the Year of Christ, 1730*, [22].
73. Barbara Smith, *Freedoms We Lost*, 90–91.
74. *Gazette*, March 30, 1738.
75. The letter was possibly a belated response to the 1736 series of popular-democratic essays by John Webbe, discussed in detail in chap. 5 in this work.
76. *Gazette*, March 30, 1738.
77. Penn, *Excellent Priviledge of Liberty & Property*.
78. *Statutes*, 3:199.
79. The *New York Gazette* was printed by William Bradford, formerly of Philadelphia, and was New York's official newspaper.
80. *New-York Weekly Journal*, September 12, 1734. The newspaper letter was soon extended and published as a pamphlet.
81. Watson, *Annals*, 1:297–98; Richard D. Brown, "Shifting Freedoms of the Press," in Amory and Hall, *History of the Book in America*, 1:368–71.
82. The narrative sold for 2s 6d in Philadelphia, the conventional price for pamphlets. *Gazette*, December 15, 1737, and April 13, 1738.
83. *Remarks on Zenger's Tryal*.
84. Fisher et al., "Andrew Hamilton, Esq.," 2.
85. *Mercury*, May 4, 1738.
86. *Gazette*, May 25, 1738. For Webbe's role in Philadelphia print culture, see chap. 5 in this work.
87. While the Zenger case left no lasting impact as a precedent, the notion that juries could decide law rather than simply establish fact remained a topic of public discussion in Philadelphia into the 1770s. See, for example, the *Pennsylvania Chronicle*, January 20 and February 3, 10, and 17, 1772.
88. Fletcher and MacCulloch, *Tudor Rebellions*, 158.
89. Chitty, *Treatise on the Game Laws*, 249, 259, 261, 333; Bowden, "Agricultural Prices, Farm Profits," 4:611–14.
90. *Provincial Council*, 1:22.
91. *Statutes*, 1:75, 2:75.
92. *Provincial Council*, 1:54. See also Weir, "Conservation, Class, and Controversy," 103–5. Penn reconfirmed the right to "fish, fowle & hunt" on private land or on lands not claimed by the proprietor in discussions over the 1701 Charter of Privileges. *Provincial Council*, 2:43.
93. *Provincial Council*, 1:54.
94. *Statutes*, 4:194–96.
95. Ibid., 263–65.

96. *Provincial Council,* 4:17–18; Weir, "Conservation, Class, and Controversy," 104.
97. *Provincial Council,* 4:284.
98. *Archives,* 1st Ser., 1:553.
99. Ibid., 553–54.
100. Quoted in Weir, "Conservation, Class, and Controversy," 104.
101. *Statutes,* 6:93–96.
102. Pearl, *Conceived in Crisis,* 48–49.
103. *To the Freemen of Pennsylvania.*
104. Thayer, "Town into City," in Weigley, *Philadelphia,* 105; *Common Council,* 590–92; *Statutes,* 5:215–19.
105. *Common Council,* 419–25; Watson, *Annals,* 1:212.
106. *Common Council,* 512–13; Watson, *Annals,* 1:212.
107. *Statutes,* 5:111–28.
108. *Common Council,* 561.
109. James Murphey also petitioned for remittance of a fine for assaulting the watch at the same meeting. *Common Council,* 576. For additional examples of assaults against watchmen and constables, see Mayor's Court Docket, May Session, 1760, PCA. See also Quarter Sessions Court Docket, March 3, 1755, and June 5, 1758, PCA.
110. More, *American Country Almanack for the Year 1754.*
111. Noble, *Terror to Some Lawyers.*
112. *Provincial Council,* 1:38.

4. "A GROWING EVIL IN THE CITY"

1. George Fox claimed execution for stealing was "contrary to the law of God in the old time," and in the 1690s the Friend and social reformer John Bellers opposed the death penalty altogether. Fitzroy, "Punishment of Crime," 244; Marietta and Rowe, *Troubled Experiment,* 7.
2. *Statutes,* 3:199–200. Between 1688 and 1820 the number of crimes designated as capital offenses in England increased from fifty to more than two hundred, creating what scholars call the "bloody code." Historiography on crime and criminal law in early modern England is substantial, but see Gaskill, *Crime and Mentalities;* T. Hitchcock and Shoemaker, *London Lives;* Beattie, *Policing and Punishment in London.*
3. Ekirch, *Bound for America,* 1, 26–27, 114.
4. Cropping involved nailing the offender's ear to the pillory, followed by the cutting of the ear from the head, leaving it "cropped."

5. Marietta and Rowe, *Troubled Experiment,* 75–78.
6. As many as eighty thousand soldiers and sailors were demobilized in the years immediately following the war. Rogers, *Mayhem,* 5, 36, 46, 108. Philadelphia's three newspapers by this time were the *Mercury, Gazette,* and the new *Pennsylvania Journal.*
7. Ekirch, *Bound for America,* 206–8. See also G. Morgan and Rushton, *Eighteenth-Century Criminal Transportation,* 99; Ziegler, *Harlots, Hussies,* chap. 7.
8. For Quakers' adoption of nonviolence, see Reay, *Quakers and the English Revolution,* 83–84, 88–91.
9. Soderlund, *William Penn and the Founding,* 103–4.
10. *Provincial Council,* 1:38–39; Staughton, *Charter to William Penn,* 112–13, 121, 144.
11. *Provincial Council,* 1:31; Marietta and Rowe, *Troubled Experiment,* 10–12; Smolenski, *Friends and Strangers,* 50, 65–70.
12. *Statutes,* 1:110.
13. *Assembly,* 1:50, 51; *Statutes,* 1:117–18; *Provincial Council,* 1:163; Nicholas More to William Penn, December 1, 1684, in M. M. Dunn, *Papers of William Penn,* 2:608.
14. *Statutes,* 1:114, 118.
15. *Assembly,* 1:163–64.
16. *Provincial Council,* 1:527.
17. Ibid., 527–30.
18. *Statutes,* 2:6–12, 21–23, 54–56.
19. *Statutes,* 1:254–55; Staughton, *Charter to William Penn,* 274–75.
20. *Statutes,* 1:380–81. For contemporary laws in New York and the West Indies on which Pennsylvania legislators drew see *Collections of the New-York Historical Society for the Year 1912,* 37–38; Shaw, *Everyday Life in the Early English Caribbean,* 37–38.
21. Tomlins, *Freedom Bound,* 494–95.
22. Ibid., 495; *Statutes,* 2:77–79.
23. *Statutes,* 2:8, 77–79.
24. Ibid., 490, 491.
25. Tomlins, *Freedom Bound,* 495–96.
26. *Provincial Council,* 2:405–6.
27. Gaskill, *Crime and Mentalities,* 126, 132.
28. The classic work is K. Scott, *Counterfeiting in Colonial America.*
29. *Provincial Council,* 1:84–88. The method used by the group, whereby a merchant like Pickering supplied silversmiths with silver to be turned into coin, was a common one. For a similar counterfeiting ring in New York, see K. Scott, *Counterfeiting in Colonial America,* 18–21, 24; and Geobel and Naughton, *Law Enforcement in Colonial New York,* 95, 97.

30. *Provincial Council,* 1:85, 88.

31. For Pickering, see Bronner, "Philadelphia County Court of Quarter Sessions and Common Pleas, 1695," 177; *Assembly,* 1:111; *To the Representatives of the Free-Men of this Province.* For Fenton's counterfeiting career, see K. Scott, *Counterfeiting in Colonial America,* 24.

32. *Provincial Council,* 1:236.

33. Johnson, "What Must Poor People Do?," 132.

34. It is possible White and Jerome's case was settled out of court, as Elizabeth's relatives John White and Daniel Lunt provided recognizances of twenty pounds guaranteeing White's court appearance. Bronner, "Philadelphia County Court of Quarter Sessions," 91.

35. Grand Jury Presentments of John Sable and John Simes, 1702, Ancient Records, HSP; Johnson, "What Must Poor People Do?," 133; Salinger, *Taverns and Drinking,* 231–32, 300n.59.

36. *Common Council,* 98–99. For women, counterfeiting, and taverns in early New York, see Zabin, *Dangerous Economies,* esp. 16–21.

37. Influential residents like Jonathan Dickinson and James Logan also expressed concern at the number of immigrants arriving in Philadelphia and Pennsylvania. *Provincial Council,* 3:29, 32–34, 40–43; *Assembly,* 2:1238–39; Marietta and Rowe, *Troubled Experiment,* 21, 63.

38. *Statutes,* 3:167–71, 199–221; Marietta and Rowe, *Troubled Experiment,* 21.

39. The only discussion appears to have been Keith's recommended amendments, which were quickly approved. *Assembly,* 2:1266, 1277–78. The statute was written by the lawyer and longtime antiproprietary assemblyman David Lloyd. Marietta and Rowe, *Troubled Experiment,* 22.

40. *Provincial Council,* 3:109–10.

41. New York's first bills of credit were issued in 1709. In 1713 counterfeited New York money was passed in Philadelphia, and alleged counterfeiter James Marks was apprehended in Philadelphia and repatriated to New York. *Provincial Council,* 2:566; K. Scott, *Counterfeiting in Colonial America,* 32–33.

42. *Assembly,* 3:1806–7; Johnson, "What Must Poor People Do?," 139–40; K. Scott, *Counterfeiting in Colonial America,* 72–76.

43. *Gazette,* December 19, 1732. For this episode, see also Johnson, "What Must Poor People Do?," 136–37; K. Scott, *Counterfeiting in Colonial America,* 78–79; P. Thompson, *Rum Punch and Revolution,* 88–89.

44. *Gazette,* June 21, 1733, January 18, 1734.

45. *Statutes,* 4:358; *Provincial Council,* 4:274–76; Johnson, "What Must Poor People Do?," 140; K. Scott, *Counterfeiting in Colonial America,* 70.

46. *Archives,* 1st ser., 1:578–81, 619–21; *Provincial Council,* 4:422, 429; K. Scott, *Counterfeiting in Colonial America,* 6, 87–92.

47. Brick's story was corroborated by a husband or brother named William. *Archives*, 1st ser., 1:619–23; Johnson, "What Must Poor People Do?," 141–42; *Provincial Council*, 4:429.
48. *Common Council*, 279.
49. Ibid., 285–86, 300–301, 319, 358.
50. *Assembly*, 3:2503, 2504.
51. The Transportation Act gave British courts more flexibility in sentencing: for example, allowing transportation for seven years for pardoned felons. For the text of the act, see Ziegler, *Harlots, Hussies*, appendix 4.
52. *Statues*, 3:264–68.
53. In the following decades the Pennsylvania legislature regularly updated the law in an effort to exclude transported felons and needy immigrants alike. *Statues*, 4:135–40, 164–71; *Archives*, 1st Ser., 1:306, 325–26; *Provincial Council*, 5:48, 66, 101.
54. *Assembly*, 3:2528.
55. *Provincial Council*, 4:47; *Gazette*, May 13, 1736. Edith Ziegler notes that of 233 women sentenced to death at London's Old Bailey between 1718 and 1743, 47 (20.2 percent) received respites because of pregnancy. Another 97 (41.6 percent) received conditional pardons; most of these were transported. *Harlots, Hussies*, 26.
56. *Gazette*, May 26 and July 7, 1737.
57. *Assembly*, 3:2530, 2536.
58. Ibid., 2542, 2544.
59. *Common Council*, 458–59, 460.
60. *Gazette*, April 22, 1736, May 26 and July 14, 1737; *New-York Weekly Mercury*, May 10, 1736; *Provincial Council*, 4:47, 5:155, 157–58, 210–11.
61. Marietta and Rowe, *Troubled Experiment*, 77–78, 80; Beattie, *Policing and Punishment in London*, 304, 343, 432–33, 435; Greenberg, *Crime and Law Enforcement in New York*, 130–31.
62. *Common Council*, 310. Jones stood in the pillory for an hour with an Indian named Glascow for his crime, after which they were whipped through town at the cart's tail. The same day Margaret Cash received twenty-one lashes at the whipping post for theft. *Gazette*, November 12, 1730.
63. Marietta and Rowe, *Troubled Experiment*, 93.
64. *Statutes*, 4:59–64.
65. J. Scott, *Weapons of the Weak*, xvi, 29, 248, 249; Guha, *Elementary Aspects of Peasant Insurgency*, 139–42; Beckles, *White Servitude and Black Slavery in Barbados*, 102, 109.
66. *Provincial Council*, 4:243–44.
67. MacMillan, *Stories of True Crime*; Kinney, *Rogues, Vagabonds*.

68. *Gazette,* June 17, 1731, and March 14, 1738.
69. Burke, *Popular Culture in Early Modern Europe,* 165–66; Gaskill, *Crime and Mentalities,* 135, 168–69; Waldstreicher, *Runaway America,* 22–23.
70. *Mercury,* March 8, 24, and April 7, 21, 1719, and June 16, July 23, and September 22, 1720.
71. *Gazette,* October 1 and November 2, 15, 1728.
72. *Mercury,* January 2, 1722; *Statutes,* 3:264–68.
73. *Blood will out, or, an Example of Justice in the Tryal, Condemnation, Confession and Execution of Thomas Lutherland.*
74. There was widespread popular hostility to George I and his new Whig ministry; a series of riots broke out in southern and western England at his accession in October 1714. Nearly fifteen hundred rebels were taken at Preston, many of them, like Hunt, transported to the colonies. For Jacobite risings in 1715 and 1745, see Szechi, *The Jacobites,* chap. 3.
75. *Mercury,* November 24, 1720.
76. Ibid. See also Johnson, "What Must Poor People Do?," 134–35; Meranze, *Laboratories of Virtue,* 39.
77. Beattie, *Policing and Punishment in London,* 343, 432–35.
78. Of seventeen sentenced to be hanged in the colony between 1718 and 1729, eight (47 percent) were executed; of twenty sentenced between 1730 and 1739, five (25 percent) were killed; fourteen of twenty-three (63 percent) were executed in the 1750s; twenty-six of thirty-four (76.5 percent) in the 1760s; and fifty-one of eighty-eight (57.9 percent) were executed in the 1770s. Marietta and Rowe note that between 1682 and 1800, 58.2 percent of those accused of capital crimes were killed in Pennsylvania. *Troubled Experiment,* 78. The rising rates of execution after midcentury follow trends discovered by Douglas Greenberg in New York. *Crime and Law Enforcement in New York,* 223.
79. *Provincial Council,* 3:110, 240, 244; *Common Council,* 279; K. Scott, *Counterfeiting in Early America,* 54–55.
80. *Gazette,* December 30, 1729.
81. I have been able to locate only one pardon in Philadelphia at this time—that of James Smith, sentenced to death for burglary. *Provincial Council,* 3:370.
82. *Gazette,* January 13, 27, 1730. See also Meranze, *Laboratories of Virtue,* 41–43; Waldstreicher, *Runaway America,* 95–96.
83. *Gazette,* November 10, 1730, and June 3, 1731.
84. S. Bullock, "Mumper among the Gentle"; Waldstreicher, "Reading the Runaways."
85. *Gazette,* March 4, 1735.
86. Ibid., March 27, 1735.
87. *Provincial Council,* 3:240; *Gazette,* December 22, 1737.

88. G. Morgan and Rushton, *Eighteenth-Century Criminal Transportation*, 181.

89. Poulter, *Discoveries of John Poulter*, 28; Ziegler, *Harlots, Hussies*, 44.

90. Carew, *Life and Adventures*, 83–84, 103–6.

91. Ibid., 109, 111–18.

92. *Boston Post-Boy*, March 4, 1751; *Pennsylvania Gazette*, April 21, 1773; *New-York Gazette and the Weekly Mercury*, January 18, 1773; *Norwich Packet or, the Chronicle of Freedom*, March 25, 1784; *Independent Ledger and the American Advertiser*, May 24, 1784.

93. S. Bullock, "Mumper among the Gentle," 232.

94. *Gazette*, June 16, 1743, July 12, 1744, and September 14, 1749; NYWPB, November 5, 1744, and April 14, 1746.

95. *Gazette*, September 14, 1749.

96. The main returned transport is Ben Budge, who with Matt the Mint argues Robinhood-like for theft in the interests of wealth redistribution. Gay, *Beggar's Opera*, act 2, scene 1, 2627–29. For the opera in New York, see O. Johnson and Burling, *Colonial American Stage*, 139.

97. See Rogers, *Mayhem*, chap. 7.

98. *Gazette*, August 20, 1752; Bullock, "Mumper among the Gentle," 255–56.

99. Within a year of the peace of Aix-la-Chapelle, approximately forty thousand seamen and marines were demobilized; some forty thousand more found themselves unemployed by 1753. Though more servicemen (157,000) were actually demobilized after the Treaty of Utrecht in 1713, Nicholas Rogers attributes the crime panic in England to the growing importance of the press, particularly newspapers as well in the works of authors like Henry Fielding. Rogers, *Mayhem*, 5, 36, 41–44, 108–9. For rising crime rates following wars, see Beattie, *Policing and Punishment in London*, 335, 339, 370; Ziegler, *Harlots, Hussies*, 12.

100. *Journal*, December 20, 27, 1748.

101. NYWPB, August 21 and September 4, 18, 1749; *Gazette*, August 24, 31, and September 7, 14, 1749; *Journal*, September 7, 1749. The two men executed for housebreaking were John Gillespie and John Roach. *Journal*, June 22, 1749.

102. *Journal*, September 28, 1749; *Gazette*, September 28, 1749; *Provincial Council*, 5:413–14.

103. *Journal*, October 5, 12, 19, 26, 1749; NYWPB, October 2, 9, 23, 1749.

104. Shoemaker, "Street Robber and the Gentle Highwayman."

105. *Gazette*, November 1 and December 25, 1750, and January 1, 8, 15, 1751; NYWPB, November 5 and December 24, 31, 1750.

106. *Gazette*, January 22, 1751. See also NYWBP, January 28, 1751.

107. *Journal*, January 23 and February 5, 19, 1751; *Gazette*, January 23 and February 5, 1751.

108. Journeymen workers earned between four and five pence per day at this time. For the chapbook's ad, see the *Gazette*, February 19, 1751.

109. *Account of the Robberies Committed by John Morrison*, 3–5.

110. Ibid., 5–11.

111. *NYWPB*, February 25, 1751; *Journal*, March 5, 1751.

112. *Gazette*, April 4, 1751.

113. Ibid., April 11, 1751.

114. Ibid., May 9, 1751.

115. Ibid., April 11, 1751; *NYWPB*, April 15, 1751.

116. *Gazette*, February 25, 1752, and February 19, 1754.

117. Thomas Penn to James Hamilton, July 29, 1751, and March 9, 1752, Correspondence of Thomas and Richard Penn with James Hamilton, 1741–71, American Philosophical Society.

118. Rosencrantz, *Life and Confession*.

119. Typical by this time was a public whipping of twenty-one lashes along with restitution, payment of courts costs, and the posting of sureties for good behavior. See Philadelphia Court of Quarter Sessions, 1753–60, PCA; Philadelphia Mayor's Court Docket, 1759–64, PCA.

120. Philadelphia Mayor's Court Docket, July 1759, PCA.

121. See sessions dockets in the years 1756–59, Quarter Sessions Court Docket, Philadelphia County, 1753–60, PCA.

122. Quoted in Watson, *Annals*, 1:361.

123. Mittelberger, *Journey to Pennsylvania*, 67, 72–73.

124. Gottlieb, "Class and Capital Punishment"; Greenberg, *Crime and Law Enforcement in New York*, 223.

125. *Independent Reflector*, March 15, 1753.

5. THE URBAN BATTLE OF IDEAS

1. *Gazette*, February 12, 1741. For a contemporary New York essay addressing similar issues, see *Independent Reflector*, November 1, 1753.

2. For urban order in Europe, see Friedrichs, *Early Modern City*, 245–74; Cowan, *Urban Europe*, 181–84.

3. Wrightson, *Earthly Necessities*, 335; E. P. Thompson, "Moral Economy of the English Crowd."

4. Thomas, *Man and the Natural World*; Beier, *Social Thought in England*.

5. For the understudied urban vision, see Musselwhite, *Urban Dreams, Rural Commonwealths*.

6. Smolenski, *Friends and Strangers*.

7. Middleton, *From Privileges to Rights*; McConville, *These Daring Disturbers*; Schultz, *Republic of Labor*.

8. Habermas, *Structural Transformation of the Public Sphere*; Warner, *Letters of the Republic*; Amory and Hall, *History of the Book in America 1*.

9. Economic, social, and technological transformations resulted in agricultural expansion, commercialization, and urbanization in the tenth and eleventh centuries, which put new pressures on traditional organicist theories of a static society of orders. Duby, *The Three Orders*; Dyer, *Making a Living*; Arnold, *Belief and Unbelief.*

10. From The *Book of Common Prayer*, reprinted in Aughterson, *English Renaissance*, 21.

11. Somerset, *Four Wycliffite Dialogues*; Barbara Johnson, *Reading* Piers Plowman *and* Pilgrim's Progress, 75–76.

12. Spufford, *World of Rural Dissenters*; Hill, *World Turned Upside Down.*

13. Como, *Blown by the Spirit*; Hill, *World Turned Upside Down.*

14. Hughes, *Gangraena and the Struggle for the English Revolution.*

15. Baxter, *Quakers Catechism.*

16. The Colchester minister Henry Glisson claimed in 1656 that Quaker leader James Parnel's views on sin, perfection, and the last days proved he was a disciple of Familist Henry Niclaes, whose works were published in England in 1574 and 1649. Davies, *Quakers in English Society*, 131.

17. Penn, *Preface*, [8].

18. N. Smith, *Collection of Ranter Writings*, 8–9; Hill, *World Turned Upside Down*, chaps. 9, 10. For evidence of self-identified Ranters in colonial New Jersey, see McConville, "Confessions of an American Ranter."

19. Fox, *Several Papers*, 10, 16, 17.

20. Baxter, *Quakers Catechism*, preface, 2, 4.

21. Billing, *Mite of Affection.*

22. Reay, "Quakers and 1659," 106.

23. Barclay, *Anarchy of the Ranters*, iii, 3.

24. Penn, *Brief Examination and State of Liberty Spiritual*, 8.

25. Budd, *Good Order Established in Pennsilvania*, 1.

26. Thomas, *Historical and Geographical Account of Pensilvania*, reprinted in Myers, *Narratives*, 331, 333.

27. In the early 1650s James Nayler and George Fox opposed using universities to train ministers, and Quakers were prominent figures in early modern movements for educational reform. For literacy and education among early Quakers, see Davies, *Quakers in English Society*, chap. 9.

28. Wall, "William Bradford, Colonial Printer"; Green, "Book Trade in the Middle Colonies," 200.

29. Green, "Book Trade in the Middle Colonies," 201–5.

30. *To the Representatives of the Free-Men of this Province of Pennsylvania.*

31. Butler, "Gospel Order Improved"; Butler, "Into Pennsylvania's Spiritual Abyss"; Smolenski, *Friends and Strangers*, chap. 4.

32. Hostilities descended to the level of a street brawl in 1693, after Keithians harangued Friends from a gallery outside the Philadelphia meeting house. P. Thompson, *Rum Punch and Revolution*, 123–24.

33. P. Thompson, *Rum Punch and Revolution*, 124; Smolenski, *Friends and Strangers*, 161.

34. G. Keith, *George Keith's Account of a National Church, and the Clergy, &c.*; G. Keith, *Refutation of a Dangerous & Hurtful Opinion*; G. Keith, *Doctrine of the Holy Apostles & Prophets*.

35. Colley, *Britons*, 20.

36. Stowell, "American Almanacs and Feuds," 276. See also Eisenstadt, "Almanacs and Disenchantment."

37. Capp, *English Almanacs*; Stowell, "American Almanacs and Feuds"; Pencak, "Politics and Ideology in Eighteenth-Century Almanacs," 157–96.

38. Atkins, *Kalendarium Pennsilvaniense*; Green, "Book Trade in the Middle Colonies," 201.

39. Leeds, *Almanack for the Year of Christian Account 1687*; Pencak, "Politics and Ideology in Eighteenth-Century Almanacs," 158.

40. In 1688 Bradford also published Leeds's *Temple of Wisdom* in Philadelphia, a philosophical treatise largely concerned with the work of the German mystic Jacob Boehme (1575–1624), another influence on early radical Quaker thought and further evidence of the diversity of ideas circulating in and around the town in the late seventeenth century.

41. See, for example, How, *Sufficiencie of the Spirits Teaching*.

42. Talbot and Leeds, *Great Mistery of Fox-Craft Discovered*, 7 (quote).

43. For Pusey's response, see Smolenski, *Friends and Strangers*, 230–31.

44. Stowell, "American Almanacs and Feuds," 279–81.

45. Taylor, *Almanack for the Year 1705*, n.p.

46. Birkett, *Almanack for the Year of Christ, 1730*.

47. Shields, "Eighteenth-Century Literary Culture," 465–66.

48. *Archives*, 2nd Ser., 7:15–16.

49. I. Norris, *Friendly Advice to the Inhabitants of Pensilvania*; Smolenski, *Friends and Strangers*, 193.

50. For English monetary debates, see Appleby, "Locke, Liberalism and the Natural Law"; Wennerlind, *Casualties of Credit*.

51. Rawle, *Some Remedies Proposed*.

52. *Provincial Council*, 3:143, 145.

53. *Mercury*, February 16, 1720.

54. In the early 1770s an agricultural writer noted Pennsylvania country gentlemen lived similarly to those in England, but "little Freeholders" were far more numerous than in the home country. *American Husbandry*, 1:185–86.

55. *Mercury*, February 20, 1722.

56. Ibid., May 31, 1722.

57. Ibid., June 21, 1722.

58. *Assembly*, 2:1459–60.

59. Logan, *Charge Delivered from the Bench*, 3–5, 7–8, 11–12.

60. *Mercury*, December 31, 1723.

61. Green, "Printing in the Age of Franklin," 251–52.

62. According to Gary Nash, forty-six political pamphlets were published between 1721 and 1729. See *Urban Crucible*, 149.

63. Keith, *Speech of William Keith*.

64. Logan, "The Antidote," 486–87.

65. *Triumvirate of Pennsylvania*.

66. *Revisal of the Intreagues of the Triumvirate*.

67. *The Establishment*, Dedicatory [9]. See also Burke, "Renaissance Dialogue."

68. Defoe, *Vindication of the Press*, 17.

69. Logan, *Dialogue Shewing what's therein to be found*, 29–30. See also P. Thompson, *Rum Punch and Revolution*, 127–28, 134.

70. *The Craftsman*, quoted in Wilson, *Sense of the People*, 130.

71. Logan, *Dialogue Shewing what's therein to be found*, 12–13.

72. Rawle, *A Just Rebuke to a Dialogue betwixt Simon and Timothy*.

73. W. Keith, *Observator's Trip to America*, 7, 9–12, 17.

74. Ibid., 10 (quote), 35; P. Thompson, *Rum Punch and Revolution*, 127–28.

75. Keith was removed from the governor's office in 1726, and after serving as a representative of the city in the assembly, the former governor left Philadelphia for England in 1728.

76. *Advice and Information to the Freeholders and Freemen of the Province of Pennsylvania; To the Freeholders and Freemen*. For a response that characterizes the author of the above pamphlets as a condescending "schoolmaster," see *Remarks on the Advice to the Freeholders*.

77. *Triumvirate of Pennsylvania; Revisal of the Intreagues of the Triumvirate; View of the Calumnies Lately Spread*.

78. *Franklin Papers*, 1:143–44, 149.

79. *Assembly*, 3:2049.

80. Green, "Printing in the Age of Franklin," 255–56; Shields, "Eighteenth-Century Literary Culture," 434–76.

81. Bushman, *Refinement of America*; Breen, *Marketplace of Revolution*.

82. *Gazette*, February 1, 1739.

83. Mandeville, *Fable of the Bees*; Tolles, *Meeting House and Counting House*, 177–78.

84. Butler, *Awash in a Sea of Faith*, 90–91.

85. J. Morgan, *Nature of Riches,* 3–5, 7–9.
86. Ibid., 5–6, 14.
87. Quoted in Butler, *Awash in a Sea of Faith,* 91.
88. *Advice to the Free-Holders and Electors of Pennsylvania,* 2, 7.
89. *Gazette,* March 25, April 1, and April 8, 1736. For the similarity of Webbe's arguments with those of the Levellers, see Schultz, *Republic of Labor,* 26–27.
90. *Gazette,* April 22, 1736.
91. In 1736 inhabitants of Philadelphia, Chester, and Bucks Counties sent separate petitions to the House opposing the court. *Assembly,* 3:2302, 2307, 2309–13, 2320.
92. *Gazette,* April 22, 1736.
93. *Mercury,* April 8, 22, 1736.
94. *Gazette,* April 22, 1736. Webbe acknowledged authorship of the Z essays in the *Gazette* in July 1737. He would write for the *Mercury* in later years, after having a falling out with Franklin in 1740. *Franklin Papers,* 2:145–46, 264–69, 270–74, 277–81.
95. *Gazette,* April 8, 1736.
96. Ibid., March 30, 1738.
97. Most printers' careers were short-lived, and they did not attempt to compete with Franklin or Bradford, instead setting up outside the city and in some cases printing in German. Green, "Printing in the Age of Franklin," 271–73. See also James Raven, "The Importation of Books in the Eighteenth Century," in Amory and Hall, *A History of the Book in America,* 1:183–98.
98. Green, "Printing in the Age of Franklin," 259–61.
99. Shields, "Eighteenth-Century Literary Culture," 438; Scribner, *Inn Civility,* 29–33.
100. Duché quoted in Wolf, *Book Culture,* 130.
101. Wolf, *Book Culture,* 79, 99–100, 115–21.
102. Hamilton, *Gentleman's Progress,* 18, 29. See also P. Thompson, *Rum Punch and Revolution,* 82–83, 120.
103. Quoted in Wolf, *Book Culture,* 130.
104. Franklin did try to appeal to Protestant Irish and the "warlike" and "brave" Germans of Pennsylvania, however. Franklin, *Plain Truth,* 5–7, 10–12, 13–14, 17–21.
105. Burgh, *Britain's Remembrancer,* 8–9, 14–17, 20, 39–47. The *Remembrancer* was also sold in Boston, New York, and Williamsburg by the end of the decade.
106. Tennant, *Late Association for Defence Encourag'd;* S. Smith, *Necessary Truth;* J. Smith, *Doctrine of Christianity.*
107. Penn quoted in Lemay, *Life of Benjamin Franklin,* 49.
108. *Provincial Council,* 6:1–3, 319; *Franklin Papers,* 6:266–67.

109. *Franklin Papers*, 6:297–301.

110. W. Smith, *Brief State of the Province of Pennsylvania*, 19, 36–37, 40–42.

111. *Tit for Tat, Or the Score Wip'd off.*

112. *Journal*, March 25, 1756, quoted in Ketcham, "Benjamin Franklin and William Smith," 148.

113. *Journal*, March 11 and May 20, 1756, quoted in ibid., 147–48, 150.

114. *Journal*, April 22, 1756, quoted in ibid., 149.

115. *True and Impartial State of the Province of Pennsylvania*, 9–12, 29, 40.

116. *To the King's Most Excellent Majesty in Council.*

6. POLITE SPACES AND NURSERIES OF VICE

1. Woodward, *Rise and Progress of the Religious Societies*; Bushman, *Refinement of America*; Shoemaker, "Reforming the City."

2. Thomas Holme, "A Short Advertisement upon the Scituation and Extent," in Myers, *Narratives*, 243; Dunn and Dunn, "The Founding," 7–10; Milroy, "For the like Uses, as the Moore-fields"; P. Thompson, *Rum Punch and Revolution*, 8.

3. Bullivant, *Glance at New York in 1697*, 18; Fontaine, *Journal*, 119.

4. P. Thompson, *Rum Punch and Revolution*; Roney, *Governed by a Spirit of Opposition*. For clubs in the colonies generally, see Shields, *Civil Tongues and Polite Letters*, chap. 6; and for England, see Brewer, *Pleasures of the Imagination*, 41–50.

5. Morrison, *Early American Architecture*, 537.

6. *Gazette*, June 4 and September 28, 1752, November 1, 1753; Wainwright, "Scull and Heap's East Prospect."

7. For taverns, see P. Thompson, *Rum Punch and Revolution*; Salinger, *Taverns and Drinking*. For lighting city streets, see Thayer, "Town into City," in Weigley, *Philadelphia*, 69; Watson, *Annals*, 1:211–12.

8. *Statutes*, 5:111. The statute was largely copied from a similar street-lighting act in the much larger city of London in 1736. For the significance of night in the early modern era, see Ekirch, *At Day's Close*; Koslofsky, *Evening's Empire*.

9. Though at various times Port Royale, Boston, and New York each could plausibly lay claim to being the British Atlantic's most disorderly city, Philadelphia's comparatively dramatic growth, embodied in the everyday tumults and disputes explored below, make it a major contender.

10. Dunn and Dunn, "The Founding," 7; Milroy, "For the like Uses, as the Moore-fields," 261; P. Thompson, *Rum Punch and Revolution*, 8.

11. J. R. Wordie estimates that three quarters of England was enclosed by 1760. "Chronology of English Enclosure." See also Greer, "Commons and Enclosure in North America."

12. Slack, *Invention of Improvement*; Thirsk, *Economic Policy and Projects*.

13. Penn, *A Further Account of the Province of Pennsylvania*, reprinted in Myers, *Narratives*, 260–62, 269–72.

14. This was an early source of argumentation during the Reformation between "radical" and "magisterial" reformers. See the documents collected in Baylor, *Radical Reformation*.

15. *Provincial Council*, 1:41.

16. For changing ideas about animals and the natural world, see Thomas, *Man and the Natural World*.

17. Penn, *Further Account of the Province of Pennsylvania*, reprinted in Myers, *Narratives*, 260.

18. Watson, *Annals*, 1:171; P. Thompson, *Rum Punch and Revolution*, 22.

19. *Provincial Council*, 1:163; Penn, "Letters of William Penn," 310.

20. Penn, "Letters of William Penn," 310.

21. *Archives*, 2nd Series, 19:11, 218; *Archives*, 3rd Ser., 3:385; P. Thompson, *Rum Punch and Revolution*, 31; Salinger, *Taverns and Drinking*, 171–72.

22. Presentments of John Simes et al., February 1702, Ancient Records, HSP. Peter Thompson notes that Simes was able to keep his tavern license, though he and his wife, Anne, ran into trouble with the law on multiple occasions in subsequent years. *Rum Punch and Revolution*, 47. See also Johnson, "Profane Language, Horrid Oaths," 1–2.

23. Watson, *Annals*, 1:257; Scharf and Westcott, *History of Philadelphia*, 1:157; Salinger, *Taverns and Drinking*, 231–32.

24. Hutton, *Rise and Fall of Merry England*, 8–9.

25. Bourne, *Antiquitates Vulgares*, 147–50.

26. Harris, "Problematising Popular Culture," in Harris, *Popular Culture in England*, 21.

27. *Archives*, 1:1, 155–56; *Statutes*, 2:186–87, 360–61.

28. Rath, *How Early America Sounded*; Johnson, "Profane Language, Horrid Oaths."

29. *Provincial Council*, 1:41; *Colonial Laws of New York*, 1:174–75; Shoemaker, "Reforming the City," 102.

30. Presentments of John Simes et al., February 1702, Ancient Records, HSP.

31. *Statutes*, 1:30, 69, 151, 153, 2:49, 99, 185.

32. Presentment of William Orion, Court of Quarter Sessions, 1685, Court Records of Philadelphia, 1685–86 (Am.3092), HSP.

33. Grand Inquest Presentment of George Robinson, 1702, Ancient Records, HSP; Bronner, "Philadelphia County Court of Quarter Sessions," 88, 176.

34. Johnson, "Profane Language, Horrid Oaths," 10.

35. Court Records of Philadelphia, 1685–86 (Am.3092), HSP; Grand Jury Presentments, 1702, Ancient Records, HSP. Peter Thompson notes that before

1771, though women ran approximately a quarter of Philadelphia taverns, nearly half of the prosecutions for keeping bawdy houses were against women. *Rum Punch and Revolution,* 45. For women tavernkeepers in early America in general, see Salinger, *Taverns and Drinking.*

36. Grand Jury petition, 1717, and Presentment of Mary Hutchins, 1722, Ancient Records, HSP; Bronner, "Philadelphia Court of Quarter Sessions," 89. For "scolding women" in New England, see Kamensky, *Governing the Tongue.*

37. This was not due to a reluctance on the part of magistrates to corporally punish women, however. John Smolenski notes that Pennsylvania officials were increasingly likely to whip women and African men in the first decade of the eighteenth century. *Friends and Strangers,* 198.

38. Hamilton, *Gentleman's Progress,* 29.

39. Smolenski, *Friends and Strangers,* 73–74, 131.

40. Anthony Moore plea of trespass against Elizabeth Hardin, 1709, Philadelphia Court Cases, 1710–13 (Am.3047), HSP.

41. For the lack of precision concerning what constituted privacy in the seventeenth century, see Norton, *Founding Mothers and Fathers,* 20–24, 402–3.

42. *Statutes,* 1:88, 176.

43. *Statutes,* 1:32; Norton, *Founding Mothers and Fathers,* 347–50; Block, *Rape and Sexual Power.*

44. Presentment of John Rambo, Court of Quarter Sessions, 1685, Philadelphia Court Records, 1685–86, HSP.

45. Indictments of Martha Wilbins and John Moon, ibid.

46. Bronner, "Philadelphia County Court of Quarter Sessions," 89–92.

47. *Statutes,* 2:5–7. In 1705 the statute was amended, with servants giving birth required to serve between one and two years, leaving it up to county justices to estimate the proper term. *Statutes,* 2:182.

48. Watson, *Annals,* 1:308–9; *Common Council,* 75, 85, 163, 678.

49. Raymond fled service after his conviction, a fact that angered Dodd as much as the prosecution. *Common Council,* 45.

50. See the indictments in the Court of Quarter Sessions Court Dockets, 1753–60, PCA; and Mayor's Court Docket, 1759–64, PCA. In 1762 John Clark's petition for the remission of his fine for fornication was rejected by the common council, and as late as 1774 inhabitants like Abraham Cornog were fined ten pounds for fornication. *Common Council,* 678, 794. For sex in the revolutionary era, see Lyons, *Sex among the Rabble.*

51. A. Fox, "Food, Drink and Social Distinction," 165–87.

52. Bullivant, *Glance at New York,* 17–18; A. Fox, "Food, Drink and Social Distinction," 180–81, 183.

53. Moraley, *Infortunate*, 68.

54. Bullivant, *Glance at New York*, 17–18; Scharf and Westcott, *History of Philadelphia*, 2:853; Morrison, *Early American Architecture*, 503.

55. Scharf and Westcott, *History of Philadelphia*, 2:856.

56. Bullivant, *Glance at New York*, 17–19.

57. Watson, *Annals*, 1:350, 353.

58. *Common Council*, 47, 51, 57, 59, 72; *Assembly*, 2:961; Scharf and Westcott, *Philadelphia*, 1:187.

59. *Archives*, 2nd Ser., 7:41; *Common Council*, 87–88.

60. *Common Council*, 227.

61. Ibid., 47, 51, 59, 72, 78, 79, 221–22.

62. In the city government's view this "Advantage" should have accrued to the corporation rather than to private individuals; it therefore ordered the building of new market spaces in the expectation of more municipal revenue. *Common Council*, 155.

63. Hucksters would meet sellers on the way to market, purchase ("engross") a provision, and later resell at a higher price. *Common Council*, 279–80, 293.

64. Burke, *Popular Culture in Early Modern Europe*; Johnson, "Profane Language, Horrid Oaths."

65. Ligon, *True & Exact History of the Island of Barbados*, 48.

66. Godwyn, *Negro's & Indians Advocate*, 144.

67. Sloane, *Voyage to the Islands Madera, Barbados, Nieves*, xlviii–li; Rath, "African Music in Seventeenth-Century Jamaica."

68. *Collections of the New-York Historical Society for the Year 1912*, 37–38.

69. *Provincial Council*, 1:380–81; Bronner, "Philadelphia County Court of Quarter Sessions," 92; Grand Jury Petition to the Mayor and Commonalty, 1702, Ancient Records, HSP; Petition of the Grand Inquest, 1717, Ancient Records, HSP.

70. *Franklin Papers*, 1:211–12; Waldstreicher, *Runaway America*, 93–94.

71. *Common Council*, 314, 326, 342, 376–77.

72. "To the worshipful the Mayor Recorder & Aldermen of the City of Philadelphia, January 1735/6," Records of Philadelphia County, 1671–1855 (Collection 1014) box 1, folder 14, HSP.

73. *Franklin Papers*, 1:212.

74. *Gazette*, March 5, 1751.

75. Shoemaker, "Decline of Public Insult in London," 114–16, 125.

76. *Gazette*, June 20, 1754. See also Fatherly, *Gentlewomen and Learned Ladies*.

77. *Gazette*, December 10, 1747.

78. Ibid., September 28, 1732.

79. The jury had made similar complaints in previous years. "Notes and Queries," 497–98.

80. "Notes and Queries," 498.

81. *Gazette*, September 1, 1737.

82. *New-York Weekly Journal*, March 7, 1736; Johnson, "Profane Language, Horrid Oaths," 17–19.

83. The *Mercury's* coverage was especially extensive between June and early August, 1741.

84. For speech, as well as frolics and music, see Horsmanden, *New York Conspiracy*, xii, 82, 94, 141, 227, 233, 256, 260, 330.

85. *Common Council*, 405.

86. "Notes and Queries," 498; P. Thompson, *Rum Punch and Revolution*, 42–43; B. Smith, *"Lower Sort,"* 21–22.

87. Watson, *Annals*, 1:383; Borsay, *English Urban Renaissance*; Bushman, *Refinement of America*.

88. Watson, *Annals*, 1:396. It was around this time that William Moraley stated wages for journeymen in Philadelphia hovered around five shillings per day. *Infortunate*, 89.

89. Pencak, Dennis, and Newman, *Riot and Revelry in Early America*, 6. The "fish dam riot" of 1738, discussed in chap. 3 of this work, might be considered evidence of such strains in Philadelphia County.

90. The following account of the tanners' controversy draws on Johnson, "Hot-Heads, Gentlemen." See also McMahon, "'Publick Service' versus 'Mans Properties.'"

91. Garzoni and Ameyden are quoted in Amelang, *Flight of Icarus*, 98.

92. Withington, *Politics of Commonwealth*, 29–30, 68, 106.

93. Johnson, "Hot-Heads, Gentlemen," 346; Glenn, "William Hudson," 336–39; *Common Council*, 128, 133. The yards of less prosperous tanners were located on the city's fringes.

94. The process of loosening hair from hides involved the soaking of hides in urine for long periods, which partly explained the noxious smells that emanated from tanyards. Johnson, "Hot-Heads, Gentlemen," 346; Finger, *Contagious City*, 3.

95. *Assembly*, 3:2487.

96. *Minutes of the Common Council of New York*, 1:21–25; Middleton, *Privileges to Rights*, 84–85.

97. *Gazette*, August 16, 1739.

98. See chap. 1 for complaints against tanners from other tradesmen.

99. Though local readers were often aware of the identity of anonymous authors, convention mandated a republican pretense of selfless anonymity, a practice broached by the *Gazette*.

100. *Gazette*, August 30, 1739.

101. *Mercury,* September 13, 1739.

102. *Gazette,* October 18, 1739.

103. For the yellow fever epidemic in 1699, see Finger, *Contagious City,* 35.

104. *Gazette,* October 18, 1739.

105. Ibid.

106. Johnson, "Hot-Heads, Gentlemen," 359; Pearl, *Conceived in Crisis,* 48; Olton, "Philadelphia's First Environmental Crisis," 92.

107. The only full-length article treatment of the controversy is Pencak, "Beginning of a Beautiful Friendship."

108. *Mercury,* September 28, 1738.

109. Bronner, "Village into Town," in Weigley, *Philadelphia,* 48–49.

110. Pencak, "Beginning of a Beautiful Friendship," 200; Nash and Soderlund, *Freedom by Degrees,* 29.

111. *Gazette,* May 1, 1740.

112. Pencak speculates that the writer was the Anglican priest Richard Peters. "Beginning of a Beautiful Friendship," 204.

113. *Gazette,* May 8, 1740; Pencak, "Beginning of a Beautiful Friendship," 201–2.

114. The inclusion of the letter in Franklin's *Gazette* testifies to a commitment to presenting opposing views, though it is also possible Franklin planned a rebuttal—and was aware that controversy made good copy.

115. *Gazette,* May 15, 1740.

116. Ibid., May 22, 1740.

117. Also included were intermeddling "Busy-bodies" who railed against innocent amusements, yet another reference to Franklin's identity. Pencak, "Beginning of a Beautiful Friendship," 207.

118. *Mercury,* May 22, 1740.

119. For print and the public in the seventeenth century, see Zaret, *Origins of Democratic Culture.*

120. *Assembly,* 4:2827–30; *Gazette,* October 7, 1742.

121. *Gazette,* October 7, 1742.

122. *Provincial Council,* 620–22; *Assembly,* 4:2983, 2984.

123. *Assembly,* 4:2830, 2834, 2843.

124. P. Thompson, *Rum Punch and Revolution,* 129–31; *Assembly,* 4:2846.

125. *Assembly,* 4:2981, 3003.

126. More than three months after the riot Cribb and Lester remained jailed, unable to pay a ten-pound fine for their involvement in the affair. *Common Council,* 419–20.

127. The theater's first production, *The Fair Penitent,* was attended by a "numerous and polite Audience." *Gazette,* April 25, 1754. In 1759 the powerful Quaker merchant and justice William Allen informed protesting Quakers that he

found more morality at plays than in sermons. Scharf and Westcott, *History of Philadelphia*, 2:864–65.

128. Scharf and Westcott, *History of Philadelphia*, 2:869–70.

129. *Common Council*, 463–64.

130. Gordon, "Journal of an Officer's Travels," 410–11.

131. Success was measured primarily by reductions in the costs of public relief. *Account of Several Work-Houses for Employing and Maintaining the Poor.*

132. Nash, "Poverty and Poor Relief"; Wulf, *Not All Wives*, 156–61.

133. *Franklin Papers*, 5:284–86. See also *Statutes*, 5:128–30.

134. For additional examples, see *Gazette*, July 19, 1739, February 2, 1744, and April 3, 1746.

135. *Gazette*, August 31, 1749.

136. Levy, "Levelers and Fugitives," 20–21.

137. *Gazette*, June 27, 1734. Similar markings were evident some years later when Nell of East Jersey, formerly of New York City and who was suspected to be harbored in the region, was noted for the diamonds on either side of her face and forehead. *NYWPB*, April 23, 1753.

138. *Gazette*, June 27, 1734; *New-York Weekly Journal*, June 24 and July 1, 1734. For tattooing among sailors in early republican Philadelphia, see S. Newman, *Embodied History*, chap. 5.

139. *Account of Several Work-Houses for Employing and Maintaining the Poor,* 25, 34–35, 53–54, 69.

140. *Whereas the Number of Poor in and around this City;* Nash, "Poverty and Poor Relief," 14.

141. Nash, "Poverty and Poor Relief," 26; Foner, *Tom Paine and Revolutionary America*, 46–47.

142. *Gazette*, August 20, 1741. Alan Tully suggests the burning of Penn's effigy was a response to the proprietor's land policy as well as his support for Governor Thomas during the war controversy of 1740–41. *Forming American Politics*, 264.

143. B. Smith, *"Lower Sort,"* 82, 104, 125, 163; P. Thompson, *Rum Punch and Revolution*, chap. 5.

CONCLUSION

1. Townspeople could also purchase a reprinted defense of Wilkes. See *Account of the Proceedings against John Wilkes, Esq.*

2. *New-Year Verses of the Printers Lads.*

3. *Imported in the Last Vessels from Europe.*

4. Egnal, "Economic Development of the Thirteen Colonies," fig. 1 (206).

5. *True and Impartial State of the Province of Pennsylvania*, ii.

6. John Smith is quoted in Woolman, *Journal and Major Essays*, 139–40.

7. Ibid., 118–19, 146–51.

8. Williamson, *Life and Curious Adventures*, 10–11.

9. Allen, *Life, Experience, and Gospel Labours*, 6.

10. One key difference, however, was that by the early nineteenth century writers like Watson could idealize slavery in the Quaker city—albeit in traditional terms of reciprocity and deference. Watson, *Annals*, 1:176–77.

11. Bouton, *Taming Democracy*; Stewart, *Redemption from Tyranny*.

BIBLIOGRAPHY

MANUSCRIPTS

HISTORICAL SOCIETY OF PENNSYLVANIA

Ancient Records of Philadelphia
Collection 1684–1854
James Hamilton Collection
James Logan Papers, 1670–1749
James T. Mitchell Collection
John A. H. Shober Collection
Joseph B. Francus Collection
Joseph Richardson Papers
Miscellaneous Collection, 1676–1937
Philadelphia County Records, 1671–1855
Philadelphia Court Records, 1676–1825
Prophecy and Dream, 1757–68

PHILADELPHIA CITY ARCHIVES

Mayor's Court Docket, 1759–64
Quarter Sessions Court Docket, 1753–60

PERIODICALS

American Weekly Mercury
Independent Reflector
New-York Gazette
New-York Journal or General Advertiser
New-York Mercury
New-York Weekly Journal and Post-Boy
Pennsylvania Chronicle
Pennsylvania Gazette
Pennsylvania Journal

PRINTED EPHEMERA

(Place of publication Philadelphia unless otherwise noted)

An Account of the Proceedings against John Wilkes, Esq; Member of Parliament for Aylesbury, and late colonel of the Buckinghamshire militia. 1763.

An Account of the Robberies Committed by John Morrison, And his Accomplices, in and near Philadelphia, 1750. 1751.

Advice and Information to the Freeholders and Freemen of the Province of Pennsylvania, and particularly to those of the County and City of Philadelphia. 1727.

Advice to the Free-holders and Electors of Pennsylvania. 1735.

Atkins, Samuel. *Kalendarium Pennsilvaniense, Or, America's Messinger.* 1685.

Barclay, Robert. *The Anarchy of the Ranters and other Libertines, the hierarchy of the Romanists, and other pretended churches, equally refused and refuted in a two-fold apology for the church and people of God called in derision Quakers.* London, 1676.

Baxter, Richard. *The Quakers Catechism; Or, the Quakers Questioned.* London, 1655.

Benezet, Anthony. *A Caution and a Warning to Great Britain and Her Colonies, in a short representation of the calamitous state of the enslaved Negroes in the British dominions: Collected from various authors, and submitted to the serious consideration of all, more especially of those in power.* 1766.

———. *A Short Account of that Part of Africa, Inhabited by the Negroes; with respect to the fertility of the country; the good disposition of many of the natives, and the manner by which the slave trade is carried on.* 1762.

Billing, Edward. *A Mite of Affection, Manifested in 31. Proposals offered to all the sober and free-born people within this common-wealth; tending and tendred unto them for a Settlement in this Day and hour of the Worlds Distraction and Confusion* London, 1659.

Birkett, William. *An Almanack for the Year of Christ, 1730.* 1729.

Blackwell, John. *An Essay Towards Carrying on the Present War with France.* London, 1695.

Blood will out, or, an Example of Justice in the Tryal, Condemnation, Confession and Execution of Thomas Lutherland, who barbously murthered the body of John Clark of Philadelphia, and was executed at Salem in West-Jarsey the 23d of February, 1691/2. 1692.

A Brief Dolorous Remonstrance: Or, the pittiful Complaint, Outcry, and Request of poor destroyed Prisoners for Debt, unto all compassionate free-born Englishmen. London, 1648.

Budd, Thomas. *Good Order Established in Pennsilvania & New-Jersey in America.* 1685.

Bullock, William. *Virginia Impartially examined, and left to publick view, to be considered by all Iudicious and honest men.* London, 1649.

Burgh, James. *Britain's Remembrancer: Or, the danger not over.* 1747.

Burrough, Edward. *Answers to Severall Queries put forth to the Despised People called Quakers, by Philip Bennet.* London, 1654.

Chew, Samuel. *The Speech of Samuel Chew, Esq; chief justice of the government of New-Castle, Kent and Sussex upon Delaware: delivered from the bench to the grand-jury of the county of New-Castle, Nov. 21. 1741; and now published at their request.* 1741.

A Dialogue between Mr. Robert Rich and Roger Plowman. 1725.

Englands Dolefull Lamentation: Or, the cry of the oppressed and enslaved Commons of England. London, 1647.

The Establishment, Or, A Discourse tending to the setling of the Minds of Men, about some of the chiefe Controversies of the present Times. London, 1654.

Fox, George, and James Naylor. *Several Papers; Some of them given forth by George Fox; others by James Nayler.* London, 1654.

Franklin, Benjamin. *Plain Truth: Or, Serious Considerations on the Present State of the City of Philadelphia and Province of Pennsylvania.* 1747.

How, Samuel. *The Sufficiencie of the Spirits Teaching, without Humane-Learning.* London, 1640.

The Humble Remonstrance and Complaint of many Thousands of Poore Distressed Prisoners in the Prisons in and about the Citie of London committed for debt and other uncapitall Offences. London, 1643.

Imported in the Last Vessels from Europe, and Sold by David Hall at the New Printing-Office in Market Street, Philadelphia, the following Books &c. 1763.

The Innocent Assemblies, and Good Order of the People of God (called Quakers) Vindicated from the gross Aspersions Calumnies and Slanders of Two Clamorous Jeering Pamphlets. London, 1669.

Keith, George. *The Doctrine of the Holy Apostles & Prophets, the Foundation of the Church of Christ, as it was Delivered in a Sermon at Her Majesty's Chapel, at Boston in New-England, the 14th of June 1702.* Boston, 1702.

———. *An Exhortation & Caution to Friends Concerning buying or keeping of Negroes.* 1693.

———. *Mr. George Keith's Account of a National Church, and the Clergy, &c., Humbly Presented to the Bishop of London.* London, 1701.

———. *A Refutation of a Dangerous & Hurtful Opinion Maintained by Mr. Samuel Willard, an Independent Minister at Boston.* New York, 1702.

Keith, William. *The Observator's Trip to America.* 1726.

———. *The Speech of William Keith, Bart., Governour of the Province of Pennsylvania, and the Counties of New-Castle, Kent and Sussex upon Delaware, to the Representatives of the Freemen of the Said Province of Pennsylvania, in General Assembly met, January 5, 1724–5.* 1725.

Leeds, Daniel. *An Almanack for the Year of Christian Account 1687.* 1686.

Lloyd, David. *A Vindication of the Legislative Power.* 1725.

Logan, James. *The Charge Delivered from the Bench to the Grand-Jury.* 1723.

——. *A Dialogue Shewing What's therein to be found.* 1725.

Mather, Cotton. *A Brief Discourse on the Necessary Properties & Practices Of a Good Servant.* Boston, 1696.

More, Thomas. *The American Country Almanack for the Year of Christian Account 1754.* 1753.

Morgan, Joseph. *The Nature of Riches.* 1732.

The Nature and Importance of Oaths and Juries. New York, 1747.

Naylor, James. *A Vindication of Truth, as held forth in a Book, Entitled Love to the Lost.* London, 1656.

New-Year Verses of the Printers Lads, who Carry the Pennsylvania Gazette *to the Customers.* 1764.

Noble, William. *A Terror to Some Lawyers.* 1749.

Norris, Isaac. *Friendly Advice to the Inhabitants of Pensilvania.* 1710.

——. *The Speech Delivered from the Bench in the Court of Common Pleas held for the City and County of Philadelphia, the 11 day of September, 1727.* 1727.

Penn, William. *A Brief Examination and State of Liberty Spiritual both with respect to persons in their private capacity and in their church society and communion.* London, 1681.

——. *The Excellent Priviledge of Liberty & Property, Being the Birth-Right of the Free-born Subjects of England.* 1687.

——. *The Preface, Being a Summary Account of the Divers Dispensations of God to Men, from the beginning of the world to that of our present age, by the minstry and testimony of his faithful servant George Fox, as an introduction to the ensuing Journal.* London, 1694.

Petition of divers of the Inhabitants of the County of Chester, To the Honourable Representatives of the Freemen of the Province of Pennsylvania, in General Assembly met. 1764.

Poulter, John. *The Discoveries of John Poulter, alias Baxter.* Sherborne, 1774.

A Prophecy, Lately Discovered; In which are Predicted Many Great and Terrible Events. 1763.

Rawle, Francis. *A Just Rebuke to a Dialogue betwixt Simon and Timothy.* 1726.

——. *Some Remedies Proposed for the Restoring the Sunk Credit of the Province of Pennsylvania.* 1721.

Remarks on the Advice to the Freeholders, &c. 1727.

Remarks on Zenger's Tryal, Taken out of the Barbados Gazettes; For the Benefit of the Students in Law, and Others in North-America. 1737.

A Revisal of the Intreagues of the Triumvirate. 1729.

Rosencrantz, Herman. *The Life and Confession of Herman Rosencrantz; executed in the city of Philadelphia, on the 5th day of May, 1770, for counterfeiting and uttering the bills of credit of the province of Pennsylvania.* 1770.

Sandiford, Ralph. *The Mystery of Iniquity; in a brief Examination of the Practice of the Times.* 1730.

Smith, John. *The Doctrine of Christianity, as held by the People called Quakers, Vindicated.* 1748.

Smith, Samuel. *Necessary Truth: Or, Seasonable Considerations for the Inhabitants of Philadelphia and Pennsylvania.* 1748.

Smith, William. *A Brief State of the Province of Pennsylvania.* London, 1755.

Talbot, John, and Daniel Leeds. *The Great Mistery of Fox-Craft Discovered.* New York, 1705.

Taylor, Jacob. *An Almanack for the Year 1705.* 1704.

Tennant, Gilbert. *The Late Association for Defence Encourag'd; Or, the lawfulness of a Defense War.* 1747.

Tit for Tat, Or the Score Wip'd off. 1755.

To the Freeholders and Freemen: A Further Information. 1727.

To the Freemen of Pennsylvania, and more especially to those of the City and County of Philadelphia. 1755.

To the King's Most Excellent Majesty in Council, the Petition of the Freeholders and Inhabitants of Pennsylvania. 1764.

To My Respected Friend I.N. 1727.

To the Representatives of the Free-Men of this Province of Pennsilvania and Counties Annexed, in Assembly Convened at Philadelphia the 10th of the 3d Month, 1692. 1692.

The Tripple-Plea. 1723.

The Triumvirate of Pennsylvania, In a Letter to a Friend in the Country. 1725.

A True and Impartial State of the Province of Pennsylvania. 1759.

A View of the Calumnies Lately Spread. 1729.

Webbe, John. *A Discourse Concerning Paper Money.* 1743.

Whereas Great Quantities of English Copper . . . 1741.

Whereas the Number of Poor in and around this City . . . 1764.

Woodward, Josiah. *An Account of the Rise and Progress of the Religious Societies in the City of London, &c. And the Endeavours for Reformation of Manners that have been made therein.* London, 1698.

Woolman, John. *Considerations on Pure Wisdom, and Human Policy; On Labour; On Schools; And on the Right Use of the Lord's Outward Gifts.* 1768.

PUBLISHED PRIMARY SOURCES

An Account of Several Work-Houses for Employing and Maintaining the Poor; Setting forth the Rules by which they are Governed, their great Usefulness to the Publick, and in particular to the Parishes where they are Erected. London, 1725.

An Act to Incorporate the Carpenters' Company of the City and County of Philadelphia. Philadelphia, 1873.

Allen, Richard. *The Life, Experience, and Gospel Labours of the Rt. Rev. Richard Allen.* Philadelphia: Martin & Boden, 1833.

American Husbandry, Containing an Account of the Soil, Climate, Production and Agriculture, of the British Colonies in North-America and the West-Indies. 2 vols. London, 1775.

Archer, Ian W., and F. Douglas Price, eds. *English Historical Documents.* 10 vols. New York: Routledge, 2011.

Aughterson, Kate, ed. *The English Renaissance: An Anthology of Sources and Documents.* New York: Routledge, 1998.

Bacon, Francis. *The Major Works.* Edited by Brian Vickers. New York: Oxford University Press, 2002.

Baylor, Michael G., ed. and trans. *The Radical Reformation.* New York: Cambridge University Press, 1991.

Blackwell, John. *A Model for Erecting a Bank of Credit*, in *Colonial Currency Reprints, 1682–1751.* Edited by Andrew McFarland Davis, 154–88. Boston, 1910.

Bourne, Henry. *Antiquitates Vulgares; Or, the Antiquities of the Common People.* Newcastle, 1725.

Brinklow, Henry. *Henry Brinklow's Complaynt of Roderyck Mors.* Edited by J. Meadows Cowper. London: Trübner and Co., 1874.

Bronner, Edwin B., ed. "Philadelphia County Court of Quarter Sessions and Common Pleas, 1695." *American Journal of Legal History* 1, nos. 1, 3 (January 1957): 79–95, 236–50.

Bullivant, Benjamin. *A Glance at New York in 1697: The Travel Diary of Dr. Benjamin Bullivant.* Edited by Wayne Andrews. New York: New York Historical Society, 1956.

Burnaby, Andrew. *Travels through the Middle Settlements in North-America, In the Years 1759 and 1760.* Dublin, 1775.

Caesar, Philipp. *A General Discovrse Against the damnable sect of Vsurers grounded vppon the vvorde of God, and confirmed by the auctoritie of doctors both auncient, and newe; necessarie for all tymes, but most profitable for these later daies, in which, charitie being banished, couetousnes hath gotten the vpper hande.* London, 1578.

Carew, Bampfylde-Moore. *The Life and Adventures of Bampfylde-Moore Carew.* London, 1793.

Child, Josiah. *A New Discourse of Trade, Wherein is Recommended Several Weighty Points Relating to Companies of Merchants.* London, 1692.

Chitty, Joseph. *A Treatise on the Game Laws, and on Fisheries.* London, 1812.

Coke, Roger. *A Discourse of Trade in Two Parts.* London, 1670.

Collections of the New-York Historical Society for the Year 1912: Proceedings of the General Court of Assizes, held in the City of New York, October 6, 1680, to October 6, 1682. New York: New-York Historical Society, 1913.

Colonial Laws of Massachusetts: Reprinted from the Edition of 1660, with Supplements to 1672; Containing also, the Body of Liberties of 1641. Edited by William Henry Whitmore. Boston: William H. Whitmore, Rockwell and Churchill, 1889.

Colonial Laws of New York from the Year 1664 to the Revolution. 5 vols. Edited by Charles Z. Lincoln et al. Albany: James B. Lyon, 1894.

Danckaerts, Jasper. *Journal of Jasper Danckaerts, 1679–1680.* Edited by Bartlett Burleigh James and J. Franklin Jameson. New York: Charles Scribner's Sons, 1913.

Defoe, Daniel. *The Great Law of Insubordination Consider'd.* London, 1724.

——. *A Vindication of the Press; Or, An Essay on the Usefulness of Writing.* London, 1718.

Documents Relative to the Colonial History of the State of New York. 15 vols. Edited by John Romeyn Brodhead, Berthold Fernow, and E. B. O'Callaghan. Albany: Weed, Parsons, 1853–87.

Dunn, Mary Maples, et al., eds. *The Papers of William Penn.* 5 vols. Philadelphia: University of Pennsylvania Press, 1982.

Ecclesiastical Records, State of New York. 7 vols. Edited by Hugh Hastings. Albany: J. B. Lyon, 1901.

Elyot, Thomas. *The Boke Named the Governour.* London: Ridgeway and Sons, 1834.

Exquemelin, Alexander O. *Bucaniers of America: Or, a True Account of the Most Remarkable Assaults Committed of late Years upon the Coasts of the West-Indies.* London, 1684.

Fernow, Berthold, ed. *New York State Library Calendar of Council Minutes, 1668–1783.* Albany: University of the State of New York, 1902.

"The First Charter of the City of Philadelphia, 1691." *Pennsylvania Magazine of History and Biography* 18, no. 4 (1894): 504–9.

Fontaine, John. *The Journal of John Fontaine.* Edited by Edward Porter Alexander. Charlottesville: University of Virginia Press, 1972.

Fortescue, John. *On the Laws and Governance of England.* Edited by Shelley Lockwood. New York: Cambridge University Press, 1997.

Franklin, Benjamin. *The Autobiography of Benjamin Franklin.* Edited by Leonard B. Larabee et al. New Haven, CT: Yale University Press, 1964.

——. *The Papers of Benjamin Franklin.* 43 vols. Edited by Leonard B. Larabee, W. B. Willcox, Claude A. Lopex, Barbara B. Oberg, and Ellen R. Cohn. New Haven, CT: Yale University Press, 1959–2018.

——. *Poor Richard's Almanack.* 1732.

——. "The Way to Wealth." In *The Heath Anthology of American Literature,* edited by Paul Lauter et al., 808–13. Boston: Houghton Mifflin, 2006.

Gay, John. *The Beggar's Opera.* In *The Norton Anthology of English Literature,* edited by Stephen Greenblatt et al., 2613–55. New York: Norton, 2006.

Godwyn, Morgan. *The Negro's & Indians Advocate, Suing for their admission into the Church. Or, a persuasive to the instructing and baptizing of the Negro's and Indians in our plantations.* London, 1680.

Gordon, Lord Adam. "Journal of an Officer's Travels in America and the West Indies, 1764–1765." In *Travels in the American Colonies.* Edited by Newton D. Mereness, 367–453. New York: Macmillan, 1916.

Gouge, William. *Of Domesticall Duties: Eight Treatises.* London, 1622.

Hakluyt, Richard. *A Discourse of Western Planting.* In *Envisioning America: Plans for the Colonization of North America, 1580–1630,* edited by Peter Mancall, 45–61. Boston: Bedford/St. Martin's, 1995.

Hamilton, Alexander. *Gentleman's Progress: The Itinerarium of Dr. Alexander Hamilton, 1744.* Edited by Carl Bridenbaugh. Chapel Hill: University of North Carolina Press, 1948.

Harrington, James. *The Commonwealth of Oceana and A System of Politics.* Edited by J. G. A. Pocock. New York: Cambridge University Press, 1992.

Hazard, Samuel, ed. *Hazard's Register of Pennsylvania,* 7 vols. Philadelphia, 1828–35.

Horne, Robert A. "A Brief Description of the Province of Carolina, by Robert Horne, 1666." In *Narratives of Early Carolina, 1650–1708,* edited by A. S. Salley, 63–73. New York: Charles Scribner's Sons, 1911.

Horsmanden, Daniel. *The New York Conspiracy, by Daniel Horsmanden.* Edited by Thomas J. Davis. Boston: Beacon Press, 1971.

John of Salisbury, *Policraticus.* Edited and translated by Cary J. Nederman. New York: Cambridge University Press, 1990.

Johnson, Odai, and William J. Burling, eds. *The Colonial American Stage, 1665–1774: A Documentary Calendar.* Madison, NJ: Fairleigh Dickinson University Press, 2001.

Kalm, Peter. *Travels in North America.* 2 vols. New York: Dover, 1964.

Kinney, Arthur F., ed. *Rogues, Vagabonds, and Sturdy Beggars: A New Gallery of Tudor and Early Stuart Rogue Literature.* Amherst: University of Massachusetts Press, 1990.

Lay, Benjamin. *All Slave-Keepers, that keep the Innocent in Bondage, Apostates.* 1737.

"Letters of William Penn." *Pennsylvania Magazine of History and Biography* 33, no. 3 (1909): 303–18.

Ligon, Richard. *A True & Exact History of the Island of Barbados, Illustrated with a Mapp of the Island, as also the Principall Trees & Plants there, set forth in their due Proportions and Shapes, drawne out by their severall and respective Scales.* London, 1657.

Locke, John. *Two Treatises of Government.* New York: Cambridge University Press, 1988.

Logan, James. "The Antidote. In some Remarks on a Paper of David Lloyd's, called A vindication of the legislative power. Submitted to the all the Freemen of Pennsylvania." *Pennsylvania Magazine of History and Biography* 38, no. 4 (1914): 463–87.

Mackraby, Andrew. "Philadelphia Society before the Revolution." *Pennsylvania Magazine of History and Biography* 11, no. 4 (January 1888): 491–94.

MacMillan, Ken, ed. *Stories of True Crime in Tudor and Stuart England.* New York: Routledge, 2015.

Mancall, Peter, ed. *Envisioning America: Plans for the Colonization of North America, 1580–1630.* Boston: Bedford/St. Martin's, 1995.

Mandeville, Bernard. *The Fable of the Bees and Other Writings.* Edited by E. J. Hundert. Indianapolis, IN: Hackett, 1997.

Minutes of the Common Council of the City of New York, 1675–1776. 8 vols. New York: Dodd, Mead, 1905.

Minutes of the Common Council of the City of Philadelphia: 1704–1776. Philadelphia: Crissey & Markley, 1847.

Minutes of the Council and General Court of Colonial Virginia, 1622–1632, 1670–1676. Edited by H. R. McIlwaine. Richmond: Virginia State Library, 1924.

Minutes of the Provincial Council of Pennsylvania: From the Organization to the Termination of the Proprietary Government. Edited by Samuel Hazard. Philadelphia: J. Severns, 1851–53.

Mittelberger, Gottlieb. *Journey to Pennsylvania.* Edited by Oscar Handlin. Cambridge, MA.: Harvard University Press, 1960.

Moraley, William. *The Infortunate: The Voyage and Adventures of William Moraley, an Indentured Servant.* Edited by Susan E. Klepp and Billy G. Smith. University Park: Pennsylvania State University Press, 1992.

More, Nicholas, and James Claypoole. "The Articles, Settlement, and Offices of the Free Society of Traders in Pennsilvania." *Pennsylvania Magazine of History and Biography* 5, no. 1 (1881): 37–50.

More, Thomas. *Utopia.* In *The Norton Anthology of English Literature,* edited by Stephen Greenblatt et al., 521–89. New York: Norton, 2006.

Myers, Albert Cook. *Narratives of Early Pennsylvania, West New Jersey and Delaware, 1630–1707.* New York: Charles Scribner's Sons, 1912.

"Notes and Queries." *Pennsylvania Magazine of History and Biography* 22, no. 4 (1898): 493–508.

"Notes and Queries: Philadelphia Exports, 1759–1763." *Pennsylvania Magazine of History and Biography* 4, no. 4 (1880): 508–16.

"Notes and Queries: Two Letters of Governor George Thomas to John Penn, November 4, 1740." *Pennsylvania Magazine of History and Biography* 45, no. 1 (1921): 98–100.

Nourse, Timothy. *Campania Fœlix. Or, A Discourse of the Benefits and Improvements of Husbandry.* London, 1700.

O'Callaghan, E. B., ed. and trans. *Laws and Ordinances of New Netherland, 1638–1674.* Albany, NY: Weed, Parsons, and Co., 1868.

"Original Letters and Documents." *Pennsylvania Magazine of History and Biography* 6, no. 3 (1882): 355–67.

Pennsylvania Archives. 138 vols. Philadelphia: J. Severns, 1852–1935.

Ray, John. *A Compleat Collection of English Proverbs; Also the most celebrated proverbs of the Scotch, Italian, French, Spanish, and other languages.* London, 1768.

Reay, Barry, ed. "The Quakers and 1659: Two Newly Discovered Broadsides by Edward Burrough." *Journal of the Friends Historical Society* 54, no. 2 (1977): 101–11.

A Report from the Committee Appointed to Enquire into the State of the Gaols of this Kingdom: Relating to the Marshalsea Prison; and Farther Relating to the Fleet Prison. London, 1729.

Revel, James. "The Poor Unhappy Transported Felon's Sorrowful Account of His Fourteen Years Transportation at Virginia in America." *Virginia Magazine of History and Biography* 56, no. 2 (April 1948): 180–94.

Sidney, Algernon. *Discourses Concerning Government.* Edited by Thomas West. Indianapolis, IN: Liberty Fund, 1990.

Sloane, Hans. *A Voyage to the Islands Madera, Barbados, Nieves, S. Christophers and Jamaica, with the Natural History of the Herbs and Trees, Four-footed Beasts, Fishes, Birds, Insects, Reptiles, &c.* London, 1707.

Smith, Nigel, ed. *A Collection of Ranter Writing: Spiritual Liberty and Sexual Freedom in the English Revolution.* 2nd ed. London: Pluto Press, 2014.

Smith, Thomas. *De Republica Anglorum.* London: Cambridge University Press, 1906.

———. *A Discourse of the Common Weal of this Realm of England.* London: Cambridge University Press, 1929.

Soderlund, Jean, et al., eds. *William Penn and the Founding of Pennsylvania, 1680–1684: A Documentary History.* Philadelphia: University of Pennsylvania Press, 1983.

Somerset, Fiona, ed., *Four Wycliffite Dialogues.* New York: Oxford University Press, 2009.

The Statutes at Large of Pennsylvania from 1682 to 1801. Edited by James T. Mitchell et al. Harrisburg, PA: Clarence M. Busch, 1896.

The Statutes at Large of Virginia, from the first session of the legislature, in the year 1619. Edited by William Waller Hening. Richmond, VA: Samuel Pleasants, 1809–23.

Staughton, George, et al., eds. *Charter to William Penn, and Laws of the Province of Pennsylvania, passed between the Years 1682 and 1700.* Harrisburg, PA: Lane S. Hart, State Printer, 1879.

Tawney, R. H., and Eileen Power, eds. *Tudor Economic Documents: Being Select Documents Illustrating the Economic and Social History of Tudor England.* 3 vols. London: Longmans, 1924.

Votes and Proceedings of the House of Representatives of the Province of Pennsylvania. In *Pennsylvania Archives,* eighth series. 8 vols. Edited by Gertrude MacKinney et al. Harrisburg, PA: Hood, 1931–35.

Watson, John F., comp. *Annals of Philadelphia, and Pennsylvania, In the Olden Time.* 3 vols. Philadelphia: Edwin S. Stuart, 1899.

Williamson, Peter. *The Life and Curious Adventures of Peter Williamson, who was carried off from Aberdeen, and Sold as a Slave.* Aberdeen, 1826.

Woolman, John. *The Journal and Major Essays of John Woolman.* Edited by Phillips P. Moulton. Richmond, IN: Friends United Press, 1971.

SECONDARY SOURCES

Abulafia, David. *The Discovery of Mankind: Atlantic Encounters in the Age of Columbus.* New Haven, CT: Yale University Press, 2008.

Almbjär, Martin. "The Problem with Early-Modern Petitions: Safety Valve or Powder Keg?" *European Review of History/Revue* 26, no. 6 (February 2019): 1–27.

Amelang, James S. *The Flight of Icarus: Artisan Autobiography in Early Modern Europe.* Stanford, CA: Stanford University Press, 1998.

Amory, Hugh, and David D. Hall, eds. *A History of the Book in America.* Vol. 1, *The Colonial Book in the Atlantic World.* New York: Cambridge University Press, 2000.

Amussen, Susan Dwyer. *Caribbean Exchanges: Slavery and the Transformation of English Society, 1640–1700.* Chapel Hill: University of North Carolina Press, 2007.

Appelbaum, Robert, and John Wood Sweet, eds. *Envisioning an English Empire: Jamestown and the Making of the North Atlantic World.* Philadelphia: University of Pennsylvania Press, 2005.

Appleby, Joyce Oldham. *Economic Thought and Ideology in Seventeenth-Century England.* Princeton, NJ: Princeton University Press, 1978.

———. "Locke, Liberalism and the Natural Law of Money." *Past and Present* 71 (May 1976): 43–69.

Armitage, David. *The Ideological Origins of the British Empire.* New York: Cambridge University Press, 2000.

Arnold, John H. *Belief and Unbelief in Medieval Europe.* London: Bloomsbury, 2005.

Baker, Caroline. "An Exploration of Quaker Women's Writing Between 1650–1700." *Journal of International Women's Studies* 5, no. 2 (2004): 8–20.

Beattie, J. M. *Policing and Punishment in London, 1660–1750: Urban Crime and the Limits of Terror.* New York: Oxford University Press, 2001.

Beckles, Hilary McD. *White Servitude and Black Slavery in Barbados, 1627–1715.* Knoxville: University of Tennessee Press, 1989.

Beier, A. L. *Social Thought in England, 1480–1730.* New York: Routledge, 2016.

Berlin, Ira. *Many Thousands Gone: The First Two Centuries of Slavery in North America.* Cambridge, MA: Harvard University Press, 1998.

Billings, Warren M., and Brent Tarter, eds. *"Esteemed Bookes of Lawe" and the Legal Culture of Early Virginia.* Charlottesville: University of Virginia Press, 2017.

Blackburn, Robin. *American Crucible: Slavery, Emancipation and Human Rights.* London: Verso, 2011.

———. *The Making of New World Slavery: From the Baroque to the Modern, 1492–1800.* New York: Verso, 1997.

Block, Sharon. *Rape and Sexual Power in Early America.* Chapel Hill: University of North Carolina Press, 2006.

Bonnell, Victoria E., ed. *Beyond the Cultural Turn: New Directions in the Study of Society and Culture.* Berkeley: University of California Press, 1999.

Borsay, Peter. *The English Urban Renaissance: Culture and Society in the Provincial Town, 1660–1770.* New York: Oxford University Press, 1989.

Bouton, Terry. *Taming Democracy: "The People," the Founders, and the Troubled Ending of the American Revolution.* New York: Oxford University Press, 2007.

Bowden, Peter. "Agricultural Prices, Farm Profits, and Rents." In *The Agrarian History of England and Wales,* vol. 4, *1500–1640,* edited by Joan Thirsk, 593–695. New York: Cambridge University Press, 1967.

Bradburn, Douglas, and John C. Coombs, eds. *Early Modern Virginia: Reconsidering the Old Dominion.* Charlottesville: University of Virginia Press, 2011.

Braddick, Michael. *State Formation in Early Modern England, c. 1550–1700.* New York: Cambridge University Press, 2000.

Breen, T. H. *The Marketplace of Revolution: How Consumer Politics Shaped American Independence.* New York: Oxford University Press, 2004.

Brewer, John. *The Pleasures of the Imagination: English Culture in the Eighteenth Century.* New York: Farrar, Straus and Giroux, 1997.

Brooks, Christopher. "Apprenticeship, Social Mobility and the Middling Sort, 1550–1800." In *The Middling Sort of People: Culture, Society and Politics in England, 1550–1800,* edited by Jonathan Barry and Christopher Brooks, 52–83. Basingstoke, UK: Palgrave Macmillan, 1994.

Brown, Vincent. *Tacky's Revolt: The Story of an Atlantic Slave War.* Cambridge, MA: Harvard University Press, 2020.

Brunsman, Denver. *The Evil Necessity: British Naval Impressment in the Eighteenth-Century Atlantic World.* Charlottesville: University of Virginia Press, 2013.

Brunt, P. A. *Social Conflicts in the Roman Republic.* New York: Norton, 1972.

Bucholz, Robert O., and Joseph P. Ward. *London: A Social and Cultural History, 1550–1750.* New York: Cambridge University Press, 2012.

Bullock, Steven. "A Mumper among the Gentle: Tom Bell, Colonial Confidence Man." *William and Mary Quarterly* 55, no. 2 (April 1998): 231–58.

Burke, Peter. *Popular Culture in Early Modern Europe.* New York: Harper & Row, 1978.

———. "The Renaissance Dialogue." *Renaissance Studies* 3, no. 1 (March 1989): 1–12.

———. *A Social History of Knowledge: From Gutenberg to Diderot.* Malden, MA: Blackwell, 2000.

Bushman, Richard L. *The Refinement of America: Persons, Houses, Cities.* New York: Knopf, 1992.

Butler, Jon. *Awash in a Sea of Faith: Christianizing the American People.* Cambridge, MA: Harvard University Press, 1990.

———. "'Gospel Order Improved': The Keithian Schism and the Exercise of Quaker Ministerial Authority in Pennsylvania." *William and Mary Quarterly* 31, no. 3 (July 1974): 431–52.

———. "Into Pennsylvania's Spiritual Abyss: The Rise and Fall of the Later Keithians, 1693–1702." *Pennsylvania Magazine of History and Biography* 101, no. 2 (April 1977): 151–70.

Canny, Nicholas. *The Elizabethan Conquest of Ireland: A Pattern Established, 1565–76.* New York: Barnes & Noble, 1976.

Capp, Bernard. *English Almanacs, 1500–1800: Astrology and the Popular Press.* Ithaca, NY: Cornell University Press, 1979.

Carey, Brycchan. *From Peace to Freedom: Quaker Rhetoric and the Birth of American Antislavery, 1657–1761.* New Haven, CT: Yale University Press, 2012.

Chaplin, Joyce. "Slavery and the Principle of Humanity: A Modern Idea in the Early Lower South." *Journal of Social History* 24, no. 2 (Winter 1990): 299–315.

Chartier, Roger. *Cultural History: Between Practices and Representations.* Ithaca, NY: Cornell University Press, 1988.

———. "Culture as Appropriation: Popular Cultural Uses in Early Modern France." In *Understanding Popular Culture: Europe from the Middle Ages to the Nineteenth Century,* edited by Steven L. Kaplan, 229–53. New York: Mouton, 1984.

Cohen, Jay. "The History of Imprisonment for Debt and its Relation to the Development of Discharge for Bankruptcy." *Journal of Legal History* 3, no. 2 (1980): 153–71.

Colley, Linda. *Britons: Forging the Nation, 1707–1837.* New Haven: Yale University Press, 1992.

Collinson, Patrick. *Elizabethan Essays.* London: Hambledon Press, 1994.

Como, David R. *Blown by the Spirit: Puritanism and the Emergence of an Antinomian Underground in Pre–Civil War England*. Stanford, CA: Stanford University Press, 2004.

Cowan, Alexander. *Urban Europe, 1500–1700*. New York: Arnold, 1998.

Daunton, M. J. *Progress and Poverty: An Economic and Social History of Britain, 1700–1850*. New York: Oxford University Press, 1995.

Davies, Adrian. *The Quakers in English Society, 1655–1725*. New York: Oxford University Press, 2000.

Davis, Natalie Zemon. *Society and Culture in Early Modern France: Eight Essays*. Stanford, CA: Stanford University Press, 1975.

Desan, Christine. *Making Money: Coin, Currency, and the Coming of Capitalism*. New York: Oxford University Press, 2014.

Diamondstone, Judith M. "Philadelphia's Municipal Corporation." *Pennsylvania Magazine of History and Biography* 90, no. 2 (April 1966): 183–201.

Dickson, R. J. *Ulster Emigration to Colonial America, 1718–1775*. 3rd ed. Belfast: Ulster Heritage Foundation, 1988.

Donoghue, John. *Fire under the Ashes: An Atlantic History of the English Revolution*. Chicago: University of Chicago Press, 2013.

Dorfman, Joseph. "Captain John Blackwell: A Bibliographical Note." *Pennsylvania Magazine of History and Biography* 69, no. 3 (July 1945): 233–42.

Duby, Georges. *The Three Orders: Feudal Society Imagined*. Translated by Arthur Goldhammer. Chicago: University of Chicago Press, 1980.

Dunn, Mary Maples, and Richard S. Dunn. "The Founding, 1681–1701." In *Philadelphia: A 300-Year History*, edited by Russell F. Weigley, 1–32. New York: Norton, 1982.

Dyer, Christopher. *Making a Living in the Middle Ages: The People of Britain, 850–1520*. New Haven, CT: Yale University Press, 2005.

Egnal, Marc. "The Economic Development of the Thirteen Colonies, 1720–1775." *William and Mary Quarterly* 32, no. 2 (April 1975): 191–222.

Ehmer, Joseph, and Catherine Lis, eds. *The Idea of Work in Europe from Antiquity to Modern Times*. Burlington: Ashgate, 2009.

Eisenstadt, Peter. "Almanacs and the Disenchantment of Early America." *Pennsylvania History* 65, no. 2 (Spring 1998): 143–69.

Ekirch, A. Roger. *At Day's Close: Night in Times Past*. New York: Norton, 2005.

———. *Bound for America: The Transportation of British Convicts to the Colonies, 1718–1775*. New York: Oxford University Press, 1987.

Fatherly, Sarah. *Gentlewomen and Learned Ladies: Women and Elite Formation in Eighteenth-Century Philadelphia*. Bethlehem, PA.: Lehigh University Press, 2008.

Finger, Simon. *The Contagious City: The Politics of Public Health in Early Philadelphia*. Ithaca, NY: Cornell University Press, 2012.

Fisher, Joshua Francis, et al. "Andrew Hamilton, Esq., of Pennsylvania." *Pennsylvania Magazine of History and Biography* 16, no. 1 (April 1892): 1–27.

Fitzroy, Herbert William Keith. "The Punishment of Crime in Provincial Pennsylvania." *Pennsylvania Magazine of History and Biography* 60, no. 3 (July 1936): 242–69.

Fletcher, Anthony, and Diarmaid MacCulloch. *Tudor Rebellions.* 5th ed. New York: Routledge, 2008.

Foner, Eric. *Tom Paine and Revolutionary America.* 2nd ed. New York: Oxford University Press, 2005.

Foote, Thelma W. "'Some Hard Usage': The New York City Slave Revolt of 1712." *New York Folklore* 18, 1–4 (1992): 147–59.

Fox, Adam. "Food, Drink and Social Distinction in Early Modern England." In *Remaking English Society: Social Relations and Social Change in Early Modern England,* edited by Steve Hindle, Alexandra Shepard, and John Walter, 165–87. Rochester, NY: Boydell, 2013.

Friedrichs, Christopher R. *The Early Modern City, 1450–1750.* New York: Longman, 1995.

Fries, Sylvia Doughty. *The Urban Idea in Colonial America.* Philadelphia: Temple University Press, 1977.

Galenson, David. *White Servitude in Colonial America: An Economic Analysis.* New York: Cambridge University Press, 1982.

Gaskill, Malcolm. *Crime and Mentalities in Early Modern England.* New York: Cambridge University Press, 2000.

Geobel, Julius, Jr., and T. Raymond Naughton. *Law Enforcement in Colonial New York: A Study in Criminal Procedure, 1664–1776.* New York: Commonwealth Fund, 1944.

Gerbner, Katherine. "Antislavery in Print: The Germantown Protest, the 'Exhortation,' and the Seventeenth-Century Quaker Debate on Slavery." *Early American Studies* 9, no. 3 (Fall 2011): 552–75.

Gerona, Carla. *Night Journeys: The Power of Dreams in Transatlantic Quaker Culture.* Charlottesville: University of Virginia Press, 2004.

Gillingham, Harrold E. "Cesar Ghiselin, Philadelphia's First Gold and Silversmith." *Pennsylvania Magazine of History and Biography* 57, no. 3 (July 1933): 244–59.

Glenn, Thomas Allen. "William Hudson, Mayor of Philadelphia, 1725–1726." *Pennsylvania Magazine of History and Biography* 15, no. 3 (1891): 336–43.

Gottlieb, Gabriele. "Class and Capital Punishment in Early Urban North America." In *Class Matters: Early North America and the Atlantic World,* edited by Simon Middleton and Billy G. Smith, 185–97. Philadelphia: University of Pennsylvania Press, 2008.

Green, James N. "The Book Trade in the Middle Colonies, 1680–1720." In Amory and Hall, *A History of the Book in America* 1:199–223.

———. "English Books and Printing in the Age of Franklin." In Amory and Hall, *A History of the Book in America* 1:248–97.

Greenberg, Douglas. *Crime and Law Enforcement in the Colony of New York, 1691–1776.* Ithaca, NY: Cornell University Press, 1976.

Greene, Jack P. *Pursuits of Happiness: The Social Development of Early Modern British Colonies and the Formation of American Culture.* Chapel Hill: University of North Carolina Press, 1988.

———, and J. R. Pole, eds. *Colonial British America: Essays in the New History of the Early Modern Era.* Baltimore: Johns Hopkins University Press, 1984.

Greer, Allan. "Commons and Enclosure in the Colonization of North America." *American Historical Review* 117, no. 2 (April 2012): 365–86.

Grubb, Farley. "The Auction of Redemptioner Servants, Philadelphia, 1771–1804: An Economic Analysis." *Journal of Economic History* 48, no. 3 (September 1988): 583–603.

Guasco, Michael. *Slaves and Englishmen: Human Bondage in the Early Modern Atlantic World.* Philadelphia: University of Pennsylvania Press, 2014.

Guha, Ranajit. *Elementary Aspects of Peasant Insurgency in Colonial India.* 2nd ed. Durham, NC: Duke University Press, 1999.

Habermas, Jürgen. *The Structural Transformation of the Public Sphere: An Inquiry into a Category of Bourgeois Society.* Translated by Thomas Burger. Cambridge, MA: MIT Press, 1991.

Hall, David D. *Worlds of Wonder, Days of Judgment: Popular Religious Belief in Early New England.* Cambridge, MA: Harvard University Press, 1989.

Hanna, Mark G. *Pirate Nests and the Rise of the British Empire, 1570–1740.* Chapel Hill: University of North Carolina Press, 2015.

Harris, Tim, ed. *Popular Culture in England, c. 1500–1850.* London: Macmillan, 1995.

———. *Revolution: The Great Crisis of the British Monarchy, 1685–1720.* London: Allen Lane, 2006.

Herrick, Cheesman A. *White Servitude in Pennsylvania.* Philadelphia: John Joseph McVey, 1926.

Hill, Christopher. *Liberty Against the Law: Some Seventeenth-Century Controversies.* London: Allen Lane, 1996.

———. *The World Turned Upside Down: Radical Ideas in the English Revolution.* New York: Penguin, 1975.

Hilton, Rodney. *Bond Men Made Free: Medieval Peasant Movements and the English Rising of 1381.* 2nd ed. New York: Routledge, 2003.

Hindle, Steve. *The State and Social Change in Early Modern England, c. 1550–1640.* London: Palgrave Macmillan, 2000.

Hitchcock, David. "'He is a Vagabond that Hath No Habitation in the Lord': The Representation of Quakerism as Vagrancy in Interregnum England, c. 1650–1660." *Cultural and Social History* 15, no. 1 (Winter 2018): 21–37.

Hitchcock, Tim, and Robert Shoemaker. *London Lives: Poverty, Crime, and the Making of a Modern City, 1690–1800.* New York: Cambridge University Press, 2015.

Hodges, Graham Russell. *Root and Branch: African Americans in New York and East Jersey, 1613–1863.* Chapel Hill: University of North Carolina Press, 1999.

Horn, James. *Adapting to a New World: English Society in the Seventeenth-Century Chesapeake.* Chapel Hill: University of North Carolina Press, 1994.

Hornick, Nancy Slocum. "Anthony Benezet and the Africans' School: Toward a Theory of Full Equality." *Pennsylvania Magazine of History and Biography* 99, no. 4 (October 1975): 399–421.

Hughes, Ann. *Gangraena and the Struggle for the English Revolution.* New York: Oxford University Press, 2006.

Hunt, Lynn. *Inventing Human Rights: A History.* New York: Norton, 2008.

———, ed. *The New Cultural History.* Berkeley: University of California Press, 1989.

Hutton, Ronald. *The Rise and Fall of Merry England: The Ritual Year, 1400–1700.* New York: Oxford University Press, 1994.

Isaac, Rhys. *The Transformation of Virginia, 1740–1790.* Chapel Hill: University of North Carolina Press, 1982.

Isenmann, Eberhard. "The Notion of the Common Good, The Concept of Politics, and Practical Policies in Late Medieval and Early Modern German Cities." In *De Bono Communi: The Discourse and Practice of the Common Good in the European City, 13th–16th Centuries,* edited by Elodie Lecuppre-Desjardin and Anne-Laure van Bruaene, 107–48. Turnhout, Belgium: Brepols, 2010.

Jackson, Maurice. *Let This Voice Be Heard: Anthony Benezet, Father of Atlantic Abolitionism.* Philadelphia: University of Pennsylvania Press, 2010.

Jensen, Arthur L. *The Maritime Commerce of Colonial Philadelphia.* Madison: State Historical Society of Wisconsin, 1963.

Jewell, Helen M. *Education in Early Modern England.* New York: St. Martin's Press, 1998.

Johnson, Barbara A. *Reading* Piers Plowman *and* Pilgrim's Progress: *Reception and the Protestant Reader.* Carbondale: Southern Illinois University Press, 1992.

Johnson, Daniel. "Hot-Heads, Gentlemen, and the Liberties of Tradesmen: The Philadelphia Tanners' Affair of 1739." *Cultural and Social History* 12, no. 3 (September 2015): 343–64.

———. "'Nothing Will Satisfy You but Money': Debt, Freedom, and the Mid-Atlantic Culture of Money." *Early American Studies* 19, no. 1 (Winter 2021): 100–137.

——. "'Profane Language, Horrid Oaths, and Imprecations': Order and the Colonial Soundscape in the American Mid-Atlantic, 1650–1750." *Social History* 46, no. 3 (August 2021): 1–23.

——. "'What Must Poor People Do?': Economic Protest and Plebeian Culture in Philadelphia, 1682–1754." *Pennsylvania History* 79, no. 2 (Spring 2012): 117–53.

Jordan, Sarah. *The Anxieties of Idleness: Idleness in Eighteenth-Century British Literature and Culture.* Lewisburg, PA: Bucknell University Press, 2003.

Kamensky, Jane. *Governing the Tongue: The Politics of Speech in Early New England.* New York: Oxford University Press, 1997.

Ketcham, Ralph L. "Benjamin Franklin and William Smith: New Light on an Old Philadelphia Quarrel." *Pennsylvania Magazine of History and Biography* 88, no. 2 (April 1964): 142–63.

Klepp, Susan E. "Demography in Early Philadelphia, 1690–1860." *Proceedings of the American Philosophical Society* 133, no. 2 (June 1989): 85–111.

Koslofsky, Craig. *Evening's Empire: A History of the Night in Early Modern Europe.* New York: Cambridge University Press, 2011.

Kussmaul, Ann. *Servants in Husbandry in Early Modern England.* New York: Cambridge University Press, 1981.

Le Goff, Jacques. "The Learned and Popular Dimensions of Journeys in the Otherworld in the Middle Ages." In *Understanding Popular Culture: Europe from the Middle Ages to the Nineteenth Century,* edited by Steven L. Kaplan, 19–37. New York: Mouton, 1984.

Lemay, J. A. Leo. *The Life of Benjamin Franklin.* Vol. 3, *Soldier, Scientist, and Politician, 1748–1757.* Philadelphia: University of Pennsylvania Press, 2008.

Lemon, James T. *The Best Poor Man's Country: Early Southeastern Pennsylvania.* Baltimore: Johns Hopkins University Press, 1972.

Levy, Barry. "Levelers and Fugitives: Runaway Advertisements and the Contrasting Political Economies of Mid-Eighteenth-Century Massachusetts and Pennsylvania." *Pennsylvania History* 78, no. 1 (Winter 2011): 1–32.

——. *Quakers and the American Family: British Settlement in the Delaware Valley.* New York: Oxford University Press, 1988.

Liddy, Christian D., and Jelle Haemers. "Popular Politics in the Late Medieval City: York and Bruges." *English Historical Review* 128, no. 533 (August 2013): 771–805.

Lyons, Clare A. *Sex among the Rabble: An Intimate History of Gender and Power in the Age of Revolution, Philadelphia, 1730–1830.* Chapel Hill: University of North Carolina Press, 2006.

MacPherson, C. B. *The Political Theory of Possessive Individualism: Hobbes to Locke.* New York: Oxford University Press, 1962.

Marietta, Jack D., and G. S. Rowe. *Troubled Experiment: Crime and Justice in Pennsylvania, 1682–1800.* Philadelphia: University of Pennsylvania Press, 2006.

Mayhew, Nicholas. "Wages and Currency: The Case in Britain up to c. 1600." In *Wages and Currency: Global Comparisons from Antiquity to the Twentieth Century,* edited by Jan Lucassen, 211–20. Bern: Peter Lang, 2007.

McConville, Brendan. "Confessions of an American Ranter." *Pennsylvania History* 62, no. 2 (Spring 1995): 238–48.

———. *The King's Three Faces: The Rise and Fall of Royal America, 1688–1776.* Chapel Hill: University of North Carolina Press, 2006.

———. *These Daring Disturbers of the Public Peace: The Struggle for Property and Power in Early New Jersey.* Ithaca, NY: Cornell University Press, 1999.

McCormick, Ted. *William Petty and the Ambitions of Political Arithmetic.* New York: Oxford University Press, 2009.

McCoy, Michael Bradley. "Absconding Servants, Anxious Germans, and Angry Sailors." *Pennsylvania History* 74, no. 4 (Autumn 2007): 427–51.

McCusker, John J. *Money and Exchange in Europe and America, 1600–1775: A Handbook.* Chapel Hill: University of North Carolina Press, 1978.

———, and Russell Menard. *The Economy of British America, 1607–1789.* Chapel Hill: University of North Carolina Press, 1991.

McMahon, Michael. "'Publick Service' versus 'Mans Properties': Dock Creek and the Origins of Urban Technology in Eighteenth-Century Philadelphia." In *Early American Technology: Making and Doing Things from the Colonial Era to 1850,* edited by Judith A. McGaw, 114–47. Chapel Hill: University of North Carolina Press, 1994.

McRae, Andrew. *God Speed the Plough: The Representation of Agrarian England, 1500–1660.* New York: Cambridge University Press, 1996.

Meranze, Michael. *Laboratories of Virtue: Punishment, Revolution, and Authority in Philadelphia, 1760–1835.* Chapel Hill: University of North Carolina Press, 1996.

Middleton, Simon. *From Privileges to Rights: Work and Politics in Colonial New York City.* Philadelphia: University of Pennsylvania Press, 2006.

Miller, John. "The Crown and Borough Charters in the Reign of Charles II." *English Historical Review* 100, no. 394 (January 1985): 53–84.

Milroy, Elizabeth. "'For the like Uses, as the Moore-fields': The Politics of Penn's Squares." *Pennsylvania Magazine of History and Biography* 130, no. 4 (July 2006): 257–82.

Morgan, Gwenda. "Law and Social Change in Colonial Virginia: The Role of the Grand Jury in Richmond County, 1692–1776." *Virginia Magazine of History and Biography* 95, no. 4 (October 1987): 453–80.

———, and Peter Rushton. *Eighteenth-Century Criminal Transportation: The Formation of the Criminal Atlantic.* New York: Palgrave, 2004.

Morgan, Jennifer L. *Laboring Women: Reproduction and Gender in New World Slavery*. Philadelphia: University of Pennsylvania Press, 2004.

Morgan, Kenneth. *Slavery and Servitude in North America, 1607–1800*. Edinburgh: Edinburgh University Press, 2000.

Morgan, Philip D. *Slave Counterpoint: Black Culture in the Eighteenth-Century Chesapeake and Lowcountry*. Chapel Hill: University of North Carolina Press, 1998.

Morris, Richard B. *Government and Labor in Early America*. 2nd ed. New York: Harper & Row, 1965.

Morrison, Hugh. *Early American Architecture: From the First Colonial Settlements to the National Period*. New York: Oxford University Press, 1952.

Mulcahy, Matthew. *Hubs of Empire: The Southeastern Lowcountry and British Caribbean*. Baltimore: Johns Hopkins University Press, 2014.

Muldrew, Craig. "'Hard Food for Midas': Cash and Its Social Value in Early Modern England." *Past and Present* 170 (February 2001): 78–120.

Musselwhite, Paul. *Urban Dreams, Rural Commonwealths: The Rise of Plantation Society in the Chesapeake*. Chicago: University of Chicago Press, 2018.

Nash, Gary B. "Artisans and Politics in Eighteenth-Century Philadelphia." In *The Craftsman in Early America*, edited by Ian M. G. Quimby. New York: Norton, 1984.

———. "The Early Merchants of Philadelphia: The Formation and Disintegration of a Founding Elite." In *The Worlds of William Penn*, edited by Richard S. Dunn and Mary Maples Dunn, 337–62. Philadelphia: University of Pennsylvania Press, 1986.

———. *Forging Freedom: The Formation of Philadelphia's Black Community, 1740–1820*. Cambridge, MA: Harvard University Press, 1988.

———. "The Free Society of Traders and the Early Politics of Pennsylvania." *Pennsylvania Magazine of History and Biography* 89, no. 2 (April 1965): 147–73.

———. "Poverty and Poor Relief in Pre-Revolutionary Philadelphia." *William and Mary Quarterly* 33, no. 1 (January 1976): 3–30.

———. *Quakers and Politics: Pennsylvania, 1681–1726*. 2nd ed. Boston: Northeastern University Press, 1993.

———. "Slaves and Slaveowners in Colonial Philadelphia." *William and Mary Quarterly* 30, no. 2 (April 1973): 223–56.

———. *The Urban Crucible: Social Change, Political Consciousness, and the Origins of the American Revolution*. Cambridge, MA: Harvard University Press, 1979.

———, and Jean R. Soderlund. *Freedom by Degrees: Emancipation in Pennsylvania and Its Aftermath*. New York: Oxford University Press, 1991.

Nelson, William E. "Government by Judiciary: The Growth of Judicial Power in Colonial Pennsylvania." *SMU Law Review* 59, no. 1 (2006): 3–53.

Newman, Eric P. "Franklin Making Money More Plentiful." *Proceedings of the American Philosophical Society* 115, no. 5 (October 1971): 341–49.

Newman, Simon P. "Benjamin Franklin and the Leather-Apron Men: The Politics of Class in Eighteenth-Century Philadelphia." *Journal of American Studies* 43, no. 2 (August 2009): 161–75.

———. *Embodied History: The Lives of the Poor in Early Philadelphia*. Philadelphia: University of Pennsylvania Press, 2003.

———. *A New World of Labor: The Development of Plantation Slavery in the British Atlantic*. Philadelphia: University of Pennsylvania Press, 2013.

Norris, J. Saurin. *The Early Friends (Or Quakers) in Maryland*. Baltimore: Maryland Historical Society, 1862.

Norton, Mary Beth. *Founding Mothers and Fathers: Gendered Power and the Forming of American Society*. New York: Norton, 1996.

Offutt, William M. *Of "Good Men" and "Good Laws": Law and Society in the Delaware Valley, 1680–1710*. Champaign: University of Illinois Press, 1995.

Olton, Charles S. "Philadelphia's First Environmental Crisis." *Pennsylvania Magazine of History and Biography* 98, no. 1 (January 1974): 90–100.

Pearl, Christopher R. *Conceived in Crisis: The Revolutionary Creation of an American State*. Charlottesville: University of Virginia Press, 2020.

Pencak, William. "The Beginning of a Beautiful Friendship: Benjamin Franklin, George Whitefield, the Dancing School, and a Defense of the 'Meaner Sort.'" In Pencak, *Contested Commonwealths*, 197–212.

———, ed. *Contested Commonwealths: Essays in American History*. Bethlehem, PA: Lehigh University Press, 2011.

———. *Pennsylvania's Revolution*. University Park: University of Pennsylvania Press, 2010.

———. "Politics and Ideology in Eighteenth-Century Almanacs: Benjamin Franklin's *Poor Richard* and Nathaniel Ames, Sr.'s *An Astronomical Diary*." In Pencak, *Contested Commonwealths*, 157–96.

———, Matthew Dennis, and Simon Newman, eds. *Riot and Revelry in Early America*. University Park: Pennsylvania State University Press, 2002.

———, and John Lax. "The Knowles Riot and the Crisis of the 1740s in Massachusetts." In Pencak, *Contested Commonwealths*, 3–52.

Peterson, Mark. *The City-State of Boston: The Rise and Fall of an Atlantic Power, 1630–1865*. Princeton, NJ: Princeton University Press, 2019.

Pettigrew, William. *Freedom's Debt: The Royal African Company and the Politics of the Atlantic Slave Trade, 1672–1752*. Chapel Hill: University of North Carolina Press, 2013.

Plank, Geoffrey. *John Woolman's Path to the Peaceable Kingdom: A Quaker in the British Empire*. Philadelphia: University of Pennsylvania Press, 2012.

Prevenier, Walter. "Utilitas Communis in the Low Countries (13th–15th Centuries): From Social Mobilisation to Legitimation of Power." In *De Bono Communi: The Discourse and Practice of the Common Good in the European City, 13th–16th Centuries*, edited by Elodie Lecuppre-Desjardin and Anne-Laure van Bruaene, 205–16. Turnhout, Belgium: Brepols, 2010.

Price, Jacob. "Economic Function and the Growth of American Port Towns in the Eighteenth Century." *Perspectives in American History* 8 (1974): 123–86.

Priest, Claire. "Creating an American Property Law: Alienability and Its Limits in American History." *Harvard Law Review* 120, no. 2 (December 2006): 385–459.

———. "Currency Policies and Legal Development in Colonial New England." *Yale Law Journal* 110 (May 2001): 1303–405.

Rath, Richard Cullen. "African Music in Seventeenth-Century Jamaica: Cultural Transit and Transition." *William and Mary Quarterly* 50, no. 4 (October 1993): 700–726.

———. *How Early America Sounded*. Ithaca, NY: Cornell University Press, 2000.

Reay, Barry. *The Quakers and the English Revolution*. New York: St. Martin's Press, 1985.

Rediker, Marcus. *The Fearless Benjamin Lay: The Quaker Dwarf Who Became the First Revolutionary Abolitionist*. Boston: Beacon Press, 2017.

Rogers, Nicholas. *Mayhem: Post-War Crime and Violence in Britain, 1748–53*. New Haven: Yale University Press, 2012.

Rollison, David. *A Commonwealth of the People: Popular Politics and England's Long Social Revolution, 1066–1649*. New York: Cambridge University Press, 2010.

Roney, Jessica Choppin. *Governed by a Spirit of Opposition: The Origins of American Political Practice in Colonial Philadelphia*. Baltimore: Johns Hopkins University Press, 2014.

Ryerson, Alan. *The Revolution Is Now Begun: The Radical Committees of Philadelphia, 1765–1776*. Philadelphia: University of Pennsylvania Press, 1978.

———. "William Penn's Gentry Commonwealth: An Interpretation of the Constitutional History of Early Pennsylvania, 1681–1701." *Pennsylvania History* 61, no. 4 (October 1994): 393–428.

St. George, Robert, ed. *Possible Pasts: Becoming Colonial in Early America*. Ithaca, NY: Cornell University Press, 2000.

Salinger, Sharon V. "Artisans, Journeymen, and the Transformation of Labor." *William and Mary Quarterly* 40, no. 1 (January 1983): 62–84.

———. *Taverns and Drinking in Early America*. Baltimore: Johns Hopkins University Press, 2004.

———. *"To Serve Well and Faithfully": Labor and Indentured Servants in Pennsylvania, 1682–1800*. New York: Cambridge University Press, 1987.

Scharf, J. Thomas, and Thompson Westcott. *History of Philadelphia, 1609–1884*. 3 vols. Philadelphia, 1884.

Schultz, Ronald. *The Republic of Labor: Philadelphia Artisans and the Politics of Class, 1720–1830.* New York: Oxford University Press, 1993.

Schwartz, Sally. *"A Mixed Multitude": The Struggle for Toleration in Colonial Pennsylvania.* New York: New York University Press, 1989.

Schweitzer, Mary M. *Custom and Contract: Household, Government, and the Economy in Colonial Pennsylvania.* New York: New York University Press, 1987.

Scott, James C. *Weapons of the Weak: Everyday Forms of Peasant Resistance.* New Haven, CT: Yale University Press, 1985.

Scott, Kenneth. *Counterfeiting in Colonial America.* New York: Oxford University Press, 1957.

Scribner, Vaughn. *Inn Civility: Urban Taverns and Early American Civil Society.* New York: New York University Press, 2019.

Sewell, William H. "The Concept(s) of Culture." In *Beyond the Cultural Turn: New Directions in the Study of Society and Culture,* edited by Victoria E. Bonnell, 25–61. Berkeley: University of California Press, 1999.

Shannon, Timothy J. "King of the Indians: The Hard Fate and Curious Career of Peter Williamson." *William and Mary Quarterly* 66, no. 1 (2009): 3–44.

Shaw, Jenny. *Everyday Life in the Early English Caribbean: Irish, Africans, and the Construction of Difference.* New York: New York University Press, 2013.

Shepard, Alexandra. *Accounting for Oneself: Worth, Status, and the Social Order in Early Modern England.* New York: Oxford University Press, 2015.

Shields, David S. *Civil Tongues and Polite Letters in British America.* Chapel Hill: University of North Carolina Press, 1997.

——. "Eighteenth-Century Literary Culture." In Amory and Hall, *A History of the Book in America* 1:434–76.

Shoemaker, Robert B. "The Decline of Public Insult in London, 1660–1800." *Past and Present* 169, no. 1 (November 2000): 97–131.

——. "Reforming the City: The Reformation of Manners Campaign in London, 1690–1738." In *Stilling the Grumbling Hive: The Response to Social and Economic Problems in England, 1689–1750,* edited by Lee Davison et al., 99–120. New York: St. Martin's Press, 1992.

——. "The Street Robber and the Gentle Highwayman: Changing Representations and Perceptions of Robbery in London, 1690–1800." *Cultural and Social History* 3, no. 4 (October 2006): 381–405.

Slack, Paul. *The English Poor Law, 1531–1782.* London: Macmillan, 1990.

——. *The Invention of Improvement: Information and Material Progress in Seventeenth-Century England.* New York: Oxford University Press, 2014.

Slaughter, Thomas P. *The Beautiful Soul of John Woolman: Apostle of Abolition.* New York: New Press, 2009.

Smith, Abbott Emerson. *Colonists in Bondage: White Servitude and Convict Labor in America, 1607–1776.* Chapel Hill: University of North Carolina Press, 1947.

Smith, Barbara Clark. *The Freedoms We Lost: Consent and Resistance in Revolutionary America.* New York: New Press, 2010.

Smith, Billy G. *The "Lower Sort": Philadelphia's Laboring People, 1750–1800.* Ithaca, NY: Cornell University Press, 1990.

Smith, Charles W., and Philip L. Mossman. "Eighteenth-Century Counterfeit English and Irish Halfpence." *Numismatic Chronicle* 172 (2012): 265–76.

Smolenski, John. *Friends and Strangers: The Making of a Creole Culture in Colonial Pennsylvania.* Philadelphia: University of Pennsylvania Press, 2010.

Soderlund, Jean R. *Quakers and Slavery: A Divided Spirit.* Princeton, NJ: Princeton University Press, 1985.

Spufford, Margaret, ed. *The World of Rural Dissenters, 1520–1725.* New York: Cambridge University Press, 1995.

Starn, Randolph. "The Early Modern Muddle." *Journal of Early Modern History* 6, no. 3 (January 2002): 296–307.

Stein, Robert, Anita Boele, and Wim Blockmans. "Whose Community? The Origins and Development of the Concept of Bonum Commune in Flanders, Brabant and Holland (12th–15th Century)." In *De Bono Communi: The Discourse and Practice of the Common Good in the European City, 13th–16th Centuries,* edited by Elodie Lecuppre-Desjardin and Anne-Laure van Bruaene, 149–70. Turnhout, Belgium: Brepols, 2010.

Steinfeld, Robert J. *The Invention of Free Labor: The Employment Relation in English and American Law and Culture, 1350–1870.* Chapel Hill: University of North Carolina Press, 1991.

Stewart, Bruce E. *Redemption from Tyranny: Herman Husband's American Revolution.* Charlottesville: University of Virginia Press, 2020.

Stowell, Marion Barber. "American Almanacs and Feuds." *Early American Literature* 9, no. 3 (Winter 1975): 276–85.

Subrahmanyam, Sanjay. *Empires between Islam and Christianity, 1500–1800.* Albany, NY: SUNY Press, 2019.

Suny, Ronald Gregor. "Back and Beyond: Reversing the Cultural Turn?" *American Historical Review* 107, no. 5 (December 2002): 1476–99.

Szechi, Daniel. *The Jacobites: Britain and Europe, 1688–1788.* Manchester: Manchester University Press, 1994.

Teaford, Jon C. *The Municipal Revolution: Origins of Modern Urban Government, 1650–1825.* Chicago: University of Chicago Press, 1975.

Thirsk, Joan. *Economic Policy and Projects: The Development of a Consumer Society in Early Modern England.* New York: Oxford University Press, 1978.

Thomas, Keith. *Man and the Natural World: A History of the Modern Sensibility.* New York: Pantheon, 1983.

Thompson, E. P. *The Making of the English Working Class.* New York: Vintage, 1966.

———. "The Moral Economy of the English Crowd in the Eighteenth Century." *Past and Present* 50 (February 1971): 76–136.

Thompson, James. "Late Early Modern." *Journal for Early Modern Cultural Studies* 13, no. 2 (Spring 2013): 72–74.

Thompson, Peter. *Rum Punch and Revolution: Taverngoing and Public Life in Eighteenth-Century Philadelphia.* Philadelphia: University of Pennsylvania Press, 1999.

Tolles, Frederick B. *Meeting House and Counting House: The Quaker Merchants of Colonial Philadelphia, 1682–1763.* Chapel Hill: University of North Carolina Press, 1963.

Tomlins, Christopher. *Freedom Bound: Law, Labor, and Civic Identity in Colonizing English America, 1580–1865.* New York: Cambridge University Press, 2010.

Tully, Alan. *Forming American Politics: Ideals, Interests, and Institutions in Colonial New York and Pennsylvania.* Baltimore: Johns Hopkins University Press, 1994.

Valenze, Deborah. *The Social Life of Money in the English Past.* New York: Cambridge University Press, 2006.

Vickers, Daniel. "Competency and Competition: Economic Culture in Early America." *William and Mary Quarterly* 47, no. 1 (January 1990): 3–29.

Wainwright, Nicholas B. "Scull and Heap's East Prospect of Philadelphia." *Pennsylvania Magazine of History and Biography* 73, no. 1 (January 1949): 16–25.

Waldstreicher, David. "Reading the Runaways: Self-Fashioning, Print Culture, and Confidence in Slavery in the Eighteenth-Century Mid-Atlantic." *William and Mary Quarterly* 56, no. 2 (April 1999): 243–72.

———. *Runaway America: Benjamin Franklin, Slavery, and the American Revolution.* New York: New Press, 2004.

Wall, Alexander J., Jr. "William Bradford, Colonial Printer: A Tercentenary Review." *Proceedings of the American Antiquarian Society* (October 1963): 361–84.

Wareing, John. *Indentured Migration and the Servant Trade from London to America, 1618–1718: "There is Great Want of Servants."* New York: Oxford University Press, 2016.

Warner, Michael. *The Letters of the Republic: Publication and the Public Sphere in Eighteenth-Century America.* Cambridge, MA: Harvard University Press, 1992.

Weigley, Russell F., ed. *Philadelphia: A 300-Year History.* New York: Norton, 1982.

Weir, Robert M. "Conservation, Class, and Controversy in Early America." In *Cultures and Identities in Colonial British America*, edited by Robert Olwell and Alan Tully, 95–120. Baltimore: Johns Hopkins University Press, 2006.

Welsh, Peter C. *Tanning in the United States to 1850.* Washington, D.C.: Smithsonian Institution Press, 1964.

Wendel, Thomas. "The Keith-Lloyd Alliance: Factional and Coalition Politics in Colonial Pennsylvania." *Pennsylvania Magazine of History and Biography* 92, no. 3 (July 1968): 289–305.

Wennerlind, Carl. *Casualties of Credit: The English Financial Revolution, 1620–1720.* Cambridge, MA: Harvard University Press, 2011.

White, Jerry. "Pain and Degradation in Georgian London: Life in the Marshalsea Prison." *History Workshop Journal* 68 (Autumn 2009): 69–98.

White, Sam. *The Climate of Rebellion in the Early Modern Ottoman Empire.* New York: Cambridge University Press, 2011.

Williams, Raymond. *The Long Revolution.* New York: Columbia University Press, 1961.

Wilson, Kathleen. *The Sense of the People: Politics, Culture and Imperialism in England, 1715–1785.* New York: Cambridge University Press, 1995.

Withington, Phil. *The Politics of Commonwealth: Citizens and Freemen in Early Modern England.* New York: Cambridge University Press, 2005.

———. *Society in Early Modern England: The Vernacular Origins of Some Powerful Ideas.* Cambridge, UK: Polity, 2010.

Wokeck, Marianne S. *Trade in Strangers: The Beginnings of Mass Migration to North America.* University Park: Pennsylvania State University Press, 1999.

Wolf, Edwin. *The Book Culture of a Colonial American City: Philadelphia Books, Bookmen, and Booksellers.* New York: Oxford University Press, 1988.

Wood, Andy. *Riot, Rebellion, and Popular Politics in Early Modern England.* New York: Palgrave, 2002.

Wood, Peter H. *Black Majority: Negroes in South Carolina from 1670 through the Stono Rebellion.* New York: Knopf, 1974.

Woodfine, Philip. "Debtors, Prisons, and Petitions in Eighteenth-Century England." *Eighteenth-Century Life* 30, no. 2 (Spring 2006): 1–31.

Wordie, J. R. "The Chronology of English Enclosure, 1500–1914." *Economic History Review* 36, no. 4 (November 1983): 483–505.

Wright, Richard R., Jr. *The Negro in Pennsylvania: A Study in Economic History.* New York: Arno Press, 1969.

Wrightson, Keith. *Earthly Necessities: Economic Lives in Early Modern Britain.* New Haven, CT: Yale University Press, 2000.

———, ed. *A Social History of England, 1500–1750.* New York: Cambridge University Press, 2017.

———. "Two Concepts of Order: Justices, Constables and Jurymen in Seventeenth-Century England." In *An Ungovernable People: The English and Their Law in the Seventeenth and Eighteenth Centuries,* edited by John Brewer and John Styles, 21–46. New Brunswick, NJ: Rutgers University Press, 1980.

Wrigley, E. Anthony. "Urban Growth and Agricultural Change: England and the Continent in the Early Modern Period." *Journal of Interdisciplinary History* 15, no. 4 (Spring 1985): 683–728.

Wulf, Karin. *Not All Wives: Women of Colonial Philadelphia.* Philadelphia: University of Pennsylvania Press, 2005.

Zabin, Serena R. *Dangerous Economies: Status and Commerce in Imperial New York.* Philadelphia: University of Pennsylvania Press, 2009.

Zaret, David. *Origins of Democratic Culture: Printing, Petitions, and the Public Sphere in Early-Modern England.* Princeton, NJ: Princeton University Press, 2000.

Ziegler, Edith M. *Harlots, Hussies, and Poor Unfortunate Women: Crime, Transportation, and the Servitude of Female Convicts, 1718–1783.* Tuscaloosa: University of Alabama Press, 2014.

INDEX

Page numbers in bold italics refer to illustrations.

Experiencing Empire: Power, People, and Revolution in Early America
Patrick Griffin, editor

Citizens of Convenience: The Imperial Origins of American Nationhood on the U.S.-Canadian Border
Lawrence B. A. Hatter

"Esteemed Bookes of Lawe" and the Legal Culture of Early Virginia
Warren M. Billings and Brent Tarter, editors

Settler Jamaica in the 1750s: A Social Portrait
Jack P. Greene

Loyal Protestants and Dangerous Papists: Maryland and the Politics of Religion in the English Atlantic, 1630–1690
Antoinette Sutto

The Road to Black Ned's Forge: A Story of Race, Sex, and Trade on the Colonial American Frontier
Turk McCleskey

Dunmore's New World: The Extraordinary Life of a Royal Governor in Revolutionary America—with Jacobites, Counterfeiters, Land Schemes, Shipwrecks, Scalping, Indian Politics, Runaway Slaves, and Two Illegal Royal Weddings
James Corbett David

Creating the British Atlantic: Essays on Transplantation, Adaptation, and Continuity
Jack P. Greene

Printed in the USA
CPSIA information can be obtained
at www.ICGtesting.com
LVHW090214171223
766611LV00004B/406